D1343725

199 ways to please God

How to (re-)align your daily life with your duty of care for Creation

By Rianne C. ten Veen

ISBN: 978-184426-629-6, published in 2009

Content

Whoever does an atom's weight of good shall see it, and whoever does an atom's weight of evil, shall see it. (Al-Zilzalah/ The Earthquake [99] 7-8)

Content.. 3
Clarification of words and symbols...................................7
Foreword.. 9
About Creation.. 23
    The Bad News... 26
        Climate change...28
        Use of fossil fuels and peak oil.....................34
        Natural Resource Exploitation.......................38
        Exponential Population Growth...................... 42
        Conclusion...45
    The Good News..47
        Combating Climate change............................. 49
        Post-Oil: Renewable energy and Permaculture..........56
        Sustainable Natural Resource Use..................60
        Population control... 64
        Conclusion...67

PART 1: BELIEFS (*AQAAID*)...75
    Introduction.. 75
    Oneness, Divine Unity (*tawheed*)..............................76
        Examples of action.. 81
    God-consciousness (*taqwa*).....................................84
        Examples of action.. 87
    Mercy (*rahma*) and to do beautiful things (*ihsan*).........89
        Examples of action.. 94
    Guardianship (*khilafah*)...97
        Examples of action.. 104

Day of Judgment... 108
    Examples of action.. 109
Paradise (*Jannah*)... 112
    Examples of action.. 119

PART 2: WORSHIP (*IBADAH*).............................123
Introduction... 123
Testimony of faith (*shahada*)..........................124
    Examples of action.. 127
Prayer... 129
    Ablution (*wudu*)... 130
    Examples of action.. 138
    Bathing (*ghusl*).. 140
    Examples of action.. 143
    Prayer.. 144
    Examples of action.. 147
    Friday prayer (*jummah*)................................148
    Examples of action.. 150
    Eid... 151
    Examples of action.. 153
    Earth is my mosque....................................... 154
    Examples of action.. 156
Purifying Social Tax (*zakat*) and charity (*sadaqah*).....158
    Examples of action.. 162
Fasting.. 164
    Examples of action.. 166
    Ramadan (month of fasting)..........................168
    Examples of action.. 170
Pilgrimage (*Hajj*)...171
    Examples of action.. 177

PART 3: TRANSACTIONS (*MUAMALAT*)....................181
Introduction... 181

Shopping..182
  Examples of actions...............................191
Toiletries 195
  Examples of actions...............................201
Cleaning... 202
  Examples of actions...............................206
Banking, Saving and Investment.............209
  Examples of actions...............................213
Pensions..214
  Examples of actions...............................215
Gifts...217
  Examples of actions...............................217
Utilities...218
  Examples of action............................... 224
Charitable endowments (*waqf*)..............227
  Examples of action............................... 229
Leisure..230
  Examples of action............................... 242

PART 4: MORAL CHARACTER (*AKHLAQ*)................245
Introduction.. 245
  Examples of action............................... 250
Purification of the soul (*tazkiyah*)............251
  Examples of action............................... 254
Supplication (*dua*)..................................256
  Examples of action............................... 259
Remembrance of God (*dhikr*)................260
  Examples of action............................... 263
Education and cultivation (*tarbiyah*)...........265
  Examples of action............................... 268
Etiquette of eating.................................. 271
Etiquette of eating: quantity.....................272
  Examples of action............................... 278

Etiquette of eating: quality...............................280
   Examples of action..................................291
Etiquette of eating: type..................................292
   Fish...303
   Genetic modification (GM).........................307
   Plant-based foods..................................313
   Examples of action 315
Etiquette of drinking......................................322
   Examples of action..................................324
Etiquette of dress...325
   Examples of action..................................327
Etiquette of the road/ travel.............................329
   Car..334
   Cycling/ Public transport..........................336
   Walking..339
   Examples of action..................................340
Man's natural state (*fitra*).............................343
   Examples of action..................................345
Balance (*mizan*)...346
   Examples of action..................................348

Epilogue...353
Sources & Resources.......................................356
About the author..362

Praise be to God ("Say, 'Call Him God, or call Him the Most Gracious; whichever name you use, to Him belongs the best names.", Al Isra/The Night Journey [17] 110). I bear witness that there is no god but God, and I bear witness that Muhammad is His messenger.

Clarification of words and symbols

ﷺ   *sallallahu alehi wasallam* – may the peace and blessings of God be upon him, customarily said by Muslims after hearing the name of Prophet Muhammad or any of the other prophets, which include Jesus, Abraham and Moses

رضى الله عنه   *radhiallahu anhu* - may God be pleased with him/ her, customarily said by Muslims after hearing the name of any of the key companions of the Prophet, including his wife Aisha and Umar ibn Al-Khitab

بسم الله الرحمن الرحيم   *bismillah rahman raheem* - in the name of God, most gracious, most merciful

Hadeeth   saying of the Prophet ﷺ

Mudd   a measure equal to some 0.51 litres

Sa   equal to 4 *mudd*, that is some 2.03 litres

Sunnah   literally means 'trodden path', and therefore, the *sunnah* of the Prophet ﷺ means 'the way of the Prophet'.

Friend   in the book I refer to numerous incidents and anecdotes. For ease of reading, while maintaining privacy and confidentiality, I do not mention names but use the term 'friend'.

CE	Common Era, used as more neutral reference for calendar years than *Anno Domini* (AD, in the year of our Lord, referring to start or counting of calendar from birth of Prophet Jesus ﷺ), and more generally understood in the West than *After Hijra* (AH, referring to Islamic calendar which started from the migration of Prophet Muhammad ﷺ in 622 CE)
Halal	a term designating any object or an action is permissible to use or engage in according to Islamic law. It is the opposite of *haram*. In the Quran halal is always followed by 'and wholesome' (*wa tayyeb*)
Haram	a term designating any object or an action is impermissible to use or engage in according to Islamic law. It is the opposite of *halal*. In between haram and halal there are three shades in the middle: *makrouh* (something that is not liked at all, offensive); *mashbooh* (quite questionable or doubtful); *mushtabahat* (questionable)

Foreword

Islam is reputedly a faith that produces guidelines for every aspect of existence. Then, how was it that care for the environment has somehow been missed out? We have come to the conclusion that it wasn't as there is much, both in the *Qur'an* and Shariah, to instruct Muslims concerning their relationship with the natural world. The next obvious question would be, then why are Muslims not aware of these teachings? This book attempts to answer the first question by cleverly summarising Islamic teachings in relation to this subject and answers the second by bridging the knowledge gap that palpably exists amongst Muslims today when it comes to environmental issues.

There are no references to the environment in the *Qur'an*, as we understand it today. The word nature, which is an abstraction, cannot be found in the *Qur'an* either and the closest one gets to is the word bi'a in modern Arabic usage which connotes a habitat or a surrounding. The *Qur'an* also speaks of creation (*khalq*) and it contains two hundred and sixty one verses where this word is used in its various grammatical forms derived from the root *kh l q*. These verses contain references to the human world; to the natural world of the planet from trees to turtles, from fish to fowl; and to the sun, stars and skies.

But how do Islamic environmental teachings express themselves in the daily lives of Muslims? The answer is that it expresses itself in personal behaviour. It is supposed to be an integral part of life, an expression of existence in submission to the will of the Creator in harmony with the cosmic pattern, unfettered by the trappings of career and consumerism. As there was an Islamic code of conduct that governed inter-personal behaviour and an individual's rights and responsibilities within a community, so there was a code of conduct governing an individual's behaviour towards other sentient beings and the rest of the natural world.

Muslim interaction with the environment evolved into a range of rules and institutions, as an expression of life in all its manifestations embodying what is truly holistic. As Islam expanded out of its sparse desert environment, it was confronted by many challenges, one of which was relative abundance. This brought about other problems like over exploitation and waste. The Qur'an asks us to be just to our natural surroundings, "We did not create the heavens and earth and everything between them, except with truth" (Quran, Al-Hijr/ Stoneland [15] 85). Thus a Muslim's behaviour towards the environment is based on the imperatives laid down in the Qur'an. They come under numerous headings but they could be distilled into three categories bearing in mind public good to be the immediate purpose. They are to do what is right, forbid what is wrong and act with moderation at all times: "Let there be a community among you who call to the good, and enjoin the right and forbid the wrong. They are the ones who have success" (Quran, Al-Imran/ Family of Imran [3] 104).

Taken as a whole as it was intended to be, caring for Planet Earth our only home was integrated within the framework of the Islamic value system. This was an everyday concern for the Muslim, which the Qur'an draws attention to thus, "We have not omitted anything from the Book" (Quran, Al

Anam/ Livestock [6] 39) and "He said 'Our Lord is He Who gives each thing its created form and then guides it'" (Quran, Taha [20] 49).

Yes, by Pleasing God we preserve the environment and Rianne ten Veen has shown us 199 different ways of doing it.

Fazlun Khalid
Founder
Islamic Foundation for Ecology & Environmental Sciences (IFEES)

Introduction

"And the servants of the Beneficent are they who walk on earth in humbleness; and when the ignorant address them they say, peace" (Al-Furqan/ The Criterion [25] 63)

When I was some six years old I moved into a 'Shell compound' in *Dock Sud*, Buenos Aires, Argentina (my father was in the oil business). Inside the compound we had a swimming pool with private guard, a decent house, large garden, lots of green, everything. I will never forget the road leading to the gated compound entrance, however: on the left side an empty, extremely smelly, disused harbour with heavy tar on all sides, on the other side of the road what was referred to as *'villa miseria'* (misery village), people living on top of a garbage dump under some corrugated sheets. Though I was no Muslim at the time and too young to comprehend things, I believe this experience is the source for my *jihad* (struggle) for justice, for people and the environment. Writing this book is part of my humble attempts to raise awareness of the state of our environment and our duty to look after God's Creation, especially amongst Muslims, and share some practical ways in which we can redress the balance of living in harmony with our surroundings.

As in the case of Lord Headley al-Farooq Churchward also known as Sir Rowland George Allanson (1855 - 1929 CE), "[i]t is possible some of my friends may imagine that I have been influenced by Muslims; but this is not the cause, for my present convictions are solely the outcome of many years of thought. My actual conversations with educated Muslims on the subject of religion only commenced a few weeks ago, and need I say that I am overjoyed to find that all my theories and conclusions are entirely in accord with Islam.", though in my case the "few weeks" has now reached several years and that is where my parallel with Lord Headley probably ends.

Islam is a complete way of life. God (or *Allah* in Arabic, as also used by Jews and Christians in Arabic speaking countries), the Creator of humanity, has given us guidelines affecting many different aspects of our lives. The love of God is not something inert or lifeless. A believer in God has to make a good deal of effort with a view to pleasing God. He has to purify his soul from all evil thoughts (the *big jihad*) and fancies so that the love of God should reside in it.

A general misconception seems to be that of thinking of the *shahada* (proclamation of faith), prayer, fasting, *zakat* (purifying social tax, translation as suggested by Tariq Ramadan), *hajj* (pilgrimage) – the 5 religious pillars - to be good acts whereas the day to day activities hold little value of weight. Islam is not only limited to direct worship, however, it is a combination of both direct and indirect worship. Islam commands us to, as Joe Ahmed Dobson, youth and community development worker in London (UK), puts it "[…] when I make decisions about most things in life, from small things like whether I should do the washing up to big things like career decisions, I am guided by Allah."

In life, Muslims are guided by *Shariah*, body of law based on Quran and *sunnah*. The very objective of the *Shariah* (which apparently literally means "path to the water source") is to promote the welfare of the people in all times, not just current generation, which lies in the safeguarding of faith, life, intellect, prosperity and wealth. According to Al-Ghazali, whatever ensures the safeguarding of these five serves public interest and is desirable. The basis of the Shariah is wisdom and welfare of the people in this world as well as the hereafter. According to Ibn al-Qayyim Al-Jawziyya (1292- 1350 CE) this welfare lies in complete justice, mercy, well-being and wisdom. Anything that departs from justice to oppression, from mercy to harshness, from welfare to misery and from wisdom to folly, has nothing to do with Shariah.

When speaking with Muslims about environmental matters I was surprised at the frequency with which I seemed to encounter what Abdal-Hakim Murad, also known as Timothy Winter refers to as 'Mallarmé–effect': "It is said that the 19th century French poet Mallarmé can only be fully understood by those who are not French, because they read him more slowly. Converts to Islam, the subject of this essay, can perhaps claim the same ambiguous advantage in their reading of the Islamic narrative." I am of course not claiming any superiority in knowledge, but referring to how different we all sometimes interpret any verse from the Quran. Having been an environmentalist for far longer than a Muslim, I would perhaps naturally read about Islam through 'green lenses' as opposed to perhaps a more inherited Arab or Asian cultural experience. And there are now several things coming together: immense population growth, direct destruction of the environment (illegal logging etc), peak oil and the effects of climate change. As the UN Secretary General Ban Ki-moon stated after visiting

Antarctica in November 2007: "I'm not here to frighten you, I'm not scaremongering […] But the world is changing, the glaciers are melting ... the change is now progressing much faster than I had thought. It's alarming."

Regularly our excuse not to try better is because "we are busy" or "society does not support us". However, when I hear this response or I want to relax myself, I think about how busy could we ever be, or how much opposition do we really face compared to the Prophet ﷺ? As Karen Armstrong states in her biography of the Prophet ﷺ: "to create a literary masterpiece, to found a major religion and a new world power are not ordinary achievements. But to appreciate his [Prophet Muhammad ﷺ] genius to the full, we must examine the society into which he was born and the forces with which he contended". Against that, what excuse do we have left? And as the Prophet ﷺ himself reminded us in his last sermon: "Beware of Satan, for the safety of your religion. He has lost all hope of that he will be able to lead you astray in big things, so beware of following him in small things." So have we got it right about the small things? Do we *live* Islam? If so, then why do speakers/ authors regularly have to distinguish between Islam and Muslims, as for example mentioned by Safei-Eldin Hamed PhD on *Seeing the environment through Islamic eyes: application of Shariah to natural resources planning and management* for Texas Tech University: "It should be pointed out that there is a distinction between "Islamic" and "Muslim", as used throughout this paper. "Islamic" refers to what pertains to Islam as a paradigm or a body of knowledge, an ideology and a system of life, while "Muslim" refers to the existing practices of societies that are conventionally known as Muslim people or Muslim countries. This paper deals with "Islamic" and not "Muslim"." Let us change this, by our actions, by *living* Islam.

The book is arranged according to recognisable aspects of the faith of Islam and aims to give some useful righteous deeds per topic. A small deed that is continuous is better than a big deed that is not done regularly. Continuity in righteous deeds strengthens faith (*iman*). The Prophet ﷺ was asked: "Which deed is most beloved to God?" He said, "The one that is continuous, even if it is little." This book contains examples on how to do your bit to avoid catastrophe and please God because the Prophet ﷺ said: "religion is very easy and whoever overburdens himself in his religion will not be able to continue in that way. So you should not be extremists, but try to be near to perfection...". According to another report, he ﷺ said: "be moderate, and you will reach what you want.". What I personally found most helpful to avoid being overwhelmed by the task and opportunities is to make a list and every month or so pick one action from that list: change bank account to more ethical bank, subscribe to vegetable box, buy a bicycle, put a water saver in the cistern....

I am not a scholar, nor do I pretend to be one. This book is the result of my best efforts over several years, which has also been a tremendously useful learning experience for me. I pray it will be also of some use and interest to the reader. As this book is aimed at a non-Arabic speaking readership (and that includes myself in this respect) I have used English equivalents of Islamic terms and simplified spelling of Arabic names. As this is not a scholarly work, I pray readers will forgive me the impossibility to thus be hundred per cent accurate as non-Arabic languages will always only be able to give an approximate version of the meaning of Quranic verses; I have used a variety of English translations. Many tips include relevant links and programmes. They are usually most relevant for those in the UK (where I am based), though I would be surprised if there were no similar programmes in at least some other countries (and I have tried to include resources in several other countries too). Note though that especially with websites, addresses sometimes change. Also, I mention the ideas as 'examples of action' as I believe the opportunities are endless so this book could only scratch the surface. I am convinced readers can adapt the suggested ideas to best suit their circumstances and knowledge.

By the way, some food for thought to start off with: poverty and wars are generally regarded as man-made problems, but equally man-made destruction and abuse of nature is generally referred to as an environmental problem, allowing us, by choice of words, to distance ourselves from our responsibility. But as Elizabeth May, a committed Christian and Leader of the Green Party in Canada, clarifies: "it is an environmental issue, in the same way that drowning is a "water issue." It surely is that, but it is much more."

We may think that the earth cannot be as ruined as 'the environmentalists' say, because we surely would have been replaced, but "If God were to punish people according to what they deserve, He would not leave on the back of the (earth) a single living creature: but He gives them respite for a stated term: when their term expires, verily God has in

His sight all His servants." (Fatir/ The Angels [35] 45). According to UN Population Fund (UNFPA) in 2008, for the first time, more than half of the' world's population will be living in urban areas. This unprecedented shift could enhance development and promote sustainability – or it could deepen poverty and accelerate environmental degradation. So another reason to look after Creation.

Sometimes people are reluctant to take green action as "it's something for sandal wearing hippies". Well, firstly I believe we should first and foremost think what God would be expecting from us (show submission and work on our guardian role to, God willing, 'earn' Paradise), not what the 'fashionistas' or 'the neighbours' might think. Secondly, I believe it is a myth that many environmentalists are "unemployed lefties": you have 'green grannies', 'green corporates', green IT security specialists, a World Business Council for Sustainable Development (www.wbcsd.org), and from green Sisters (US catholic nuns) to green Sisters (women in Greece) etc. Also, it is not just a Western fashion (to be replaced by a new fashion soon), but something that inspires people from all walks of life to take genuine action for the sake of pleasing God and/ or looking ahead at what we may leave for generations after us: Muhammad A. Shaban for example is an environmental activist based in Dar es Salaam, Tanzania. In 2001 he launched *The Environmental Club* (www.environmental-club.org), an online "environmental care club which aims to educate people about various issues on the environment". Their motto is *For Sustainable Living and Development*. He is also the author of a book on the environment: *THE QUEST*

For a Greener, Cleaner, Better & Peaceful World. Plus, he is an optician in his day job.

Those who stand to lose most from accepting climate change science are known to use 'tricks' with an aim to confuse us, for example by stating – untruthfully – that there is no scientific consensus (there *is* consensus amongst relevant scientists) or that we can solve it all with 'business as usual'. But remember: "And do not follow (blindly) any information of which you have no (direct) knowledge. (Using your faculties of perception and conception, you must verify it for yourself. (In the Court of your Lord,) you will be held accountable for your hearing, sight, and the faculty of reasoning." (Al-Isra/ The Night Journey [17] 36). Check www.lobbywatch.org or www.sourcewatch.org to see how companies use money and resources to lobby those in power to have their way (not the way in our collective best interest).

Jarir relates that the Prophet ﷺ said: "Whoever initiates a good practice in Islam and is emulated by others in doing so will get the reward of it and the reward of all those who act upon it without their rewards being diminished in any respect. And whosoever initiates an evil practice in Islam and is emulated by others will bear the sin of it and the sin of all those who act on it without their burden being diminished in the least." None of the narrations of this *hadeeth* give the identity of the man. This shows that he was likely not a prominent person in the community, though he took the initiative in the presence of Abu Bakr ﵁, Umar ﵁, and other pre-eminent emigrants. According to scholars this should make it clear to us that *no one should see himself as too unimportant to set a good precedent*. That man did not let the presence of those esteemed Companions keep him from being the first to do something good. Due to his taking the initiative, he received the reward of all those who followed his example, even those who spent far more than he did.

Though this book contains some frightening and disconcerting facts, it is not meant as a despairing book, because much is in our (albeit sometimes collective) hands. I believe we *can* change the world, starting with ourselves, today. Or as Aldous Huxley, the English novelist and critic, best known for his dystopian novel, *Brave New World* put it: "there's only one corner of the universe you can be certain of improving, and that's your own self". Or as the Prophet ﷺ stated: "[e]very person goes forth in the morning trading in his own self. He either earns its freedom or consigns it to perdition." And please do not just pray that the world leaders will make the right decisions and change the world: "when I was a young man, I wanted to change the world. I found it was difficult to change the world, so I tried to change my nation. When I found I could not change the nation, I began to focus on my town. I could not change the town and as an older man, I tried to change my family. Now, as an old man, I realise the only thing I can change is myself, and suddenly I realise that if long ago I had changed myself, I could have made an impact on my family. My family and I could have made an impact on our town. Their impact could have changed the nation and I could indeed have changed the world." (anonymous)

According to the last verse of Chapter 99 of the Quran 'Whoever does an atom's eight of good will see it then, and

21

who ever has done an atom's weight of evil will see it then also'. Apparently early commentators of the Quran explained the phrase 'an atom's weight' as a mosquito or a particle of dust which could be seen only when exposed to the light of the sun. So, as an African proverb goes: "If you think you are too small to make a difference, try sleeping in a room with a mosquito". I pray that this book might in a small way inspire to contribute to what Idris Tawfiq mentions: "the best and fastest way of acquainting the world with the true image of Islam is to set a good example in real life."

About Creation

"Assuredly the creation of the heavens and the earth is greater than the creation of mankind; but most of mankind know not." (Ghafir or Al-Mumin/ Forgiver or The Believer [40] 57)

According to Fazlun Khalid (Founder Director, Islamic Foundation for Ecology and Environmental Sciences, IFEES) "[t]he word nature, which is an abstraction, cannot be found in the Qur'an and the closest modern Arabic usage is the word *bi'a*, which connotes a habitat or a surrounding. […] The Qur'an speaks of creation (*khalq*) and it contains two hundred and sixty one verses where this word is used in its various grammatical forms derived from the root *kh l q*. These verses contain references to the human world; to the natural world of the Earth, from trees to turtles, from fish to fowl; and to the sun, stars and skies." Creation was created for the benefit of humanity, and humanity was created to know and worship God, demonstrating it in belief and deed. In his Eighteenth *Khabar* (58) Muhammad Ibn Arabi (1165 -1240 CE) states: "God, ever mighty and majestic is He, says: 'O child of Adam, I have created you for My sake, and I have created things for your sake. So do not disgrace that which I have created for Myself with that which I have created for you.'"

In the foreword to Muhammad Al-Ghazali's (1917-1996 CE) thematic commentary on the Quran, the International Institute of Islamic Thought (IIIT) London remarks: "Muslims are enjoined, along with the rest of humanity, to 'read' the two great books of Revelation and Creation, i.e. the Qur'an and the natural world. Reading one without the other will result in an imbalance detrimental to the existence (and prosperity) of humanity on earth, indeed to the divine purpose of the cosmos." Syed Ali Ibnul Hussain Baqri in his article *Quran penetrates all the faculties of life* says something similar: "I see that there are two books of Allahtaala [God]. One is Quran, a transcendental spiritual Holy Book. We revealed this Quran and we will protect this. Yes this is a spiritual and transcendental book, and the other one is perceptual and physical book. And the skies and the earth is cover of that perceptual and physical book, and what are in between are the verses of this Book. Now you see the suns, the moons, the planets, the stars, the galaxies, the birds, the gardens, the ocean, seas, rivers, cattle, the animal, the men, the women, the camels, horses, donkeys, elephants, trees, plants, mountains, fountains, flowers, stones, and every thing that you see is the *Ayat* [sign], the verse of this perceptual book." When doing this, according to Muslih al-Din Sadi Shirazi (1213-1293 CE), "[e]very leaf of the tree becomes a page of the sacred scripture once the soul has learnt to read."

Human well-being is highly dependent on ecosystems and the benefits they provide such as food and drinkable water, no matter how much we are forgetting this by living more and more in concrete cities detached from direct contact with the other "nations". And as Ibn Rushd (Averroes, 1126 – 1198 CE) inspires by naturally combining revelation and reason for the best understanding of existential questions, so do we need to learn about what we are doing to God's Creation. For example, how often do we reflect that one fifth of the chapters of the Quran are named after parts of nature, from cow (chapter 2) to daybreak (chapter 113).

And as according to Jalal al-Deen Al-Suyuti (1445-1505 CE) "[i]t has been proven that the names of the *surahs* [chapters of the Quran] have all been given by means of *tawqeef* (Divine guidance through revelation)", I believe God meant to bring our attention regularly to parts of Creation, and not just for the sake of it: "When the earth is shaken with its earthquakes and the earth yields up its burdens, and man says: 'What is the matter with it?' That day it shall proclaim its news, for your Lord will have inspired it." (A-Zilzalah/ The Earthquake [99] 1-5). Prophet Muhammad ﷺ asked: "Do you know what the earth's news is? Its news is that it will bear witness about every man and woman as to what they did upon it. It will say: 'He did such and such on such and such day.' That is its news."

As Charles Le Gai Eaton (Hasan le Gai Eaton or Hassan Abdul Hakeem) (1921– CE) poignantly remarks: "It might be said that we leave our fingerprints upon all that we touch, and they remain in place long after we have gone on our way. We forget so much of the past, but the past is still there and cannot be wiped out, unless God - under His Name "the Effacer" (*Al-Afu*) - chooses to erase it from our records."

According to Khurram Murad what we must remember is that "to live by the Qur'an requires a major decision on your part: we have to completely alter the course of our life, irrespective of what may be the dominant thought-patterns around us, of what our society may be dictating, or what others may be doing. This decision requires major sacrifices. But unless we, as believers in the Qur'an being the word of God, are prepared to take the plunge, not much good will come out of the time you spend with the Qur'an."

Weather differs month to month, day to day, even hour to hour. Climate is weather over the longer term. According to journal Science (July 2007) the coldest period in the past 800,000 years occurred around 20,000 years ago, during the last glacial maximum, when the ice sheets were at their peak. The scariest bit is that it was then only ten degrees colder than today, so though large weather temperature differences are normal and pleasant, major differences in climate are not.

Hereunder the bad news in a nutshell. For all the bad news, however, there is fortunately much good happening as well. Unfortunately this does not mean that 'business as usual' is an option. From personal experience I know environmentalists are regularly accused of being doom-mongerers, looking at 'glass-half empty' only, unrealistic people. The message (the facts) are depressing, I totally agree, but beware of 'blaming the messenger', it only distracts from working on solving the challenges. The aim of this book is to serve as a reminder for myself and hopefully for the reader to remember what we, as guardians of Creation, have done to God's Creation, but more so be an inspiration in what we *can* all do, should do, together and as individuals, for the sake of pleasing God and those who get to live on God's Creation after us and for the sake of our record on Day of Judgment…because, as I read on a banner at the Camp for Climate Action (www.climatecamp.org.uk) in August 2007: "this planet has no emergency exits".

The Bad News
"Corruption has appeared in the land and sea for that men's own hands have earned, that God may let them taste

26

some part of what they have done [...]" (Ar-Rum/ The Romans [30] 41)

According to Iyad Abumoghli (Senior Environment and Knowledge Management Adviser, United Nations Development Programme) "[t]he Qur'anic term *"fasad"* [corruption] includes destruction of both the environment as well as man's own destruction." He adds: "Corruption is a serious matter in Islam where it represents the mismanagement and destruction of the balanced system God created. The Prophet ﷺ has requested Justice, as part of a good governance system, in several occasions: 'If you rule people, rule in justice'."

The bad news is that several major issues are coming to a head and, left unchecked, could threaten the future viability of the planet, of God's Creation for which we have been left in charge. They are climate change, peak oil, natural resource overexploitation and major population growth. As Velma Cook muses on her website (www.islamicgarden.com): "When I first came to Cairo I used to stand at my seventh floor balcony and look over the misty, polluted sky containing an endless horizon of cement buildings. It made me feel somewhat depressed and often claustrophobic! So I'd think about the past of this place and the beauty that man's hand turned into ugliness. Yet hope remains if we, as Muslims, can align our lives with Islam and rise above the evil that surrounds us." Or as Seyyed Hossein Nasr puts it "the environmental crisis has deep spiritual, philosophical, and religious roots and causes." The metaphor that will bring the message home most graphically, however, is that as presented by Abdalhamid Evans (Director of Research and Intelligence, KasehDia,

27

Malaysia) in a talk at a conference in 1987 about just trade: "Let us imagine that we are looking at the body of a crime victim. Multiple injury, heavy duty GBH [Grievous Bodily Harm, as used in English criminal law], rape and robbery of an unprecedented nature. The victim's condition is serious, critical, but there is still life. It's not yet time for an autopsy, but it soon will be, if something is not done. [...] The victim is the planet and its inhabitants, the people, animals, plants, oceans, forests, the air, earth and water. Life itself."

Climate change

"Behold, your Lord said to the angels: "I will create a vicegerent on earth." They said: "Will You place therein one who will make mischief therein and shed blood? - while we do celebrate Your praises and glorify Your holy (name)?" He said: "I know what you know not."" (Al-Baqarah/ The Cow [2] 30)

Human activity - particularly the burning of fossil fuels - has made the blanket of greenhouse gases around the earth 'thicker'. The resulting increase in global temperatures is altering the complex web of systems that allow life to thrive on earth, such as cloud cover, rainfall, wind patterns, ocean currents, and the distribution of plant and animal species. The complexity of the climate system means predictions vary widely, but even the minimum changes forecast could mean frequently flooded coastlines, disruptions to food and water supplies, and the extinction of many species. This is not just the conclusion of some extremist green groups but of the United Nations' Intergovernmental Panel on Climate Change (UN's IPCC). It has taken six years to compile, draws on 29,000 pieces of research analysed by 2,500 scientists from over 130 countries. Or as the UK Royal

Society succinctly puts it: "We know from looking at gases found trapped in cores of polar ice that the levels of carbon dioxide in the atmosphere are now 35 per cent greater than they have been for at least the last 650,000 years. From the radioactivity and chemical composition of the gas we know that this is mainly due to the burning of fossil fuels, as well as the production of cement and the widespread chopping down (and burning) of the world's forests" (according to the UN Food and Agricultural Organisation [FAO], during the 1990s the world's total forest area shrank by 9.4 million ha - about three times the size of Belgium - each year). Note that 650,000 years includes some ice ages, so small changes in average global temperatures make a huge difference... and this time we are going for the opposite of an ice age.

Very worryingly, according to peace group International Alert, a total of 46 nations and 2.7 billion people are now at high risk of being overwhelmed by armed conflict and war because of climate change. A further 56 countries face political destabilisation, affecting another 1.2 billion individuals. Much of Africa, Asia and South America will suffer outbreaks of war and social disruption as climate change erodes land, raises seas, melts glaciers and increases storms, it concludes. Or as UN Secretary General Ban Ki Moon exemplified in June 2007 "amid the diverse social and political causes, the Darfur conflict began as an ecological crisis, arising at least in part from climate change."

And even according to NASA (again, not an extremist 'greeny') in May 2007 found that human-made greenhouse gases have brought the Earth's climate close to critical tipping points, with potentially dangerous consequences for the planet. If global emissions of carbon dioxide continue to rise at the rate of the past decade, this research shows that there will be disastrous effects, including increasingly rapid sea level rise, increased frequency of droughts and floods, and increased stress on wildlife and plants due to rapidly shifting climate zones. While the researchers say it is still possible to achieve an 'alternative scenario' they note that significant actions will be required to do so. Emissions must begin to slow soon. With another decade of 'business-as-usual' it becomes impractical to achieve the 'alternative scenario' because of the energy infrastructure that would be in place. Research by the Netherlands Environmental Assessment Agency, in collaboration with the Joint Research Centre (JRC) of the EU, showed that global emissions of the six Kyoto greenhouse gases increased by 75 per cent between 1970 and 2004 to about 45,000 megaton CO_2 equivalents.

There have been successful efforts at land reclamation (the creation of new land where there was once water). Notable examples are the *polders* of the Netherlands, the southern Chinese cities of Hong Kong and Macau and the city state of Singapore. It is, however, an expensive and risky undertaking. It is thus often only considered in places that are densely populated and/ or flat land is scarce. A related practice is the draining of swampy or seasonally submerged wetlands to convert them to farmland. While this does not create new land exactly, it allows productive use of land that would otherwise be restricted to wildlife habitat. In some parts of the world, new reclamation projects are restricted or no longer allowed, due to environmental protection laws. For example, draining wetlands for ploughing is a form of habitat destruction and ignores other misunderstood purposes of wetlands, such as 'flood busters'.

The Millennium Ecosystem Assessment (MA) Synthesis Report published in March 2005 (a five-year study by 1,360 scientists from 95 countries) estimates that up to sixty per cent of the ecosystems that support life on earth are being degraded or used unsustainably. As the report makes clear, most of this damage has been done in the last 50 years. "Human activity is putting such a strain on the natural functions of earth that the ability of the planet's ecosystems to sustain future generations can no longer be taken for granted," the report says. Between 1960 and 2000, the world population doubled from three billion to six billion. At the same time, the global economy increased more than six-fold, the production of food and the supply of drinking water more than doubled, and the consumption of timber products increased by more than half. There is little better news for the state of the soil: the UN estimate that at present 70 per cent of drylands and about 25 per cent of the total land area of the world is undergoing desertification ("land degradation in arid, semi-arid and dry sub-humid areas resulting mainly from adverse human impact.").

According to the IPCC there are multiple mitigation options, for example in the transport sector, but their effect may be counteracted by growth in the sector. And mitigation options are faced with many barriers, such as consumer preferences and lack of policy frameworks. According to research by the US Government's National Oceanic and Atmospheric Administration (NOAA) every month for the last 10 years was hotter than the average for the entire period between 1880 and 2007. Not 51 per cent, 90 per cent or 99 per cent of them. Every single month.

We might feel smug as it is China, not us, being the worst polluter in the world...but that is partly as they have 1.3 billion souls (so their per capita pollution is still nowhere near that of the UK, let alone US) and secondly much of what they produce, we buy and by blaming China for the pollution we are, according to a New Economics Foundation published in October 2007, turning China into our "environmental laundry" with devastating consequences for the planet.

Pioneered by William Rees (1943– CE) and Mathis Wackernagel (1962- CE) in 1996, the ecological footprint approach has become one of the most widely referenced sustainability analysis tools around the globe. Ecological footprint analysis (EFA) is used to calculate the land area needed to sustain human consumption and absorb its ensuing wastes. Comparing the footprint of a given population in a discrete area with the amount of biologically productive space available to that population provides a way to estimate whether or not a population's consumption is sustainable. Ecological footprints and bio-capacity are expressed in "global acres." Each unit corresponds to one acre of biologically productive space with "world average productivity." To calculate a nation's footprint, EFA use official statistics tracking consumption and translate that into the amount of biologically productive land and water area required to produce the resources consumed and to assimilate the wastes generated on an annual basis. Because people use resources from all over the world, and affect faraway places with their pollution, the footprint is the sum of these areas wherever they are on the planet. And if this footprint is larger than the earth's 'carrying capacity', it is just like somebody who goes into overdraft with his bank. While he will not immediately think he is in financial trouble, if he continues to stay in overdraft (and worse so, continually increases his overdraft), his bank will ultimately take him to court and have him declared bankrupt. So too Muslims as guardians of the Earth, if we neglect to keep up our duty may not immediately feel repercussions for running up an 'ecological debt', but if we continue like this could easily be replaced by a new people (like happened to the people of Ad and Thamud before us and is mentioned in the Quran, apparently some 22 times, as a warning for us - both were powerful tribes in their respective times and lands - Ad were "endowed abundantly with power" and Thamud were "settled firmly on earth" - but they arrogantly abused the power given to them by God, and were destroyed by an environmental cataclysm.). The destruction of the She-Camel in itself is not the reason God destroyed the nation. Rather, it is the destruction of His Special Sign which had been sent to them, such destruction symbolising their utter denial of God as the One to whom they will return, and *tawheed* (unity of Creation) as the religion that he ordained.

The annual number of natural disasters has more than doubled in the past decade. In the 1990s, an annual average of 354 natural disasters occurred throughout the world. Between 2000 and 2004, this figure more than doubled to an annual average of 728. The number of people who are forced to migrate as a consequence of these environmental disasters (that is, environmental refugees) already approximates, and may soon dwarf, the number of people who are forced to migrate for political reasons (that is, the UNHCR 'persons of concern', currently estimated to be 20.8 million people). Indeed, research by the International Federation of the Red Cross and Red Crescent Societies indicates that more people are now displaced by environmental disasters than war. And according to a paper drafted for the European Council in March 2008, there are three main threats posed by climate change that will impact the EU significantly: conflict over resources, increased migration, and what happens to oil, gas and fishing resources if borders and territories change, or disappear beneath the sea? How to assess and adjudicate territorial claims, political tensions are bound to rise.

And though the world's richest countries have together pledged nearly $18 billion or £12.5 billion in the last seven years to help the poorest countries cope with the consequences of climate change, despite world leaders' rhetoric that the finance is vital, less than $0.9 billion of that pledge has been disbursed.

Use of fossil fuels and peak oil

"To whom I granted resources in abundance, And sons to be by his side! To whom I made (life) smooth and comfortable! Yet is he greedy-that I should add (yet more); By no means! He has been stubborn to Our revelations. Soon will I visit him with a mount of calamities! For he thought and he plotted; And woe to him! How he plotted! Yes, Woe to him; How he plotted!" (The Cloaked One [74] 12-19)

Fossil fuels are energy resources that come from the remains of plants (reminds me of: "He who produces for you fire out of the green tree, so that, lo! you kindle [your fires] therewith" Yaseen/ Yaseen [36] 80) and animals. These remains are millions of years old. There are three fossil fuels: petroleum oil, natural gas, and coal. Fossil fuels are a non-renewable resource as they take millions of years to develop under extreme conditions. Once they are gone, they can no longer be part of our energy mix. This cheap and abundant supply of energy changed the world in then unimaginable ways, leading to the rapid expansion of industry, transport, trade and agriculture. The peak of oil discovery was passed in the 1960s, and the world started using more than was found in new fields in 1981. The gap between discovery and production has widened since. According to Colin Campbell (40 years experience in oil business), "[t]he term Peak Oil refers to the maximum rate of the production of oil in any area under consideration, recognising that it is a finite natural resource, subject to depletion." For the gas industry, peak gas output could come sooner than expected, "maybe not too different from peak oil," Shell executive vice president John Mills told delegates at a conference in Abu Dhabi in November 2008.

And what I find incomprehensible, is that we seem collectively suicidal (which is against Islam: "...Nor kill [or destroy] yourselves: for verily God has been to you Most Merciful!", Al-Nisa/ The Women [4] 29) as current subsidies on oil products in non-OECD countries are estimated at over \$90 billion annually. Some of these subsidies are presented as development aid, but as End OilAid, a diverse coalition of organisations working together to end oil aid and address the issues at the intersection of oil dependence, climate change, and international debt, states: "For more than 25 years, wealthy countries have been using aid and other foreign assistance to subsidize the expansion of the international oil industry, a practice known as "Oil Aid" [...] Our international development dollars should be spent on climate change adaptation, alleviating poverty, or clean renewable resources, not on subsidizing a profitable and polluting industry."

As first expressed in Hubbert peak theory (after M. King Hubbert, 1903- 1989 CE), peak oil is the point or timeframe at which the maximum global petroleum production rate is reached. After this timeframe, the rate of production will by definition enter terminal decline. According to the Hubbert model, oil production will follow a roughly symmetrical bell-shaped curve. Though of course the only reliable way to identify the timing of peak oil will be in retrospect, most peak-oil experts state this will be between 2007 and 2020. Numerous observers believe that because of the high dependence of most modern industrial transport, agricultural and industrial systems on inexpensive oil, the post-peak production decline and possible resulting severe price increases will have negative implications for the global economy. After 'cheap oil' there are 'unconventional sources'. Experts say that this extra oil supply is likely to come from expensive and environmentally damaging unconventional sources within 15 years, according to a detailed study published in February 2007 by Wood Mackenzie, respected adviser to the energy industry for over 30 years. Unconventional sources, such as heavy crude oil, tar sands, and oil shale are not counted as part of oil reserves until oil companies can book them as proven reserves after they finish a strip mine or thermal facility to extract them. Worse, according to Matthew Simmons, an industry banker: "it takes vast quantities of scarce and valuable potable water and natural gas to turn unusable oil into heavy low-quality oil. In a sense this exercise is like turning gold into lead". He said this in February 2007, at the International Petroleum Week in London.

Sadad al-Huseini (former Head of Exploration and Production, Saudi Aramco) in October 2007 stated that global production had hit its maximum sustainable plateau and that output would start to fall within 15 years, by which time the world's oil resources would be "very severely depleted". Even Jeroen van der Veer (Chief Executive, Royal Dutch Shell) in January 2008 acknowledged that the end of the oil era is almost upon us, and sooner than you might think: "Shell estimates that after 2015 supplies of easy-to-access oil and gas will no longer keep up with demand." This was just over a week before Shell announced annual *profits* (not turnover) of £13.9 billion, a record for a British company.

The International Energy Agency (IEA) in its World Energy Outlook 2008 (published in November 2008) estimates that world energy demand will increase by some 45 per cent between 2006 and 2030 if policies remain unchanged. Nobuo Tanaka, Executive Director of the IEA, stated at the launch: "[c]urrent trends in energy supply and consumption are patently unsustainable – environmentally, economically and socially – they can and must be altered. [...] the growing concentration of production in a small number of countries, would increase our susceptibility to supply disruptions and sharp price hikes. At the same time, greenhouse-gas emissions would be driven up inexorably, putting the world on track for an eventual global temperature increase of up to 6°C." But with more than 50 of the 100 largest economic entities in the world being companies (whose aim is profit), *not* countries; and of the 10 largest companies, 5 selling cars and 3 selling oil, you can imagine that Upton Sinclair's "It is difficult to get a man to understand something when his salary depends on his not understanding it." comes to mind.

I am interested in the link drawn between slavery and cheap fossil fuels/ tackling climate change: J.F. Mouhot (research fellow, Birmingham University, UK) amongst others has studied the double parallelism between a) the convenience brought to us by fossil fuel powered machines and the convenient life slaves brought to slave owners and b) the moral assessment of the harm of burning fossil fuels on a large scale and of slavery: it was recognised it was bad, but reasoned away by stating that tackling slavery/ climate change would be too disruptive, thus worse than using slaves or exploiting natural resources. We survived the official abolishment of slavery (though I believe there is still too much bonded labour around to not make Islamic encouragement to free slaves outdated); I am sure we can survive our addiction to fossil fuels, if we decide to 'detox' quickly.

Natural Resource Exploitation
"When it is said to them: "Make not mischief on the earth," they say: "Why, we only want to make peace!"" (Al-Baqarah/ The Cow [2] 11)

The Quran reminds us that each species of animal is a "community" like the human community. It then stands to reason that each and every creature on earth has, as its birth-right, a share in all the natural resources. In other words, each animal is a tenant-in-common on this planet with human species. As human species we are the guardians of Creation, but within the limits of submitting to God. Instead, as always, God knows us very well, as we are using the blessings in an unsustainable way, slowly killing the goose that lays the golden eggs. This leaves us, and the rest of Creation, exposed and vulnerable to natural disasters.

According to the Worldwide Fund for Nature (WWF), if everyone in the world consumed natural resources and produced CO_2 at the rate we do in the UK, we would need three planets to support us. Obviously we only have the one. The first step in reducing our impact on the planet is to understand how our everyday lives affect the environment; our 'ecological footprint', a tool that measures how much land and water area a human population requires to produce the resources it consumes and to absorb its wastes under prevailing technology. Every action impacts the planet's ecosystems. This is of little concern as long as human use of resources does not exceed what the Earth can renew. But are we taking more? Today, humanity's Ecological Footprint is over 23 per cent larger than what the planet can regenerate. In other words, it now takes more than one year and two months for the Earth to regenerate what we use in a single year. Turning resources into waste faster than waste can be turned back into resources puts us in global ecological overshoot, depleting the very resources on which human life and biodiversity depend.

The concept of ecological debt is the basis for Ecological Debt Day (Earth Overshoot Day), the date upon which the sum of global annually renewable resources has been consumed for the year. This is calculated using the global ecological footprint: the total area required to sustainably feed consumption, divided by the global bio-capacity (the amount of area available to feed that consumption) and multiplied by 365 (the number of days in a year). The first Ecological Debt Day occurred in 1987, and has steadily been moving earlier into the year, being 9 October in 2006 and 23 September in 2008. Ecological Debt has also been applied to highlight the disparity between industrialised nations, which consume a greater share of the global resource pool, and developing nations, who despite their greater share of the global population, consume less. For more on ecological debt, check www.ecologicaldebt.org.

Some ecosystem changes such as increased food production have helped hundreds of millions of people out of poverty, but also have negative effects. Degradation of ecosystem services is harming many of the world's poorest and most vulnerable people, and is sometimes the main factor causing poverty. Poverty in turn tends to increase dependence on ecosystem services. This, plus population growth, can lead to additional pressure on ecosystems and a downward spiral of poverty and ecosystem degradation. For example, the Yemen National Biodiversity Strategy and Action Plan presented in January 2005 mentions in its summary that "[t]he medium and long-term economic development of Yemen is very much dependent upon the appropriate management and sustainability of the limited resources in the country."

From the *Rapid Environmental and Socio-Economic Assessment of Tsunami-damage in terrestrial and marine coastal ecosystems of Ampara and Batticaloa Districts of Eastern Sri Lanka* done by International Union for Conservation of Nature (IUCN) "Extensive stands of mangrove appear to have played a positive role in buffering the inland landscapes from the tsunami by reducing the energy of the incoming waves and absorbing the tsunami waters into a network of mangrove creeks and channels. Agricultural lands such as rice fields, roads, human settlements and buildings were observed to be relatively undamaged in those sections of the coastline which had continuous thick stretches of mangroves" In January 2008 the UN Food and Agriculture Organisation (FAO) published a report) stating the world has lost around 3.6 million hectares (ha) of mangroves since 1980, equivalent to an alarming 20 percent loss of total mangrove area.

United Nations University (UNU) experts in June 2007 stated the loss of soil productivity and the degradation of life-support services provided by nature pose imminent threats to international stability. One-third of all people on Earth - about 2 billion in number in 2006 - are potential victims of desertification's creeping effect. And, left unchecked, the number of people at risk of displacement due to severe desertification is an estimated 50 million over the next 10 years – a sweep of migrants worldwide equal in number to the entire population of South Africa or South Korea. According to the UNU "land use policy reform is urgently needed to halt overgrazing, over-exploitation, trampling and unsustainable irrigation practices, as are policies to create livelihood alternatives for dryland populations". The research was based on input of 200 experts from 25 countries who met in Algiers (Algeria) at the end of 2006. I heard an interesting metaphor which really brings the message home: in certain areas of Sudan, the desert is advancing at some 6-8 kilometres a year. If this were some enemy invading our country by even 500 metres, we would call for UN Resolutions and an immediate cessation of hostilities. But when it is difficult to show it on TV and it does not affect us directly, we often shrug and say 'well, stuff happens'.

Some countries, especially the poorest, are forced to overexploit their natural resources, kill their livelihoods, due to the need to raise funds in 'hard currency' to pay off international (sometimes odious) debts. So it would be hupocritical for us to tell countries like Brazil and Indonesia to just stop felling their forests; we should first see the link with international debt (the world's poorest countries pay almost $100 million every day to the rich world) and look at the bigger picture. For more information on this, check www.jubileedebtcampaign.org.uk and www.publishwhatyoupay.org

Exponential Population Growth

"There is not an animal (that lives) on the earth, nor a being that flies on its wings, but (forms part of) communities like you. Nothing have we omitted from the Book, and they (all) shall be gathered to their Lord in the end." (Al-Anam/ Livestock [6] 38)

We are monopolising the space of the earth. The human population had remained about stable at around one million for thousands and thousands of generations. Since the Industrial Revolution it has started to rise markedly: though in 1800 CE the world population had not yet reached one billion, and by 1960 the world population was still under three billion, by 2007 the world population has risen to 6.6 billion. By 2050 (within most of our lifetimes!) this is estimated to reach more than 9 billion, though with 27.4 per cent of the world's population being below 15 years of age (as according to the 2006 CIA World Factbook), some say this could be 11 billion. This means that the generation born immediately after WWII will experience the global population grow from 3 to 9 billion. I fear this will be devastating for life on earth, for the future of the survival of the rest of Creation, but do not just take my word for it. As the UK Royal Society states that while the human population has increased fourfold, in the last 50 years the global economy has quintupled in size, placing considerable pressure on the world's natural resources.

According to the United Nations World Population Fund's *State of the World Population 2007*, in 2008 the world reached an invisible but momentous milestone: for the first time in history, more than half its human population, 3.3 billion people (more than the *total* world population just over 40 years ago), are living in urban areas. By 2030, this is expected to swell to almost 5 billion. While the world's urban population grew very rapidly (from 220 million to 2.8 billion) over the 20th century in western countries, the next few decades are expected to see an unprecedented scale of urban growth in the majority world. Unfortunately cities also embody the environmental damage done by modern civilization (environmental refugees due to desertification often flee to cities). So far, world attention has centred mostly on immediate concerns, problems such as how to improve living conditions; how to generate employment; how to reduce cities' ecological footprint; and how to administer increasingly complex urban systems. These are all of course important questions, but according to the UN they shrink in comparison with the problems raised by the impending future growth of the urban population. Poor people will make up a large part of future urban growth. This simple fact has generally been overlooked, at great cost. Most urban growth now stems from natural increase (more births than deaths) rather than migration. On the issue of population, big numbers can seem just that, bit numbers. However, I realised how fast our world population is increasing when I was listening to an anniversary programme on the radio at the occasion of 60-years after partition. Just 60 years ago the population of what now is India, Pakistan and Bangladesh was 400 million. In just 60 years this has grown to 1,449 million or a multiplication of more than 3.6 times. All this on a planet which has not grown nor cannot grow. Or as the Environment Society of Oman states "The rapid population growth in many countries has resulted in too great a demand on natural resources. This is especially true of desert countries such as Oman, where fertile soil and water are severely limited."

Such continued growth is unsustainable (according to www.islamicpopulation.com there were 1.6 billion Muslims in 2007 so we are part of this) and an increasing interest is now being given to the topic. For example, the *Islamic Declaration on Sustainable Development*, presented at the first Islamic Conference of Environment Ministers held in Jeddah (Saudi Arabia) in June 2002, and issued in due time for the Earth Summit (the unofficial name of the United Nations Conference on Environment and Development, UNCED) which was held later that year in Johannesburg (South-Africa), mentions that one of the major constraints to sustainable development (article 5) is "[o]verpopulation, particularly in cities of developing countries and the deterioration of living conditions in shanty towns and an increase in the demand for resources, health and social services."

A last, but important, note on this topic is to note that a child born in the US has an eco-footprint ten times that of a child born in for example Yemen or Indonesia and a child born in the UK will put ten times more pressure on world resources than an Afghan or Bangladeshi child, so though countries can have local reasons to alleviate the burden on the environment, there are also global ones.

Conclusion

"When the Earth is shaken with a violent shaking, and the Earth throws out her burdens, and man says: 'What has befallen her?' - on that Day she shall tell her story!" (Al-Zilzalah/ The Earthquake [99] 1-4)

As observed by the Global Ethics and Religion Forum (http://gerforum.org), a closer look at the current environmental crisis reveals an underlying problem: the broken relationship of the majority of human beings (including Muslims), with the natural world. Technological solutions to protect the environment are part of the answer to the problems facing us, but cannot in themselves be sufficient. The deeper problem it seems is that the majority of humans have lost their sense of the sacredness of nature and their understanding of the interdependence of natural and human flourishing. The bad news is thus that we have lost the connection. Thus A. Karim Ahmed (Director of International Programmes and Secretary-Treasurer, National Council for Science and the Environment, USA) titled his contribution to the Forum *Nature out of balance: ecosystem degradation, poverty and human health*. A film on this, called *Sacred Planet* was due to come out in 2009 (not to be confused with a film of same name from 2004, though also worth watching)

The good news is that it is something that lies within our power to change, which this book hopes to convey and contribute to by sharing teachings, reminders and practical ideas on how to achieve a more sustainable future and, God willing, please God. Because we need to remember that ultimately, none of the five major aims (*maqasid*) of the Shariah (protection of religion, life, mind/ intellect, offspring and property) can be sustained if the world's environment – God's Creation - does not allow for survival. But though no-one can go back and make a brand new start, anyone can start from now and make a brand new end.

So, as Parvez Manzoor, a Swedish-based Muslim writer and thinker, in a review of *Touch of Midas* asks: "[c]an we...check this threat to our planet simply by introducing stricter legislation against pollution, industrial waste and nuclear spill? Can we reverse the degradation of our environment by adopting conservationist policies on both national and international levels? Or could it be that the whole ecological imbalance betokens the spiritual and teleological crisis of modern civilization itself? Does it require fundamental revision of our own way of life, our cherished goals, indeed our very conception of ourselves and the world?"

The Good News

"O mankind! There has come to you a direction from your Lord and a healing for the (diseases) in your hearts, - and for those who believe, a guidance and a Mercy." (Yunus/ Jonah [10] 57)

The best news is, the Quran and the *sunnah* give us all the guidance we might need, very nicely I believe summarised in the Prophet ﷺ saying "Live in this world as if you were going to live forever; prepare for the next world as if you were going to die tomorrow." Would we not immediately change our ways if we would live to experience more of the consequences of our actions? And as Imran narrated: I said, "O God's Messenger! Why should a doer (people) try to do good deeds?' The Prophet ﷺ said, "Everybody will find easy to do such deeds as will lead him to his destined place for which he has been created."

According to Yusuf Al-Qaradawi "[i]t is quite striking to the fair researchers how the Qur'an and *Sunnah* cared about the environment". At numerous occasions the role of the *ummah* in conservation is emphasised, for example in Indonesia in June 2005 in 'Formulating the Role of Islamic *Ummat* in Environmental and Nature Conservation', which starts with "We recognize that Islamic *ummat* are required to comprehend the importance of conserving and protecting nature, and to apply these principles in everyday life." This is especially so at these times because the Prophet ﷺ said "He who holds firm to my *sunnah* when corruption is rampant in my *ummah* will attain the reward of a hundred martyrs."

Farooq Hassan (President, Pakistan Ecology Council) says of the verse Yunus/ Jonas [10] 14 ('Then We made you heirs in the land after them, to see how you would behave!'): "I feel that this verse of the Qur'an may be said to be the simplest Magna Carta of the genesis of a law of environmental protection in Islam." His compatriot, Parvez Hassan (former Chairman of the Commission on Environmental Law of IUCN, the World Conservation Union), highlights a more elaborate and current version and states about the Earth Charter (launched in 2000): "By integrating ecological concerns with mankind's historic quest for social justice, democracy, and peace, it creates a successful environmental ethic which will resonate well beyond the constituency of environmental activists."

And Kemal Dervis, (Administrator, United Nations Development Programme, UNDP), had grounds for optimism while handing out a prize on the occasion of World Environment Day 2007: "Biodiversity is an essential resource not only in responding to climate change, but also in reducing poverty. Environments that are richly diverse in plant and animal life provide communities with a range of options with which to sustain livelihoods, while sensitive and highly biodiverse ecosystems, such as forests, bogs, and coral reefs, contain massive carbon reservoirs that contribute to regulating the global climate. Today in Berlin we honour the winners of this year's Equator Prize which recognises and rewards local communities for their work in helping to reduce poverty through the sound management of biodiversity."

For a practical holistic solution for the here and now, there are calls for some kind of green New Deal. 75 years after US President Roosevelt launched a New Deal to rescue the US from financial crisis, the UN Environment Programme launched the Green Economy Initiative (GEI, www.unep.org/greeneconomy). In the UK a group of experts in finance, energy and the environment have come together to propose a *Green New Deal* as a response to the credit crunch and wider energy and food crises, and to the lack of comprehensive, joined-up action from politicians. The aim is to "rekindle a vital sense of purpose, restoring public trust and refocusing the use of capital on public priorities and sustainability, thus also help deliver a wide range of social benefits that can greatly improve quality of life in the future". For more information, check: www.greennewdealgroup.org

Combating Climate change

"And how many populations We destroyed, which exulted in their life (of ease and plenty)! now those habitations of theirs, after them, are deserted,- All but a (miserable) few! and We are their heirs!" (Al-Qasas/ The Story [28] 58)

According to the Stern Report (headed by the former Chief Economist and Senior Vice-President of the World Bank Nicholas Stern): "If the science is wrong and we invest one per cent of GDP in reducing emissions for a few decades, then the main outcome is that we will have more technologies with real value for energy security, other types of risk and other types of pollution. However, if we do not invest the one per cent and the science is right, then it is likely to be impossible to undo the severe damages that will follow. The argument that we should focus investment on other things, such as human capital, to increase growth and make the world more resilient to climate change, is not convincing because of these irreversibilities and the scale and nature of the impact."

Combating climate change is not only a necessity for this world, but also due to God's call as the Quran quote above reminds us (see also: "How many populations that insolently opposed the Command of their Lord and of His messengers, did We not then call to account, - to severe account? - and We imposed on them an exemplary punishment" (At-Talaq/ Divorce [65] 8)). Though there is obviously much to do, it is good to hear that awareness is increasing and becoming more 'mainstream', for example *500 Experts to Participate in Environment Meet in Bahrain* (Bahrain's Society for Engineers in partnership with several Saudi environmental organisations held a three-day environment conference and exhibition in Manama in April 2007) and more and more countries have a Minister for the Environment (and though for example Saudi Arabia's rules on environmental responsibility sound good), the competent minister is also Minister of Defence and Aviation....

According to the UK Climate Impacts Programme (UKCIP) "[t]he climate change we expect in the next 30-40 years will be due to our past greenhouse gas emissions. Climate change later this century will be determined by the emissions we allow now." The United Nations Framework Convention on Climate Change (UNFCCC, http://unfccc.int) was adopted in 1992 by nations to set an overall framework for intergovernmental efforts to tackle the challenges posed by climate change; with an objective "to achieve stabilisation of greenhouse gas concentrations in the atmosphere at a low enough level to prevent dangerous anthropogenic interference with the climate system". There are currently 191 parties to the UNFCCC. As of January 2009, 183 countries (including China and India, but not the US) and one regional economic organisation (the EEC) have deposited instruments of ratification, accession, approval or acceptance regarding the Kyoto Protocol.

And according to the WWF "the technologies and sustainable energy resources known or available today are sufficient to meet this challenge, and there is still sufficient time to build up and deploy them, but only if the necessary decisions are made in the next five years." It is not about denying ourselves, but living differently, and quite likely, more happily. The European Happy Planet Index researched by the New Economics Foundation reveals that Europe is heading in the wrong direction, its carbon footprint still growing, and its level of carbon efficiency in terms of fuelling happy, long lives - lower than at any level in the last 40 years. This may sound like bad news, but it means that 'tightening the carbon belt' is not the big doom scenario of having to 'revert to the cave'. On the contrary, it will make us happy (according to the research: the unhappier the country, the larger the footprint; happier the country, the smaller the footprint). And the small country of

Bhutan has long known this: most western countries are driven by GNP (gross national product) indicators, and this translates to people being driven to make more money. We have been fed a lie – that more money is better; if we have more money we will be happy. Instead of GNP or gross domestic product (GDP), the King of Bhutan developed, more than 30 years ago, a more meaningful indicator of the country's wellbeing, Gross National Happiness (GNH) indicator. It is rooted in the Buddhist idea that the ultimate purpose of life is inner happiness. Bhutan places happiness at the very centre of development and public policy. GNH is an attempt to define quality of life in a more holistic and psychological terms than Gross National Product. More recently a regular conference is organised by the Gross National Happiness Movement (http://gnh-movement.org) is organised where in the November 2007 conference, Muhammad Shahbaz and Naveed Aamir spoke on happiness of the poor in Pakistan.

International Panel on Climate Change (IPCC) research shows that both bottom-up and top-down studies indicate that there is substantial economic potential for the mitigation of global GHG emissions over the coming decades, that could offset the projected growth of global emissions or reduce emissions below current levels. It also shows that changes in lifestyle and behaviour patterns can contribute to climate change, that mitigation across all sectors is necessary and management practices can also have a positive role. While studies use different methodologies, in all analysed world regions near-term health co-benefits from reduced air pollution as a result of actions to reduce greenhouse gas emissions can be substantial and may offset a substantial fraction of mitigation costs

In its latest scientific review (published in November 2007), the Intergovernmental Panel on Climate Change (IPCC) estimates that mitigating climate change could cost up to 3 per cent of global GDP if we act promptly. While this a huge figure, it is still less than the estimated 5-20 per cent of GDP cost if we do not do anything, according to the Stern Review Report on the Economics of Climate Change. Another good news is that countries in colder climates, like the UK and some parts of the US for example, have no need to have high CO_2 levels: much colder Sweden has per person CO_2 emissions of 5.9 metric tons compared with the British 9.4; Iceland has a 7.6 compared to Luxembourg's 22. Nor is a higher per person CO_2 necessary for development: rich Switzerland has per person emissions of 5.6; and where Qatar has 63.1, Hong Kong has 5.5.

The Centre for Alternative Technology (CAT) in July 2007 released *Zerocarbonbritain*, a blueprint for Britain to reduce its carbon emissions to zero by 2027 (www.zerocarbonbritain.com). According to Paul Allen, CAT Development Director and co-author, "zerocarbonbritain is scientifically necessary, socially possible and technically achievable - we must now make it politically thinkable." Using only existing and proven technologies, zerocarbonbritain integrates solutions to the intimately connected issues of climate change, energy security and global equity.

The implementation of only a dozen policies, as suggested by the International Energy Agency (IEA, an autonomous body within the framework of the Organisation for Economic Co-operation and Development, OECD) to implement an international energy programme), for its Alternative Policy Scenario (as opposed to Reference Scenario, continuing along current route) would result in nearly 40 per cent of avoided CO_2 emissions by 2030. And in aggregate, the new policies and measures analysed yield financial savings that far exceed the initial extra investment cost for consumers. The main obstacle the IEA sees is that "it will take considerable political will to push these policies through". But as we elect politicians and we make consumers choices, we can make it happen.

Abd-Allah ibn Masud رضى الله عنه reported that the Messenger of God ﷺ said: "Beware of sins that are seen as insignificant, for they will keep accumulating until they destroy a man." The Messenger of God ﷺ explained this by comparing them to people who stop to camp in the wilderness and decide to build a fire, so one man goes out and brings back a stick, and another man brings a stick, until they have gathered enough, then they light a fire and cook whatever they throw onto it.

Abu Al Faraj Ibn al-Jawzi (died 1201 CE) wrote in his *The Hunt of Thought* (*Sayd al-Khatir*): "Many people are too easy-going in matters which they think are not serious but which in fact destroy the bases of faith [...]", which comes to mind when, as the Stern Review mentions: "climate change threatens the basic elements of life for people around the world - access to water, food production, health, and use of land and the environment." We need to combat climate change as much as we can to support achieving the aims (*maqasid*) of Sharia (protection of life, dignity, offspring, religion and property) and these require a living planet so as the Prophet ﷺ said: "Adhere to my Sunnah." Because of the increase in climate related disasters, aid agencies have now joined environmental groups in a coalition called *Stop Climate Chaos*, www.stopclimatechaos.org.

Jafar Ibn Awn said: "there are three things which I love for myself and my brothers: this *Sunnah*, that they should learn about it and ask about it; the Quran, that they should seek to understand it and ask about it; and that they should leave people alone unless it is for a good reason." Green is the colour of Islamic civilisation, so too the dome of Prophet's ﷺ tomb is green. These are not mere coincidence; they should be seen as reflecting the importance Islam gives to greenery, nature, and trees.

The German Federal Environment Ministry has presented a long term sustainability model, which shows that renewable energy could contribute up to 58 per cent of national primary energy by 2050, supported by significantly improved energy productivity (3-5 per cent per year). Additionally the European Renewable Energy Council (EREC, www.erec-renewables.org) recently broke down the growth rates of renewable energy sources up to 2040, by decade, to show a possible 47 per cent penetration of renewables into global energy supply by 2040 under an *Advanced International Policies* (AIP) scenario. Beginning in the early 1990s, when Germany had almost no renewable energy industries and few actual applications, the German Government adopted policies intended to dramatically reduce the emission of greenhouse gases. One part of that policy was to develop renewable energy resources on a fast track. The result has been that, in just a little over 10 years, Germany leads the world in wind energy, with 14,612 MW installed by the end of 2003, and ranks second in the world in terms of photo-voltaic (PV) capacity, with 417 MWp installed by the same date. The latter is all the more remarkable given that average solar insolation in Germany is only about 50 per cent of that in the world's sunnier locations.

Doing some of the above and/ or more, combating climate change will require investments. However, let us remember that not doing something is quite likely more expensive. The Australian government's chief climate change adviser, Ross Garnaut, concluded in a report ordered by the Australian prime minister, Kevin Rudd, in July 2008 that if no action were taken, climate change would cut 4.8 per cent of gross domestic product, more than AS$400 billion (£194 billion), by the end of the century for his country alone. For the UK, the Stern review mentions that the cost of necessary action will cost some 1 per cent of GDP, but costs of extreme weather alone could reach 0.5–1 per cent of world GDP per annum by the middle of the century, and will keep rising if the world continues to warm. Uncertainty, it mentions, is an argument for a more, not less, demanding goal, because of the size of the adverse climate change impacts in the worst-case scenarios.

Post-Oil: Renewable energy and Permaculture

"To the righteous (when) it is said, "What is it that your Lord has revealed?" they say, "All that is good." To those who do good, there is good in this world, and the Home of

the Hereafter is even better and excellent indeed is the Home of the righteous." (An-Nahl/ The Bee[16] 30)

With the cost of a barrel of oil going from $63 in December 2006 to $147 in July 2008 (after having hovered around $20 per barrel – in 2007 prices – for much of the time since the 1870s CE), going for alternatives to oil are not just a must for the planet, but also makes financial sense (even if oil has, for now, come down somewhat again).

According to Prince Hassan bin Talal of Jordan (Chairman of the Governing Board of the Arab Thought Forum): "More than 40 years ago the Apollo Space Programme was launched to fulfil the old dream of taking man into outer space. Today, we have a bigger dream, to restore balance between man and his home planet, Earth. With the political will, EUMENA [European Union, Middle East and North African] countries could now launch an Apollo-like EUMENA DESERTEC Programme [deserts of the earth receive about 700 times more energy a day from the sun than humankind consumes by burning fossil fuels. Deserts are the places with the best solar radiation conditions and with the least possible impact of collector deployment onto the biosphere on earth, more information check CSP, or: www.concentratingsolarpower.info], to bring humankind back into balance with its environment, by putting deserts and technology into service for energy, water and climate security. This would be an important step towards creating a truly sustainable civilization." And do not think this is 'untreaded territory': a first such solar system was set up in Egypt in 1914, but as Tony Juniper (former Director, Friends of the Earth UK, 1997-2008), states: "the reason it is not flourishing already is because you can't make weapons of mass destruction as a by-product, or make billions out of mining rare ores as an essential feedstock". Also, if the projected annual growth rate of CSP through 2012 is maintained to 2020, according to the Earth Policy Institute, global installed CSP capacity will exceed 200,000 megawatts - equivalent to 135 coal-fired power plants.

A report published in June 2008 concludes that, with changed policies, the number of UK homes producing their own clean energy could multiply to one million (about one in every three) within 12 years, thus producing enough power to replace five large nuclear power stations, at about the same time as the first of the much-pushed new generation of nuclear reactors is likely to come on stream (energy independence? how would the uranium from Kazachstan etc make it to the UK? And even the International Atomic Energy Agency and the optimistic Organisation for Economic Cooperation and Development put the total world uranium reserves at 4.7m tonnes, with primary uranium production is falling. If the figures are roughly correct, the total of known uranium resources is expected to be exhausted by 2030). Most positively for Creation, by 2030, such 'micro-generation' would save the same amount of emissions of CO_2 as taking all Britain's lorries and buses off the road. I say less futuristic as in 2007, Germany put up 130,000 solar photovoltaic panels, which produce electricity, on homes, while Britain only managed 270.

And instead of eating food grown at the other side of the world imported out of season (remembering "eat of their fruit in their season", Al-Anam/ Livestock [6] 141), with much pesticides etc, we could go for 'permaculture' as a new *Dig for Victory* (as announced by the British Ministry of Agriculture one month after the outbreak of the Second World War where households "were encouraged to transform their private gardens into mini-allotments"). Presented by Australians Bill Mollison and David Holmgren during the 1970s as a combination of permanent agriculture as well as permanent culture, I am not sure they are Muslim, but the concept surely does: permaculture is an approach to designing human settlements, in particular the development of perennial agricultural systems, that mimics the structure and interrelationship found in natural ecologies.

Permaculture design principles extend from the position that, as Mollison put it "[t]he only ethical decision is to take responsibility for our own existence and that of our children". The intent was that, by rapidly training individuals in a core set of design principles, those individuals could become designers of their own environments and able to build increasingly self-sufficient human settlements - ones that reduce society's reliance on industrial systems of production and distribution that Mollison identified as fundamentally and systematically destroying the earth's ecosystems. While originating as an agro-ecological design theory, permaculture has developed a large international following of individuals who have received training through intensive two week long 'permaculture design courses'. This 'permaculture community' continues to expand on the original teachings, integrating a range of alternative cultural ideas, through a network of training, publications, permaculture gardens, and internet forums. In this way permaculture has become both a design system as well as a loosely defined philosophy or lifestyle ethic which I believe is in line with Islam (a key introductory book on permaculture even refers to Islam; for more useful information on this: www.permaculture.co.uk).

A Transition Initiative is a community that is unleashing its own latent collective genius to look peak oil and climate change squarely in the eye and to discover and implement ways to address this big question: "for all those aspects of life that this community needs in order to sustain itself and thrive, how do we significantly increase resilience (to mitigate the effects of Peak Oil) and drastically reduce carbon emissions (to mitigate the effects of Climate Change)?" The resulting coordinated range of projects across all these areas of life leads to a collectively designed energy descent pathway. The community also recognises two crucial points: that we used immense amounts of creativity, ingenuity and adaptability on the way up the energy upslope, and that there's no reason for us not to do the same on the downslope; and if we collectively plan and act early enough there is every likelihood that we can create a way of living that's significantly more connected, more vibrant and more in touch with our environment than the oil-addicted treadmill that we find ourselves on today.

Sustainable Natural Resource Use
"He created the earth for all creatures." (Al-Rahman/ The Beneficent [55] 10)

According to Asma Hassan and Zeinoul Abedien Cajee (both active in the National Awqaf Foundation, South Africa) in a *Message from Johannesburg 2002*:

"Sustainable development should not be a new concept to Muslims. […] The Qur'an and the *Sunnah* of our beloved Prophet Muhammad ﷺ provide the framework for the spiritual and physical well being of humanity. There are over 500 verses in the Qur'an giving us guidance on matters relating to the environment and how to deal with it. In addition, there are numerous examples from the Prophet's life and his sayings, which provide a model for justice and equity. Sadly, most of us are not aware of this rich legacy of environmental consciousness and socio-economic justice in Islam and how these relate to contemporary issues."

From a very useful two part series on *Companions of the Prophet* ﷺ by AbdulWahid Hamid, I noticed how often the author used the word 'simple' to describe the (in most cases) chosen lifestyles of the companions of the Prophet ﷺ. I learned for example that companion Abu Darda, after converting, abandoned his luxurious lifestyle, ate only what was sufficient to keep him upright and wore clothes that were simple and sufficient to cover his body; companion Abdurrahman ibn Awf ﷺ at times could not eat from fear that his reward had been bestowed on him early (in this life, while he of course preferred to be rewarded in the hereafter). I learned that companion Ubbay ibn Kab ﷺ lived simply and did not allow the world to corrupt or deceive him: "he had a good grasp of reality and knew that however a person lived and whatever comforts and luxuries he enjoyed, these would all fade away and he would have only his good deeds to his credit." That Umar ibn Abdal-Aziz ﷺ during his time as Caliph was very scrupulous about the type of persons he appointed as governors, always concerned that they "should live simply and frugally and not acquire much wealth even though this was through lawful means." Adiy ibn Hatim converted to Islam after noting the simplicity of the Prophet's ﷺ lifestyle. Said ibn Amir "lived the unique and exemplary life of the believer who has purchased the Hereafter with this world. He sought the pleasure and blessings of God above selfish desires and material comforts." Abu Dharr رضي الله عنه, a companion much liked by the Prophet ﷺ, "persisted in his simple and frugal life to the end". When I was reading about them, one of the things that struck me was: without all the pills and medical interventions we now have at our disposal to prolong our lives, several companions and historical great teachers lived to a ripe old age: Abdal Qadir Al-Jilani lived to the age of ninety, Abu Hurayrah رضي الله عنه (Companion Abdur-Rahman known under his nickname meaning 'father of the kitten'. He was called so because of a small cat that he used to feed and care for and carry with him everywhere he went) lived to 78. Is that because or in spite of living simply? My hunch it is due to the former.

Regularly when discussing reduction of consumption, the discussion (on the radio, in the newspaper, in real life etc), often quickly descends into a black and white world where there are just two options: you stay on society's bandwagon and consume whatever you fancy, the alternative is 'going back to the cave age'. However, as Bryce Gilroy-Scott states in *Handbook for Change* (www.handbookforchange.org): "reducing the amount of energy or water we use, doesn't necessarily mean a reduction in the standard of living - it means using our common sense, consuming responsibly, thinking about our actions and putting back into the earth what we take out." Let us here remember that standard of living (material wealth) is not the same as quality of life (how happy one is), and that one can therefore lessen one's material wealth while maintaining or increasing quality of life (and many have already done it). One American organisation calls this living consciously *The New American Dream* (www.newdream.org) and their magazine is even called *In Balance* (*mizan* in Islam).

The United Nations University says the main barrier to expanding isolated successes at combating desertification is "the lack of effective management policies". According to Zafar Adeel, lead author of the report, "reforming policies to combat desertification also represent one of the most expedient ways to sequester more atmospheric carbon and help address the climate change issue." For the protection of the land, forests and wildlife, the Prophet ﷺ created inviolable zones known as *hima* and *haram*. In these zones the natural resources were to be left untouched (thus avoiding desertification).

Also, sustainable resource use will support global peace. As Mohamed Sahnoun (Member, Earth Charter's International Council and former Special Adviser to the UN's Secretary General) on the Horn of Africa region states: "I am often a witness in my work of the linkage between the degradation of the environment and the spread of violent conflicts. We tend to underestimate the impact of degradation of the environment on human security everywhere. Repeated droughts, land erosion, desertification, and deforestation brought about by climate change and natural disasters compel large groups to move from one area to another, which, in turn, increases pressure on scarce resources, and provokes strong reaction from local populations. It is the issue of insecurity brought about by the prospect of exclusion from resources, or the perceived threat of starvation, that ignite most violent conflicts. This feeling of insecurity is often brought about by degradation of the environment".

Population control

"God charges no soul except to its capacity". (Al-Baqarah/ The Cow [2] 286)

Within the Muslim community, a common concern is that family planning is deemed to be a western ideology which aims to limit the size of the Muslim population. In reality, family planning as such is neither a conspiracy from the West nor foreign to Islam. Like the other two Abrahamic religions (Judaism and Christianity), Islam values the family and encourages procreation. Some Muslims have concluded from these facts that Islam does not permit family planning. Two pieces of evidence are often cited in support of this conclusion. First, that the Quran prohibited Muslims from killing their children for fear of want (Al-Isra/ The Night Journey [17] 31, Al-Anaam/ Livestock [6] 151), second, that the Prophet ﷺ exhorted Muslims to multiply. But this argument does not do justice to the complexity of the Islamic position and the totality of its teachings. Otherwise, it would be impossible to explain the established fact that the Prophet ﷺ knew that some of his companions, including his cousin Ali, practiced *al-azl* (*coitus interruptus*) and yet he did not prohibit the practice.

Muslim physicians in the medieval period conducted in depth investigations into the medical dimension of birth control, which were unparalleled in European medicine until the 19th century. Indeed, Abdullah Ibn Sina (Avicenna, 980-1037 CE) in his *Qanun* lists 20 birth control substances and physician Abu Bakr Muhammad ibn Zakariya al-Razi (865–925 CE) in his *Hawi* lists 176 birth control substances. The permissibility of contraceptive practice in Islamic history at the level of both theory and practice is abundantly evident in both its medical and legal legacies.

Islam is a religion of mercy and does not decree anything that is beyond the capacity of humankind. Fertility can be controlled for birth spacing purposes; if it compromises the quality of life of the mother or the child, or the ability of the parents to raise their children. For example, Mahmoud Shaltout (former Grand Imam of Al-Azhar, Egypt) in 1959 endorsed the use of contraception for health, social and economic reasons: "Planning in this sense is not incompatible with nature, and is not disagreeable to national conscience, and is not forbidden by Sharia'a, if not prescribed by it".

Many religious scholars and Muslim authors have supported this argument., including Abul Kalam Azad (Chairman, Masjid Council for Community Advancement [MACCA], Bangladesh). In his book published in 1992, Abdel Rahim Omran argues that: "if excessive fertility leads to proven health risks to the mother and children, and/ or if it leads to economic hardship or embarrassment for the father, or if it results in the inability of parents to raise their children according to religious traditions, and educate them socially, then Muslims would be allowed to regulate their fertility in such a way that these hardships are warded off or reduced." From *hadeeths*, the four schools of thought agreed that *coitus interruptus* is permissible, provided that the wife authorises the husband to do so. This is in accordance with the following saying of the Prophet ﷺ as narrated by Abu Huraira رضي الله عنه : "*al-azl* is not allowed without the consent of the wife". The wife has this authority because of her right of enjoyment and to have children. Omran also states: "the population in the Muslim world is growing at a rate that is not matched by economic and service development. Due to these realities [...] Muslim countries have been forced to acquire debt, import food and rely on foreign aid to cope with the needs of growing populations. The result is a vicious cycle of poverty, ill health, illiteracy, overpopulation and unemployment being compounded with social frustration, extremism and social unrest."

The four main schools of thoughts in Islam accept that any scientific means of contraception, such as the pill, condoms, injections, and intra-uterine devices, that aim to achieve the same result as *azl* is acceptable. Finally, it is important to mention that *azl* or other methods of contraception mentioned here cannot interfere with God's creation. If God wants to create a soul, nothing can stop it. In 1964, the rector of Al Azhar University in Cairo issued a *fatwa* on the acceptability of family planning, noting that "greater numbers were only required in ancient days so that Islam would survive" (in 2007 there were some 1.6 billion Muslims – 1 in 4 on the planet - so Islam is not really at risk at the moment).

An International Congress on Islam and Population Policy took place in Aceh (Indonesia) in February 1990. The *Aceh Declaration*, which contained the main conclusions of the Congress, included an emphasis on responsibility that the present generation owes to the future generations since the lifestyle and decisions of the former impact the quality of life of future generations. Similar messages were issued in the *Islamabad Declaration on Population and Development* adopted by the International Ulama Conference on Population and Development held in Islamabad, Pakistan in 2005 and the *Sanur-Bali Declaration* of the International Conference of Muslim Leaders to Support Population and Development to Achieve the MDGs in February 2007. This is what inspired Pakistan, the sixth most populous country in the world and the second most populous country with a Muslim majority, to mark World Population Day 2007 with a pledge to reduce the population growth rate to 1.3 percent by 2020.

Conclusion

"The worshipers of the Most Gracious are those who tread the earth gently, and when the ignorant speak to them, they only utter peace." (Al-Furqan/ The Criterion [25] 63)

After the will of God, all solutions are in *our* hands. And we have all the examples we need, all the opportunities to act. Or as Ibrahim Osman (Deputy Secretary General, International Federation of the Red Cross and Red Crescent Societies [IFRC]) puts it: "[w]ithin the Red Cross/ Red Crescent we believe in the power of humanity. We believe that billions of innocent actions that contribute to climate change can be changed in billions of small and bigger encouraging solutions to reverse the trend of climate change that threatens the lives of so many of us, our children and grand children."

So is being Muslim enough? Muawiya narrated: "I heard the Prophet ﷺ saying, 'A group of people amongst my followers will remain obedient to God's orders and they will not be harmed by anyone who will not help them or who will oppose them, until God's Order (the Last Day) comes upon them while they are still on the right path.'" As Goethe (1749 – 1832 CE) said: "To think is easy. To act is difficult. To act as one thinks is the most difficult of all." Some people say: 'why do something about climate change/ deforestation, I cannot make a difference' Well, why then give to charity (could your contribution solve poverty?), do any non-environment related good deed? We have duty of guardianship *khilafah*, so taking care of Creation is part of our faith. And taking care of Creation is not the same as worshipping it.

The problem is encapsulated in the language used to describe the natural world. To say nature provides human beings with 'services' is to delude ourselves that our relationship of complete dependence on the natural world is a transaction we enter into. Yet it is the absolute basis of our dependence that means we have to think of the natural world not as 'free', but as a public good that cannot be bought and sold. Until that acknowledgement is placed at the heart of our initiatives, attempts to take into account natural costs will merely create more markets and lead to further inequity and degradation.

The ultimate objective of Islamic law is the universal common good of all created beings, encompassing both our immediate welfare in the present and our ultimate welfare in the hereafter. This objective of the universal common good is a distinctive characteristic of Islamic law. It means that no species or generation may be excluded from consideration in the course of planning and administration, but that each individual Muslim as well as the Muslim community must honestly strive toward the welfare of the whole. The responsibility for right action thus lies with the individual who will be judged on the Day of Judgment for what (s)he did with his/ her life, regardless of what the governing authorities with their various administrative and municipal agencies and courts of law required of him/ her. Therefore the protection, conservation, and development of the environment and natural resources is a mandatory religious duty to which every Muslim should be committed. This commitment emanates from the individual's responsibility before God to protect himself and his community.

Religious awareness and guidance in this field is necessary so that each individual may take part in the protection and development of the environment and natural resources. Much environmental degradation is due to people's ignorance of what their Creator requires of them. People should be made to realise that the conservation of the environment is a religious duty demanded by God. God has said, " And seek by means of what God has given you the future abode, and do not neglect your portion of this world, and do good (to others) as God has done good to you, and do not seek to make mischief in the land, surely God does not love the mischief-makers." (Al-Qasas/ The Story [28] 77) "Eat and drink, but waste not by excess; verily God loves not the excessive." (Al-Araf/ The Heights [7] 31); according to Ibrahim Ozdemir "the eating and drinking in this verse refer to utilising the resources necessary for the continuation of our lives.") "And follow not the bidding of those who are extravagant, who make mischief in the land, and mend not (their ways)." (Ash-Shuara/ The Poets [26] 151- 152) "And do not cause corruption in the earth, when it has been set in order." (Al-Araf/ The Heights [7] 56). Any deliberate damage to the natural environment and resources is a kind of corruption which is forbidden by Islam. It is indeed a kind of despicable foolishness which every Muslim should shun, and which every ruler and every individual should prohibit, especially if it leads to or results in general damage. God has said, "and from among you there should be a party who invite to good and enjoin what is right and forbid the wrong, and these it is that shall be successful" (Al-Imran/ Imran [3] 104).

Religious awareness and Islamic guidance should employ all possible means at all levels to call all individuals to commit themselves to Islamic ethics, morals, and manners in dealing with nature, the environment, and the natural resources for their sustainable use and development. According to Abubakr Ahmed Bagader (author, *Environmental protection in Islam*), "[a]ll individuals should be reminded of the following religious obligations:

1. No wastage or over-consumption of natural resources [between 1996-97 and 2005-06 household waste generated per person in the UK increased by 9 per cent. In 2005-06, this was equivalent to each person generating an average of 512 kilograms, or just over half a tonne, of waste. Most of this waste

goes to landfill, a method that makes little use of waste and produces greenhouse gases, mainly carbon dioxide and methane];

2. No unlawful obstruction or destruction of any component of the natural resources;
3. No damage, abuse, soiling or distortion of the natural environment in any way;"

Sustainable development of the earth, its resources, elements, and phenomena through the enhancement of natural resources, the protection and conservation of them and of all existing forms of life, bringing new life to the land through its reclamation, and the rehabilitation and purification of the soil, air, and water.

What appeals to me as a Muslim is the personal accountability. It is not about what others did or did not do, but what you did (or not): "Unto us shall be accounted our deeds and unto you your deeds. We cannot take part in what you are doing. However our hope is that you should remain in peace and well being; but after seeing and knowing what you all are doing, we cannot join a group of ignorant people" (Al-Qasas/ The Story [28] 55). And the accountability is according to our abilities ("some ranked above others", Al-Anam/ Livestock [6] 165), as some have had more opportunities than others to achieve things, for example a president or a day labourer. Instead of waiting until we are judged, Yusuf Al-Qaradawi suggests that: "At the end of every year, a careful trader applies the brakes in order to measure his performance over the past year, and establish his financial position at the end of it. He wants to know his profit or loss, and his assets and liabilities; i.e. his claims and the claims against him. An intelligent, sensible

71

person ought to do likewise, in respect of his life. More than that, he should beseech Allah to bless his life, make his day better than yesterday, and his tomorrow better than today." This will hopefully prevent the situation as portrayed in the film *The Age of Stupid*, where an archivist in the devastated world of 2055 looking at old footage from 2008 asks: "We could have saved ourselves, but we didn't. It's amazing. What state of mind were we in, to face extinction and simply shrug it off?" I pray our time will not be referred to as Age of Stupid, but that we will follow what the Earth Charter (a declaration of fundamental ethical principles for building a just, sustainable and peaceful global society in the 21st century, the product of a decade-long, worldwide, cross cultural dialogue on common goals and shared values) suggests: "Let ours be a time remembered for the awakening of a new reverence for life, the firm resolve to achieve sustainability, the quickening of the struggle for justice and peace, and the joyful celebration of life."

And we can all do what is in our capacity, as Ibn Umar صلى الله عليه وسلم reported: I heard the Messenger of God ﷺ say: Everyone of you is a ruler and everyone of you shall be questioned about those under his rule; the king is a ruler and he shall be questioned about his subjects; and the man is a ruler in his family and he shall be questioned about those under his care; and the woman is a ruler in the house of her husband, and she shall be questioned about those under her care; and the servant is a ruler so far as the property of his master is concerned, and he shall be questioned about that which is entrusted to him."

Muhammad ﷺ used to ponder the meaning of the Quran to the greatest extent. Ibn Hibbaan said: "Ubayd-Allah ibn Umayr and I met Aisha ﵂ and Ubayd-Allah ibn Umayr said: 'Tell us of the most wonderful thing you saw on the part of the Messenger of God.' She wept and said, 'He got up one night (to pray) and said, "O Aisha, leave me to worship my Lord." I said, "By God, I love to be near you, and I love what makes you happy." He got up, purified himself and stood up to pray, and he kept weeping until his lap got wet, then he wept and kept weeping until the ground got wet. Bilaal came to call the *adhaan* [call to prayer] for him, and when he saw him weeping, he said, "O Messenger of God, are you weeping when God has forgiven all of your sins, past and future?" He said, "Should I not be a thankful slave? This night some verses have been revealed to me, woe to the one who reads them and does not think (about their meaning). Among them is: Verily! In the creation of the heavens and the earth, and in the alternation of night and day, there are indeed signs for people of understanding, those who remember God (always, and in prayers) standing, sitting, and lying down on their sides, and think deeply about the creation of the heavens and the earth..." (Al-Imran/ Family of Imran [3] 190-191).'"

Do not wait until tomorrow, or as Ibn Sinna (Avicenna, 980-1037 CE) put it: "I prefer a short life with width to a narrow one with length". Also, do not just care for the environment because environmentalists warn us about disastrous consequences (as Hasan Gai Eaton suggests "that should be the least of our worries") but because, as Mohammad Ali Shomali (Associate Professor of Philosophy and Head of the Department of Religious

73

Studies, Imam Khomeini Education and Research Institute, Iran) states "in Islam the environment is sacred and has an intrinsic value. Even if there is no threat or shortage, we must still look after natural resources, protect animals and plants and, more generally, improve and develop the environment. As the vicegerent of God, we have to channel the mercy of God to everything within our reach." Doing otherwise, as Mohammad Shomali states "[t]o misuse divine blessings or harm them, for example by destroying jungles and polluting water, are signs of ungratefulness which is severely condemned in Islam."

Lastly, "most of us believe that the only way we can change our lives is through tedious work and drastic measures-retraining ourselves, breaking habits, divorcing ourselves from others, changing jobs or even moving to a new area. But in *Change Your Thoughts-Change Your Life*, Wayne [Dyer] shows us that it is simply a matter of changing the way we think." Though I have not read this book, I do wholeheartedly, and from personal experience, agree with the quote that changing your life is only a thought away (I found it in my e-mail inbox in a newsletter on more holistic wellbeing). Let's get started. So, as the World Muslim Leaders at their Summit under the theme *Islam and a future world of peace* (December 2001, in Jakarta, Indonesia) concluded: "We pledge to be courageous defenders of peaceful teachings and interpretation of Islam and to be exemplary peacemakers in our personal, family, and social conduct of our lives. May *Allah* bless this effort and forgive our shortcomings." Peace with humanity, peace with Creation. Ameen.

PART 1: BELIEFS (*AQAAID*)

Introduction

"It is not righteousness that you turn your faces towards East or West; but it is righteousness to believe in God and the Last Day and the Angels, and the Book, and the Messengers; to spend of your substance, out of love for Him, for your kin, for orphans for the needy, for the wayfarer, for those who ask; and for the freeing of captives; to be steadfast in prayers, and practice regular charity; to fulfil the contracts which you made; and to be firm and patient in pain (or suffering) and adversity and throughout all periods of panic. Such are the people of truth, the God-conscious." (Al-Baqarah/ The Cow [2] verse 177)

Muhammad Marmaduke Pickthall (1875-1936 CE), on the occasion of *Eid* in 1919 stated in his *khutba* (sermon) in Woking (UK): "[…] do not think of that submission as the end of spiritual life. It is not an end at all, it is a state of being, and a very active state of being in obedience to the law of God". As Abdullah Omar Naseef (former Secretary General, Muslim World League) stated: "[O]nly when we submit to the Will of *Allah* can we find peace: peace within us as individuals, peace between man and man, and peace between man and nature. When we submit to the Will of *Allah*, we become aware of the sublime fact that all our powers, potentials, skills and knowledge are granted to us by *Allah*. We are His servants and when we are conscious of that, when we realise that all our achievements derive from the Mercy of *Allah*, and when we return proper thanks and respect and worship to *Allah* for our nature and creation, then we become free. Our freedom is that of being sensible, aware, responsible trustees of Allah's [God's] gifts and bounty."

Key beliefs in Islam are *tawheed*, or faith in the unity of God and of His creation, God being the undisputed supreme being; *taqwa*, the attitude of reverence, care and carefulness; that is, each person, whether man, woman, or child, each organism, no matter how insignificant is created for a purpose, and therefore none must be wantonly treated, and no life must be taken except for right; *rahma* and *ihsan*, compassion and beneficial works; and most relevant in this case, *khilafa*, or stewardship, guardianship. I will now look into each of these in more detail.

Oneness, Divine Unity (tawheed)
"And those who live in awe for fear of their Lord; And those who believe in the Signs of their Lord, And those who join not anyone [in worship] as partners with their Lord; And those who give that which they give [i.e. charity] with their hearts full of fear [whether their charity has been accepted or not], because they are sure to return to their Lord" (Al-Muminun/ The Believers [23] 57-60)

According to Ibrahim Ozdemir (Professor, Divinity School of Ankara University, Turkey) the concept of Divine unity is the basis and essence of Islam. Divine unity is apparent in the unity of humanity and of nature. God's vicegerents on the earth, the holders of His trust (us) are therefore primarily responsible for preserving the unity of creatures, the integral wholeness of the world, the flora and fauna, and wildlife and natural environment. This should not be a chore, but a privilege, remembering a poem attributed to Rabia Al-Adawiyya al-Basri (717– 801 CE) which opens

76

and closes with: "O God, Whenever I listen to the voice of anything You have [...] I hear it saying: "God is One! Nothing can be compared with God!" and the reminder of the Prophet ﷺ: "He who cuts a lote-tree (without justification), God will send him to Hellfire." (the lote-tree grows in the desert and it is very much needed in an area which has scarce vegetation). According to Yusuf Al-Qaradawi this *hadeeth* provides us with the most vivid illustration in terms of protecting the natural resources and preserving the balance that exists between the diverse elements of nature in the environment.

Some may be neglecting nature (from stamp-size garden to national park) because of the *hadeeth* as related by Aisha رضي الله عنها (Prophet's ﷺ wife): "if you displease God by pleasing the Creation, then God will be displeased with you and will make the Creation also displeased with you and if you please God by displeasing the Creation, then God will be pleased with you and will also make the Creation pleased with you." I understand, however, from my research that 'if you displease God by pleasing the Creation' refers to obeying somebody who commands you towards sin, which would result in you disobeying God (for example, obeying your husband when he tells you not to pray); this is not the same as taking care of Creation to please God (it is a means, not an end).

Unfortunately we are chopping down trees everywhere like there is no tomorrow. According to the *Global Canopy Programme*, an alliance of 29 scientific institutions in 19 countries active in understanding interactions between forests and the atmosphere in relation to climate change, the total natural forest cover that is left in the South-East Asian countries of Malaysia, Indonesia and Papua New Guinea (some 136 million hectares) is predicted to be converted into agricultural land, forest plantation and other non-forested uses before 2050. Deforestation is largely caused by billion dollar agribusiness expansion driven by western demands for cheap palm oil (found in 1 in 10 household products in supermarkets; 75 per cent of world supply comes from Indonesia and Malaysia), beef and soya (40 per cent of Brazil's beef exports are to Europe; soya is mainly to feed our farm-fed animals, not the vegans). 80-90 per cent of timber extraction is illegal under the existing laws of Brazil and Indonesia and Britain is the largest importer of illegal timber (for example in the form of Quran holders, garden furniture) in the EU. By buying it (perhaps thinking 'well, this tree was felled already, better make use of it') note you are exerting demand and thus new resources will be used to replenish the shop stocks. Fortunately there are some positive developments, like Aceh Governor Irwandi Yusuf announcing in June 2007 a total moratorium on logging in Aceh's forests for a period of 15 years, even if he was forced to do this when in 2006 deforestation hit a high of 374,327 hectares.

The key principle underlying the eco-ethic of Islam is the oneness and unity of God, or *tawheed*. According to S. Parvez Manzoor in an article in 2005, this principle is the *sine qua non* of the Islamic faith: it asserts that God is the absolute source of all values, and also the Owner and Originator of the entire Universe of which humankind is a part. Fazlun Khalid (Founder Director, IFEES) calls the *tawheed* principle the "bedrock of the holistic approach in

Islam as this affirms the interconnectedness of the natural order".

As the Quran reminds us, humans are but one of the 'communities' on earth (Al-Anam/ Livestock [6] 38: "All the creatures on earth, and all the birds that fly with wings, are communities (just) like you. We did not leave anything out of this book. To their Lord, all these creatures will be summoned."). Humans are encouraged to share the earth under the term of '*i'mar*'. Generally this term is given the translation of 'to inhabit'. However, it is important to understand the wider meaning of this word. According to Mustafa Abu-Sway (Associate Professor and Director of the Islamic Research Centre, Al Quds University, Jerusalem), in a lecture given at the Belfast Mosque in February 1998 on Islamic jurisprudence on the environment, the Quran shows that any attempt to achieve *i'mar* and prosperity away from divine revelation and guidance will certainly lead to destruction, quoting "Do they not travel through the earth; and see what was the end of those before them? In strength they tilled the soil and populated it in greater numbers than these have done: there came to them their apostles with Clear (Signs), (which they rejected, to their own destruction): it was not God who wronged them, but they wronged their own souls." (The Romans/ Ar-Rum [30] 9) The *i'mar* of the earth should thus be in areas and projects that could benefit humanity and not harm it. This means that projects and activities that destroy the environment are excluded from permissible human enterprise.

Ismail Al-Madani (Director-General, Bahrain's Environmental Protection and Ecology Department) said it was "proven beyond doubt that there was a direct link between negligence of the environment and several diseases increasingly found in human beings". He urges the need to adopt effective policies to fight pollution at the ground level instead of looking for temporary solutions after irreparable harm has been done. So back to *tawheed*: according to Taqi ad-Din Ahmad Ibn Taymiyyah (1263–1328 CE) "The perfection of *tawheed* is found when there remains nothing in the heart except God, the servant is left loving those He loves and what He loves, hating those He hates and what He hates, showing allegiance to those He has allegiance to, showing enmity to those He shows enmity towards, ordering what He orders and prohibiting what He prohibits."

Though we all seem to understand and appreciate unity (*tawheed*), how often do we stop and think, as Fazlun Khalid, Founder Director of the Islamic Foundation for Ecology and Environmental Sciences (IFEES), suggests: "where the hell are we going?" The reason he urges us to ponder on this question as "[m]ost of us are not even aware that there is a question of this nature to be asked. We enjoy the ride goaded on by the selfish short-termism of our share prices, bank balances, property values, insurance policies and life spans. Incidentally, as we become accustomed to increasing our national economies for ever and ever, nobody has noticed that Planet Earth has remained the same size for much of its life span and will continue to remain the same during the time allocated to our species on it and way beyond."

According to the Prophet ﷺ: "The example of the person abiding by God's order and restrictions in comparison to those who violate them is like the example of those persons who drew lots for their seats in a boat. Some of them got seats in the upper part, and the others in the lower. When the latter needed water, they had to go up to bring water (and that troubled the others), so they said, 'Let us make a hole in our share of the ship (and get water) saving those who are above us from troubling them. So, if the people in the upper part left the others do what they had suggested, all the people of the ship would be destroyed, but if they prevented them, both parties would be safe." Do we not draw lots on where we happen to be born? How will God respond when we do not help those with a more challenging lot to aim for what we have instead of us sharing our wealth?

Examples of action

1. Take a few minutes to stop and contemplate God's amazing Creation. As Zaid Shakir (imam) says: "[s]pirituality is very important and should be an active part of our lives, our children's lives and an active part of our educational curriculum. The heart is then more sensitive to the Creator and that enhances our attainment of education, awareness of social justice, ecological and environmental issues. By being sensitive to the Creator, we are more sensitive to the creation. Spirituality gives us an awareness of those things that guard our relationship with the Divine and that leads to a propensity to safeguard our relationship with other people and our environment." Reflect on what the options are if we do not share God's bounties equitable with the rest of Creation; we cannot say "Brother, Can You Spare Me a Planet?" (the title of an interesting

article by Robert Nadeau in *Scientific American* in March 2008). Zaid Shakir would often go into the woods, even alone and just wander and lose himself, sit down and reflect.

2. Anas ﷺ and Abdullah Ibn Masud ﷺ reported that the Prophet ﷺ said: "All creatures are the family of God. The most beloved to God, amongst His creatures, is the one who is good to His family (that is, creatures)" And according to Ahmad Ar-Raissouni (Professor of Islamic studies, Mohammed V University, Morocco) on the Quranic chapter *The Bee* (Al-Nahl): "Allah mentions the beauty of those animals, and does not reduce their worth to the food and the transportation with which they provide us." Love God, love His Creation and measure your eco-footprint (to check how justly you are sharing Creation with other species, including fellow humans). A simple one is offered for free by the World Wildlife Fund: http://footprint.wwf.org.uk or check the UK Government one: http://actonco2.direct.gov.uk.

3. Yunus Emre's, 13th century Turkish poet, reminds us: "We love all creatures for the sake of their Creator!" and more recently repeated by Iajuddin Ahmed (President, People's Republic of Bangladesh, a country challenged significantly by adverse environmental challenges) in February 2008: "Love all the creations on the earth and let them grow naturally. I advise not to harm insects, birds, animals for their natural living. Let us work unitedly for making a friendly and habitable environment for the birds and animals on the earth."

4. Saleem H. Ali, concludes in an article entitled *Indonesia's green madrassas*: "Rather than harping on the divisive rhetoric of tribe, sect and political persuasion, we have a theological and teleological imperative to "green our society." Or, with reference to the *hadeeth* above of the boat with the two decks, as Shahid Athar put it during the Earth Day Summit in the US in 2005: "Friends! We are in this boat of environmental mess together. Unless we all do something to save our earth, we will have same fate." With neighbours, local community, set up an organic allotment. According to the UN Food and Agriculture Organisation (FAO) "typically, organic agriculture uses 30-50 per cent less energy in production than comparable non-organic agriculture." It does require about a third more human labour, but this will allow to feel an integral part of Creation, God willing. Moha Mohamed achieved this in Kibera slum of Nairobi (Kenya), where a group of young local men now sell their produce to other locals.

5. Taqi ad-Din Ahmad Ibn Taymiyah (1263–1328 CE) said: "The perfection of *tawhid* is found when there remains nothing in the heart except [the remembrance of] God, the servant is left loving those He loves and what He loves, hating those He hates and what He hates, showing allegiance to those He has allegiance to, showing enmity to those He shows enmity towards, ordering what He orders and prohibiting what He prohibits." The Islamic contribution to the *Assisi Declaration* (1986) includes: "His trustees are responsible for maintaining the unity of his creation: the

integrity of the earth, its flora, and fauna, its wildlife and its natural environment. Unity cannot be had by discord, by setting one need against another or letting one end predominate over another; it is maintained by balance and harmony." How much do you love Creation for His sake and hate polluters? How do you show this? A useful source for community solutions on especially food, housing and transport is: www.communitysolution.org.

God-consciousness (taqwa)

"And we have not created the heavens and the earth and what is therein purposelessly - that is the view of those who reject [God] or who are ungrateful" (As-Saaffat [37] 27; Al-Imran [3] 191)

Having God consciousness allows a person to be constantly aware of both God's omnipresence and attributes and a reminder of their relationship and responsibility to God as his creation and servant. The scholars explain that the way to God consciousness is through obedience of God, avoiding disobedience, and striving to stay away from doubtful matters (Islam itself is translated as "submission"). Put simply, God consciousness is awareness of God's presence as one moves through life.

According to Andrew M. Watson the inhabitants of the early Islamic world were, to a degree that is difficult for us to comprehend, enchanted by greenery. This love of plants is clearly shown in a genre of poetry, the *rawdiya* or garden poem, probably of Persian origin, which came to be one of the main poetic forms in the Abbasid era from the eighth to the tenth century. In the garden poem, the author exclaimed at the coolness of the shade, the heaviness of the perfume, the music of the running water, the lushness of the foliage and so forth - in short at all the features of the artificially contrived environment which contrasted so strongly with the arid natural world. And according to M.W. Dols it was not only the rich who had large and lavish botanical gardens but also the poor with their small gardens and terraces, gardens were a distinctive cultural trait of Islamic society.

On the authority of Ubayy Ibn Kaab it is reported that God's Messenger ﷺ said: "Do not malign the wind; if you see that which displeases you, say: "Oh, God! We ask of You the good of this wind and the good that it is commanded to bring with it; and we seek refuge with You from the evil of this wind and the evil that it is commanded to bring with it." Because Islam has ordered us to be of good character and good manners, the Messenger of God ﷺ forbade the Muslims from maligning or cursing the wind; this is because the wind is one of God's creations: It does not blow or remain still, or harm or benefit except by God's command therefore vilifying it amounts to vilifying God Who sent it. Then God's Messenger ﷺ informs us that the wind may bear good or ill and that it is incumbent upon the believer to ask God for the good and to seek protection with God from the evil.

Wildlife and natural resources are protected under Shariah by zoning around areas called *hima*. In such places, industrial development, habitation and extensive grazing are not allowed. The Prophet ﷺ himself, followed by the Caliphs of Islam, established such *hima* zones as public property or common lands managed and protected by public authority for conservation of natural resources. In current day UK similar such areas are referred to 'greenbelt areas'.

I enjoyed reading Akhtaruddin Ahmad's plea in his book *Islam and the environmental crisis* (published in 1997): "The followers of all religions especially the Muslims must stop looking at themselves as if they were football club supporters, and must see themselves as worshippers of *Allah* who follow prophets". I am not sure whether that is what Ahmad was referring to, but personally it reminds me of when I was attending school in Argentina. According to my memory we would do sports (have physical education, or PE) every school day except when the weather was too bad (fortunately we always did sports outside in the fresh air). In the latter case, it seemed we always got to the watch a film of the series *Herbie* (the talking car) or the 1978 football world cup final, a match of The Netherlands versus Argentina, and the latter won (1-3). In my memory, for weeks afterwards I (with my two younger sisters the only Dutch in school) would be told "we won from you" and I would think 'we've never played against each other' (we were classmates), so what are they doing claiming credit for deeds they have not done?' (well, in those days I may have thought this in different words, but with similar gist). Actually, Ahmad does explain what he means (I paraphrase): we should stop looking at our small differences, educate ourselves on environmental issues and put the teachings we adhere to into practice in the here and now ourselves instead of only referring to Islam as sacred relic of the past.

God-consciousness and curiosity to explore God's Creation, used to be so common. For example, Abu Uthman al-Basri, known as Al-Jahiz (781 - 868 or 869 CE) wrote an encyclopaedic *Book of Animals* in which he pondered on such topics as effects of the environment on the likelihood of an animal to survive and food chains. Eighty-seven folios of the *Book of Animals* (about one-tenth of the original text) are preserved in the Ambrosiana Library in Milan (Italy). This collection (a copy of the original) dates from the 14th century and bears the name of the last owner, Abd al-Rahman al-Maghribi. Fortunately Khalifa Ezzat did recently state in a Friday sermon at London Central Mosque: "*[t]aqwa* is not a passive idea. It is not merely a feeling or an emotion. *Taqwa* is an active concept. It is about action, doing good and positive actions in preparation for the hereafter."

Examples of action

6. Make the most of your outdoor space, whether it is stamp size or acres large because as we learn from a *hadeeth* if a Muslim plants a tree, that part of its produce consumed by people will be as almsgiving for him. Any fruit stolen from the tree will also be as almsgiving for him. That which the birds eat will also be as almsgiving for him. Any of its produce which people may eat thus diminishing it, will be as almsgiving for the person who planted it. Don't have time? Then remember Massoumeh Ebtekar's (Former Vice-President of Iran, UN Champion of the Earth 2006) conclusion at the International Symposium *The Arctic: The Mirror of Life* organised by Ecumenical Patriarch Bartholomew, also known as the *Green Pope*:

"How can those who lack inner peace and spiritual prudence guide the ship of humanity through these troubled waters, to find and follow the eternal light that knows no ebb?" We still have the same 24 hours our forefathers had.

7. Ali said, "The Prophet ﷺ, was in a funeral procession and he picked up something and began to scratch the ground with it. He said, 'There is none of you who does not have his seat written either in the Fire or in the Garden.' They said, "Messenger of God, then should we not rely on what is written for us and abandon action?" "Act," he said, "Everything is easy if you were created for it." He added, "As for someone who is one of the people of happiness, it is easy for him to perform the actions of happiness. As for someone who is one of the people of wretchedness, it is easy for him to perform the actions of wretchedness." Then he recited, "As for him who gives out and has God consciousness and confirms the Good' (Al-Lail/ The Night [92] 5-10)

8. As a 'green Muslim' from *Green Muslims in the District* ("a network of Muslims in the District of Columbia [and surrounding areas] working proactively to help our communities understand and implement sustainable and eco-conscious ways of living while relating it to our deen [faith], and a holistic world-view.") mentioned on their blog "Upon discovering the truth behind our food, we must not only choose between what food production practices we indirectly support, but more importantly how they consequently contribute or detract from the wholeness of our own being. While deeming things *halal* or *haram* is an exercise in Islamic

jurisprudence set aside for those most qualified, figuring out what we decide is acceptable or unacceptable for ourselves is a practice of personal *taqwa* or God consciousness."

9. Seyyed Hossein Nasr (1933- CE) in his book *Science and Civilization in Islam* and other works, notes there was a marked difference between Islamic science, in which the pursuit of understanding nature was seen as a sacred undertaking, a way of better knowing the mind of God, and the de-sacralised scientific approach of the post-Enlightenment West in which nature is seen as mechanical, devoid of life or inherent meaning, and existing only to serve human ends. Which way do you see nature? Is that obvious in your behaviour? Do you share Creation equitably? Check your 'eco-footprint' at: www.myfootprint.org

10. In an article in *Radiance Weekly*, Rida Islam concludes: "[a]s humans, we have clearly betrayed the Divine trust which has been given to us along with a rational soul capable of seeing in advance the consequences of our actions and hence capable of acting accordingly and being responsible for them before God. Hence the "rite of atonement for the sin of excess" begins not with sorting out the garbage about us but the garbage within us." Be conscious of your duty to God and 'recycle your soul'.

Mercy (rahma) and to do beautiful things (ihsan)
"We sent you [oh Muhammad] not but as a mercy for all creatures." (Al-Anbiya/ The Prophets [21] 107)

According to Muhammad al-Mahdi, "Islam is not just about prayer, fasting and zakat – these are mercies that Allah has given human beings so that we do not forget Him and our true role as Khalifah of Allah, and so that we do not to forget to keep our hearts cleansed and our souls pure. Allah knows how forgetful we can be." According to American Umar Faruq Abd-Allah Wymann– Landgraf (1948– CE) "[t]he imperative to be merciful - to bring benefit to the world and avert harm - must underlie a Muslim's understanding of reality and attitude toward society. Islam was not intended to create a chosen people, fostering exclusive claims for themselves, while looking down upon the rest of humanity like a sea of untouchables or regarding the animate and inanimate worlds around them as fields readied for wanton exploitation. Wherever Muslims find themselves, they are called upon to be actively and positively engaged as vanguards of mercy, welfare, and well-being."

Similarly, when a man hurts any animal without just cause, he is denying one of the aspects God has ordained mankind should act on, which is mercy. When a man denies an animal (or vegetation) its right to mercy, then the right to mercy the man has from God is similarly withdrawn (see the case of the woman destined to hell-fire for not feeding a cat or letting it feed itself), and he will be punished. Furthermore, if a person intentionally performs a mercy to an animal, vegetation (or person), then God will reward him out of His mercy (see the case of the prostitute who was promised paradise after helping an animal survive). Such was the Prophet's ﷺ concern for animals that Martin Lings, a modern biographer of the Prophet ﷺ, quotes thus: "During the march on one of these days (the expedition to conquer Mecca) the Prophet saw a bitch lying by the side of the road with a litter of recently born pups which she was feeding, and he (the Prophet ﷺ) was afraid that she might be molested by one or another of the men. So he told Juayl of Damrah (a disciple) to stand on guard beside her until every contingent had passed."

Some people have understood the *hadeeth* "O Abu Umayr! What did the Nughair (a kind of bird) do?" to prove that it is acceptable for children to play with birds or to keep them in cages so they enjoy looking at them. Scholar Al-Maghrabi Al-Malki, Abu Ali Ibn Rahal clarified this issue saying: "The claim that it is acceptable to put a bird in a cage is true providing that it will not be exposed to any kind of torture, starvation or thirst even if one may neglect it through forgetfulness or by putting another bird that might stick its bill into its head as cocks in cages do to one another until they kill one another. By consensus, torturing animals is forbidden. It is to one's advantage to put the bird in a cage alone to prevent harm that may touch it, or if need be, by putting a partition between them. Moreover one should care about the bird by feeding it just as one feeds one's children! Place a perch (like a wooden perch) in the cage so it is not exposed to the cold ground. These instructions do not need verses from the Qur'an or hadiths to uphold as they are obvious. We have seen people that torture chickens in cages in different ways [see under food]. [..] The merciless only care about keeping the animal alive or if it loses weight. The merciless have no consideration for its spiritual torture. All this is forbidden and one wilt be punished for it in this life and in the Hereafter unless Allah forgives him." He continued: "This is a serious matter of recompense and punishment. It is just like the overloading of beasts of burden with weights beyond their capacity under the pretext of its being customary. All of this reflects the fact that mercy has been plucked from their hearts." Adhering to the regulations concerning taking care of animals should thus not only stem from the jurisdictions of governments, but the conscientiousness of individuals which should not allow negligence or disobedience.

Sayyid Qutb (1906– 1966 CE) mentions that "God does not ask man to suppress his desires because God knows that it is not possible for him to do so. God simply asks man to control his desires and not let them control him." And to have an idea what 'controlling our desires' means plus how seriously 'need' should be interpreted when considering taking from nature, we can learn from the first Caliph, Abu Bakr As-Sidiq رَضِيَ اللهُ عَنْهُ , when he ordered his troops: "Do not cut down a tree, do not abuse a river, do not harm animals and be always kind and humane to God's creation, even to your enemies."

When thinking of doing good things, I remember reading about 'peace parks' (more formal name is transfrontier conservation area or TFCA). A Peace Parks Foundation was established in 1997 by the now late Prince Bernhard of the Netherlands (Founder and first President of Worldwide Fund for Nature, WWF), Nelson Mandela and the now late Anton Rupert (then President of WWF South Africa, then called the Southern African Nature Foundation). According to their website "Peace parks epitomise harmony between humans and nature by using resources to create prosperity. When this happens, peace usually prevails, as economic stability is a cornerstone of peace. Furthermore, the joint management of natural resources entails the protection of these resources, which, in turn, creates job opportunities for the people living in these areas. The joint management committees also strengthen good neighbourliness." There are now seven Peace Parks in Southern Africa and more in the pipeline, God willing. In September 2007, MIT press published a book called *Peace Parks: Conservation and Conflict Resolution*, edited by Saleem H. Ali (Associate Professor of Environmental Studies at the University of Vermont's Rubenstein School of Natural Resources, USA). The book examines the ways in which environmental cooperation in multi-country conservation areas may help resolve political and territorial conflicts. Its analyses and case studies of transboundary peace parks focus on how the sharing of physical space and management responsibilities can build and sustain peace among countries.

According to Akhtaruddin Ahmad (author, *Islam and the Environmental Crisis*) the "perilous state of the environment is just one more indication of our remoteness from our Lord and our disobedience of his Messenger ﷺ" Taking care of Creation is not the same as worshipping it, but a means to show gratitude to our Creator. Doing beautiful things and showing mercy is good, no matter what the situation is: Abu Bakr رضي الله عنه, the first Caliph of Islam, even when having to send his army to Syria, warned the leader of the exhibition, Usamah bin Zaid, "do not injure the palm trees nor burn them with fire and do not cut fruit-bearing trees." A recent positive example in the area of mercy and doing beautiful things, in November 2008 representatives of several faiths agreed *The Uppsala*

Interfaith Climate Manifesto 2008, Faith traditions addressing Global Warming which includes the commitment: "As religious leaders and teachers, we want to counteract a culture of fear with a culture of hope. We want to face the climate challenge with defiant optimism to highlight the core principles of all major sacred traditions of the world: justice, solidarity and compassion. We want to encourage the best science and political leadership. We commit our communities to fostering a spirit of joy and hope in relation to the greatest gift given to us all - the gift of life!" Muslim signatories include Larbi Djeradi (Professor, University of Mostaganem, Algeria, and member of Inter-faith Action for Peace in Africa and Djanatu-al-Arif Mediterranean Foundation of Sustainable Development); Amina al-Jerrahi (President, Commission on International Relations of the Inter-religious Council, Mexico); M. Abdus Sabur (Secretary General, Asian Muslim Action Network, based in Bangkok, Thailand); Mawil Izzie Dien (Senior Lecturer in Islamic Studies, University of Wales, Lampeter, UK and collaborating with the Alliance of Religions and Conservation (ARC) to create a Centre for Islam and Ecology at the University).

Examples of action

11. The Prophet 🕌, as narrated by Abdallah bin Amr, said: "The Merciful is kind to those who are merciful. If you show compassion to your fellow creatures in this world, then those in heaven shall be compassionate toward you." Have mercy even on the small creatures: Anas ibn Malik reported that a man cursed fleas in the presence of the Prophet 🕌, and the Prophet 🕌, said, "Do not curse them. A flea woke up one of the

94

Prophets for the prayer." So, as the Prophet ﷺ said: "If you want to be loved by your Creator, love His creatures" Dedicate a session of your circle (*halaqa*) to mercy and doing good things for Creation.

12. Abu Hurayra said, "A fierce wind blew when the people were on the road to Makka while Umar was making hajj. Umar asked those around him, 'What is the wind?' They did not give any answer. I urged my camel forward and I caught up with him and said, 'I have heard that you asked about the wind. I heard the Messenger of God ﷺ, say, "The wind is from the spirit of God. It brings mercy and it brings punishment. Do not curse it. Ask God for the good of it and seek refuge from its evil." Read about the potential of wind as renewable energy source (World Wind Energy Association, www.wwindea.org) and write to your political representatives to support it more (www.writetothem.com).

13. Worship God as if you see Him, as in Gabriel's (Arabic: *Jibreel*) *hadeeth* when he said to the Messenger ﷺ: "*Ihsan* is that you worship God as if you see Him and while you see Him not yet truly He sees you". As Fazlun Khalid says: "[t]he earth then is a testing ground of the human species. The tests are a measure of our acts of worship (*ihsan*) in its broadest sense. That is living in a way that is pleasing to Allah [God], striving in everything we do to maintain the harmony of our inner and outer environments." Do like Zahid Rafiq and Rashid Hamid, who initiated *Cycle Relief* (www.cyclerelief.com) which was set-up by a group of

volunteers to organise sponsored cycle runs in an effort to raise money for a variety of humanitarian causes, including water.

14. Rev. R. Bosworth Smith stated in 1874 CE that Prophet Muhammad ﷺ was the real upholder of the liberation of animals "nor does Muhammad omit to lay stress on what I venture to think is a crucial test of a moral code, and even of a religion, as is the treatment of the poor and the weak - I mean the duties we owe to what we call the lower animals. There is no religion which has taken a higher view in its authoritative documents of animal life and none wherein the precept has been so much honoured by its practical observance." – can we still say that that is wholly true today? And can you do something to share correct knowledge of Islamic teachings, for example by contributing to internet forums or in *dawah* activities?

15. Amr ibn al-As, a Companion of the Prophet ﷺ, once said: "It doesn't take a judicious mind to tell the good from the bad, but it takes such a mind to tell what is good from what is better, and likewise to tell what is bad from what is worse." According to Salman al-Oadah of www.islamtoday.com: "One thing this entails is how we should apply our productive energies. For instance, there are many issues that we would like to address. We should give priority to the major issues that society's welfare depends upon and put aside secondary matters that can only squander our energies and bring about pointless disputes." Omar Faruk from London (UK) for example has done so by setting up *EcoMuslim*

(www.ecomuslim.com) to "change behaviours on an individual, organisational, societal, national, regional and global level to preserve the Earth's ecosystems, natural resources, beauty and environment. We are the guardians of the natural order, protecting the environment, working to reduce our individual and collective ecological footprints. We will pioneer change, lead by example and influence an eco-responsible existence of everyone who resides on our beautiful planet Earth."

Guardianship (khilafah)

"It is He who has made you (His) caretakers inheritors of the earth: He has raised you in ranks, some above others: that He may try you in the gifts He has given you: for your Lord is quick in punishment: yet He is indeed Oft-forgiving, Most Merciful." (Al-An'am [6] 165)

Hasan Zillur Rahim (editor of IQRA, bimonthly newsletter of the South Bay Islamic Association, San Jose, California, USA) wrote in 1991: "Nature is created on the principle of balance, and as a steward of God it is the human's responsibility to ensure that his or her actions do not disrupt this balance. Stewardship does not imply superiority over other living beings: because ownership belongs to God alone, stewardship invests humans with a moral responsibility in safeguarding God's creation."

F. Kamal in the chapter on *Islam & the Environment* in *Easily Understand Islam* ponders: "What is expected of a viceroy, a trustee or ruler? If those over whom one commands power are killed without cause, have their homes polluted heedlessly with toxic wastes, and have

97

deformities and diseases resulting from the careless and wasteful disposal of carcinogens, should not the ruler be asked if he is discharging his responsibilities and trust faithfully? Unfortunately, there have been altogether too many shameful, unnecessary cases of pollution that have taken their toil on the planet, the animals, and the plants that inhabit it. One wonders if man is taking his responsibilities seriously." I agree also with the author's note at the end of the chapter: "When I have on occasion visited some Muslim majority nations it has saddened me to see a sometimes cavalier (almost to a point of carelessness) attitude towards things like pollution. I really do understand that there is a lot of poverty and lack of education in these regions, but I know there are many good people there too, who if reminded of Islamic teachings, will strive for a more healthy relationship between man and his environment."

As Seyyed Mahmood Taleqani (1910-1979 CE) writes in his book *Islam and Ownership*: "…from the Quranic text, man is neither the absolute owner not the total possessor of the earth and its resources. He does not have the right to possess as much as he desires or to obtain material wealth in any way he may choose. Indeed, the earth's wealth belongs to God and man his vicegerent and servant. Indeed, because vicegerency belongs to all people, each individual is a guardian of the public trust. And, this ownership should be limited for the public welfare."

There is a very interesting Muslim fable, dating back to the tenth century from the *Ikhwan As-Safa* (Brethren of Purity or Sincerity) regarding *The Case of the Animals versus Man Before the King of the Jinn*. The fable concerns how 70 people, representing the different faiths and colours of humankind, nearly shipwrecked, discover an island where animals ruled, and began to settle on it. However, after a while mankind started oppressing and killing the animals, who, unused to such harsh treatment, complained to the King of the Jinns. The King arranged a series of debates between the humans and various representatives of the animals, such as the nightingale, the bee, and the jackal. The animals nearly defeated the humans, but a representative of the humans ends the series by pointing out that there was one way in which humans were superior to animals and so worthy of making animals their servants: they were the only ones God had offered the chance of eternal life to. The King was convinced by this argument, and granted his judgement to them, but strongly cautioned them that the same Quran that supported them also promised them hellfire should they mistreat their animals.

Seyyed Hossein Nasr states that "to be human is to be aware of the responsibility which the state of vicegerency entails". This vicegerency or guardianship must be carried out with justice and kindness to all creation. The interpretation of khalifah as master or vicegerent, trustee or tyrant is central to the eco-ethical position of Islam. Belief in the hereafter and accountability for one's actions further impresses upon the minds and hearts of Muslims that humanity will be accountable for their actions, as well as the goods in their care. As Mr Nasr also clarifies "there is no more dangerous a creature on earth than a *khalifat Allah* [guardian of God] who no longer considers himself to be *abd Allah* [slave of God] and who therefore does not see himself as owing allegiance to a being beyond himself. Such a creature is able to possess a power of destruction which is truly Satanic in the sense that 'Satan is the ape of God'; for such a human type wields, at least for a short time, a godlike by destructive dominion over the earth because this dominion is devoid of the care which God displays towards all His creatures and bereft of that love which runs through the arteries of the universe." Abu Said Khudri reported that God's Messenger ﷺ said: "The world is sweet and green (alluring) and verily God is going to install you as vicegerent in it in order to see how you act."

Contrary to perhaps popular belief, I was very pleasantly surprised to find that a country like Iran has, after the 1979 revolution, adapted the Constitution and in which article 50 now reads: "The preservation of the environment, in which the present as well as the future generations have a right to flourishing social existence, is regarded as a public duty in the Islamic Republic. Economic and other activities that inevitably involve pollution of the environment or cause irreparable damage to it are therefore forbidden." Would it not be nice if all countries had such a rule *and* lived by it?

As a humanitarian aid worker it is very heartening to see such generosity when charities launch an appeal following floods in Asia, or drought in East Africa, even if "the region's high death toll from environmental degradation can be avoided if we are determined to reverse the current trend" according to Shigeru Omi (Western Pacific Director, UN World Health Organisation) and research shows that one dollar (or pound or rupee) invested in mitigation can save seven in disaster recovery costs.

It is impossible for any of us to look after the whole earth, so I like the idea of *Neighbourhood Nature* as put forward by the Urban Wildlife Trust (www.wildlifetrust.org.uk/urbanwt): "a community based scheme which helps local people to enhance, protect and enjoy their local environment by enriching their surroundings and encouraging wildlife." A now defunct project, but I pray any reader can revive it, either in its location or replicate it in his or her neighbourhood, is *Ashram Acres* in inner city Birmingham, UK. Ashram Acres was started in 1981 by the Sparkbrook Ashram Community House (which now houses Ashiana Community Centre). Problems in the area include infrastructure decay, poor housing, discrimination and unemployment. Ashram Acres occupied 3/4 acre of back gardens behind three Victorian terraces. There were two polytunnels, a solardome, cold frames and outhouses for two goats, for milking and dairy work, and for the farm office. Apart from a few years when the project had a paid horticulturalist, the garden has been run entirely by volunteers - a member of the Community House as the main worker - and interested locals, people referred from the Birmingham Volunteer Bureau, WWOOFers (see under holidays), workers sponsored by international organisations and schools. The Employment Preparation Unit sent clients for 3-6 month placements. Local schools visited to take saplings from the plantation set up by British Trust for Conservation Volunteers (BTCV) to plant in their school yards. Women would call to pick their own vegetables and children would come to feed the animals, collect eggs and milk the goats. A management committee of subscribers met monthly and a special membership was available for those who could not pay in cash. The garden grew organic callaloo, fenugreek, spinach, pumpkin shoots, garlic leaves and much more, and kept goats for milk and hens for eggs. Produce was sold on site and at stalls at events. Ashram Acres also held work camps of young overseas volunteers and run play schemes for children from neighbouring streets. Volunteers helped maintain gardens for pensioners and disabled people and undertook gardening projects for other organisations and centres such as places of worship. The local community used to donate left over rice and chapatis for the animals and sometimes pasture the goats in their gardens to keep their weeds down. The project provided otherwise unobtainable vegetables, the opportunity to become involved in a number of activities, learn new skills and show how people can use their own backyards to produce vegetables.

A more recent initiative is *From Concrete to Coriander* supported by CSV Environment, a group of Bengali speaking ladies who turned a derelict corner of a park into bloom, and getting fit in the process. And the Women's Environmental Network (WEN, www.wen.org.uk) run a *Taste of a Better Future Network* which supports and empowers multicultural women's groups to develop their own food growing skills, together, bringing life to inner-city plots. The project offers direct support to women's groups in the London Borough of Tower Hamlets and across East London. It also offers networking and learning opportunities for groups across the UK. They have also developed the concept of 'culture kitchen' as a model for a community event centred around a meal with ingredients that people have brought along. These events stimulate conversation about food and act as a stepping stone towards engaging with sustainability.

Another example is in Balsall Heath in Birmingham (UK). It, like many inner city neighbourhoods, appeared uncared for. There are six small parks and many little, public places. There are a host of avenues and alleyways in which people dump rubbish, and walls on which others scribble graffiti. The overall effect on the eye is unpleasant. It creates the sense that nobody cares. It encourages crime and rats and more rubbish. Twenty five years (it is a work in progress, you do not change a neighbourhood around overnight) ago thus, a few "intrepid" people initiated a *Building a Better Balsall Heath* campaign. The "leading lights" included representatives from a mosque, two churches, and a voluntary organisation. They were joined by a trade unionist and some residents. Together, they made progress in changing the image of the area, forming and representing the local voice to 'the powers that be', helping organise a mid-summer carnival, starting and contributing to a community newspaper. A more recent initiative is the set up of a *Green Team*. The Green Team's task is to 'own' the neighbourhood and act as if they were its 'estate gardener'. They tend overgrown gardens, create flower beds in the parks, put planters and hanging baskets on main roads and move all the grime and graffiti which has accumulated. The Green Team's base is being turned into a Social Enterprise and a Garden Centre. One of the staff acts as a modern version of a Park Keeper. Further, the staff visit the local primary schools and persuade children and adults to help them in their task, use the bins provided and recover the sense of pride and purpose. They have compiled their lessons in a *Neighbourhood Renewal DIY Tool Kit*. To find more about their achievements and be inspired for your neighbourhood: www.balsallheathforum.org.uk. On Green Teams, Groundwork USA has an interesting Intergenerational Green Team programme (www.groundworkusa.net).

According to Ziauddin Sardar "[t]he ultimate consequence of man's acceptance of trusteeship is the arbitration of his conduct by divine judgment. To be a Muslim is to accept and practice the injunctions of the *Shariah*. Thus the *Shariah* is both a consequence of one's acceptance of *Tauhid* and it is a path." So to finish with Muhammad al-Mahdi's words, author of *On being Khalifah of Allah*: "although on the Day of Judgment we are to be judged on our deeds, but we are specifically to be judged on our deeds as *Khalifah of Allah*. And the actual judgment is made on how well we have carried out our role as *Allah's Khalifah*".

Examples of action

16. The Prophet ﷺ said: "Take the initiative to do deeds, before trials come like a piece of a dark night (unexpectedly).": apply guardianship of Creation in your own garden, check *Garden for Wildlife* (US, www.nwf.org/gardenforwildlife) or the RSPB's A to Z of a wildlife garden (UK, www.rspb.org.uk/wildlife/wildlifegarden). As Muhammad Al-Mahdi suggests: "Teach your children about their role as *Khalifah of Allah*. Do this in a way that lets them feel in their hearts how this is the most exciting, glorious honour that they could ever receive. At least several times every day find different positive

ways to remind your children that they are *Khalifah of Allah*."

17. What are you guardian over? From Umar ﷜ who said that God's Messenger ﷺ said: "Each of you is a guardian and is responsible for those whom he is in charge of. So the ruler is a guardian and is responsible for his subjects; a man is the guardian of his family and is responsible for those under his care; a woman is a guardian of her husband's home and is responsible for those under her care; a servant is the guardian of his master's wealth and is responsible for that which he is entrusted with; and a man is the guardian of his father's wealth and is responsible fore what is under his care. So each one of you is a guardian and is responsible for what he is entrusted with."

18. Take inspiration from the *Clean Medina* campaign: it intends to, as initiator Ayman Ahwal puts it, "prompt a self generating and self sustained movement to clean up the dirty, *haram* horrible inner city areas of Birmingham [UK] all which happen to be predominantly Muslim areas. At present every one blames every one else for the swirling rubbish. The council blames the people and the people blame the council. The 'Clean Medina' campaign is a spontaneous people's 'Just do it!' effort. The film of the campaign intends to pull the triggers of people- motivation which hopefully will make the campaign self sustaining. Shift the Muslim mindset from houseproud to streetproud. Bash the trash! Our Medina will be cleaner! *Allah Akbar* [God is Great]!" For a toolkit on how to go about it, see for example

Sustainable Production in Active Neighbourhoods (www.spanpartnership.org.uk) or get a *Community Garden Starter Pack* from the Federation of City Farms and Community Gardens (www.farmgarden.org.uk; motto: 'plant a seed, grow a community'); in the US there is the American Community Gardening Association (www.communitygarden.org), which organises two-day training on 'growing communities'. With climate change in mind, why not give a glance at 'Plants for a Future' (www.pfaf.org). This should also save some good cash in years to come: since the 1960s the amount of litter dropped annually in the UK has shot up by 500 per cent and via our local taxes we are now left to foot a bill of an estimated £500 million a year to clean it up.

19. Set up a green team to green your mosque or community centre grounds and follow the example of Mohammed Fahim (Chairman and head Imam, mosque and community centre, South Woodford, London, UK) in December 2007: "We are the first mosque in the country to be carbon free and we are trying to be pioneers. We are going to ensure that we promote environmentally friendly things so people will start to recycle more and not be wasteful. And people at the mosque will have to start to think about how to be carbon free in their lives as well." For a very useful step-by-step guide on how to set you're your team, check *A Guide to Developing a 'Green Team' in Your Faith Community* as developed by *Faith & the Common Good*, www.faith-commongood.net/gss/greenteamguide.asp.

20. Launch the Green Team on *Clean Up the World* weekend, the third weekend of September (www.cleanuptheworld.org). *Clean Up the World* is a community based environmental programme that "inspires and empowers individuals and communities from every corner of the globe to clean up, fix up and conserve their environment". And to get really inspired: this now global initiative, where in 2007 some 35 million people participated in 120 countries, started just seventeen years ago when "an 'average Australian bloke' had a simple idea to make a difference in his own backyard - Sydney Harbour."

21. Yusuf al-Qasim (www.islamtoday.com) states: "It should be as clear as day to us that the irresponsible conversion of farmland for biofuel production, which is causing food shortages and soaring food prices, is inhumane. It is a case of neglecting basic human needs on a global scale. Allah has subjected the Earth and its material wealth to our service. This is a trust. We should, therefore, not let the most basic needs of Earth's people be sacrificed to crass material interests." Check www.biofuelwatch.org.uk to see what you can do to stop biofuels.

22. According to V.A. Mohamad Ashrof in an article on IslamOnline (www.islamonline.net) states: "to be a slave of one's desires is actually worse than being a beast (Al-Furqan 25:43–44). No animal will overstep the limits set by God. Every animal eats what God has fixed for it; it performs only those functions that are allotted to it. A man who worships his own passions,

impulses, and desires is the most hopeless steward."
Reflect on what kind of a steward you are.

Day of Judgment

"You squandered your good things in the life of the world and sought comfort therein. Now this day you are rewarded with the doom of ignominy because you were disdainful in the land without a right, and because you used to transgress" (Al-Ahqaf/ The Dunes [26] 20)

The ones who behave as in the quote from the Quran above are addressed as 'unbelievers', so not looking after Creation as God has commanded us when appointing us Guardian I understand is a very grave matter indeed. Perhaps thus Umar ibn al-Khattab ﷺ said: "Take account of yourselves before you are called to account." And Al-Hasan said: "You will not meet a believer except he is evaluating himself." Maymoon ibn Mahraan said: "The pious person is harder on himself than a stingy partner."

Ibn Masud ﷺ stated that the Messenger of God ﷺ said, "The two feet of the son of Adam will not move from near his Lord on the day of Judgement until he is asked about five (matters) about his life - how he spent it; about his youth - how he took care of it; about his wealth - how he earned it; and where he spent it and about that which he acted upon from the knowledge he acquired." There is also a saying of the Prophet ﷺ which informs us: "The prudent one is he who takes stock of his soul and works for what comes after death, while the foolish one is he who follows his whims yet hopes in God's forgiveness."

Ibn al-Qayyim said: "Doom comes about because of neglecting to evaluate one's self and because of just following one's whims." So the Muslim must take the time to be alone and evaluate himself and check how he is doing, and what he has sent forward for the Day of Judgement, because as explained by Bediuzzaman Said Nursi (1878 – 1960 CE) said: "Man will be called to account in the hereafter for what he has done in this world. Included in this will be his treatment of the beings in the universe, animate and inanimate."

I really appreciate Tariq Ramadan's reminder in his article *Ecology and the Prophet of Islam* that "Muslim women and men, wishing to be faithful to the deepest essential teachings of Islam, should be primarily interested in the studies- and real-life experiences - which raise questions about our development and consumption models, our utilitarian relationship to nature, and our ecological carelessness." Better to read it now and use our time in this life to work on it than to ignore it and have God remind us on Day of Judgment. Because, as Zaki Jalil reminds us in an article for the reading group in Singapore on *How green is Islam*: "[t]hat the Earth will ultimately be destroyed does not diminish our responsibility as stewards of God's Creation". And "If being spiritual is doing what is pleasing to God, does that not make caring for His creation a spiritual activity?" (which will weigh on our record on Day of Judgment, God willing).

Examples of action

23. The Prophet ﷺ said: "He who takes pity (even) on a sparrow and spares its life, God will be merciful on him

on the Day of Judgement." And better to take this advice to heart as: "[i]ndeed in the Messenger of God ﷺ you have an excellent example to follow for him who hopes in (meeting with) God and the Last Day, and remembers God much." (Al-Azhab/ The Coalition [33] 21). Umar ibn al-Khattab, as Caliph, took this to heart when he said: "I swear by God! If a sheep were to stumble in Iraq, I would expect God to call me to account for it on the Day of Judgment, asking: Why did you not make the roads suitable for it, O Umar!" Support petitions to stop cruelty to animals and support indigenous communities. For a free e-mail address and starting point for petitions go to www.care2.com.

24. Why wait until Day of Judgment to plant a tree (the Prophet ﷺ said: "Even when the Day of Judgement comes upon you, if any one has a palm-shoot in hand, he should plant it.")? As Kenyan Wangari Maathai (Nobel Peace Prize winner) muses: "Every one of us can make a contribution. And quite often we are looking for the big things and forget that, wherever we are, we can make a contribution. Sometimes I tell myself, I may only be planting a tree here, but just imagine what's happening if there are billions of people out there doing something. Just imagine the power of what we can do." Since taken up by the UNEP her initiative has planted more than three billion trees (www.unep.org/billiontreecampaign).

25. Check your record for Day of Judgement as the Prophet ﷺ said: "Whoever wants to know what God has prepared for him, then he should look to what he has

prepared for God." As Abu Nadra said, "One of our men called Jabir or Jubayr said, 'I went to Umar while he was Khalif to ask for something which I needed. I reached Medina during the night and went straight to him. I am someone with intelligence and a ready tongue or he said speech (meaning eloquence). I had looked at this world and thought little of it. I had abandoned it as not being worth anything. At Umar's side there was a man with white hair and white clothes. When I had finished speaking, he said, "All that you have said is correct except for your attack on this world. Do you know what this world is? This world is that in which we reach (or he said, 'where our provision is') the Next World. It contains our actions for which we will be rewarded in the Next World." He said, "A man who knows this world better than I do worked in it." I asked, "Amir al-Muminin, who is this man at our side?" He replied, 'The master of the Muslims, Ubayy ibn Kab.'"

26. Mohamed Hyder (Chairman, Muslim Civic Education Trust) states: "The Qur'an says that humanity's role is to be *Khalifa* - the vice regent on earth for God. Our role is to protect all life and to use it thoughtfully and carefully so that on the Day of Judgement we can report back to God that we have been true and faithful *Khalifas*." What will your report contain? A good opportunity on what to look out for is to get involved with the Earth Charter (whose Preamble includes "[t]he protection of Earth's vitality, diversity, and beauty is a sacred trust."): www.earthcharter.org, now available in at least 35 languages, including Arabic and Bangla. There is also an Earth Charter Youth Initiative (ECYI) which is

convinced that "urgent action is required to bring about a just, sustainable, and peaceful world": www.earthcharterinaction.org.

Paradise (Jannah)

"(Here is) a Parable of the Garden which the righteous are promised: in it are rivers of water incorruptible; rivers of milk of which the taste never changes; rivers of wine, a joy to those who drink; and rivers of honey pure and clear. In it there are for them all kinds of fruits; and Grace from their Lord. (Can those in such Bliss) be compared to such as shall dwell for ever in the Fire, and be given, to drink, boiling water, so that it cuts up their bowels?" (Muhammad [47] 15)

According to the New Oxford American dictionary the word 'paradise' entered English from the French *paradis*, inherited from the Latin *paradisus*, which was in turn borrowed from the Greek *paradeisos* (royal garden). The root of the Greek word comes from an Eastern Old Persian word *pairidaêza*, meaning 'a walled enclosure'. *Jannah* is the Arabic word often used to refer to paradise and means 'Garden'. We all aspire to go to paradise…so what does paradise look like? Beautiful descriptions of paradise (in the Quran more often than not the word Garden is used): nice and green etc…that is what God likes…but why we do not appreciate it so much? We want to go to Paradise, we know God loves green, but it then seems so contradictory that we ruin God's Creation in this world and thus also our chances of making it to Heaven. "What is the example [i.e., description] of Paradise promised to the righteous like? It has rivers flowing under it, and its foodstuffs and cool shade never fail. That is the final fate *of those who have done their duty*. But the final fate of the disbelievers is the Fire." (Ar-Rad/ The Thunder [13] 35)

Natural beauty and greenery are among Paradise's wonderful blessings. Mansions built in gardens, right next to springs, are another beauty. Paradise, in which there is "neither burning sun nor bitter cold" (Al-Insan/ Man [76] 13), has such a pleasant climate that no one is made uncomfortable. It contains no exhausting sweaty heat or freezing cold. In Paradise, God will admit believers into "cool, refreshing shade" (An-Nisa/ Women [4] 57). The expression "refreshing shade" along with revealing that the climate will be comfortable and just as a person would want it, points out that Paradise's environment and conditions have been designed to give the human spirit true satiety and comfort. Every thing and condition in Paradise will be just as a believer desires. One of the natural beauties most mentioned by God in the Quran is that of "outpouring water" (al-Waqia/ The Inevitable [56] 31).

As we observe in this earthly life, the human spirit derives great pleasure from water, especially flowing water. Lakes, rivers, waterfalls, and streams flowing in a forest all speak to the human spirit. The sight and sound of flowing water comfort and gladden the human heart. The sight and sound of water falling from above give pleasure and are a means whereby people can give thanks to God and praise His name. Especially if the water flows in the hills, among trees and greenery or runs over stones, it is a really impressive sight. It either collects in the place where it falls, or forms pools and flows from one place to another. Continually flowing water is a sign of endless and inexhaustible plenty.

As we learn in Quran Al-Hijr [15] 45: "The heedful will be amid Gardens and Springs."

Another natural beauty is the gardens. For example, the "lush meadows of the Gardens" mentioned in chapter Ash-Shu'ara/ The Poets [26] 22 have been prepared only for believers who do good deeds. One of their particular features is the harmony of natural beauty contained therein. Within them grow a never-ending variety of plants, similar to the most delicate and sweet-smelling ones on Earth, and several species of animals, both known and unknown to us. The gardens are adorned with various fruit and other types of trees, plains of "deep viridian green" (Ar-Rahman [55] 64) plants and flowers, and, in some places, pools and fountains. Al-Waqia/ The Event [56] also mentions "fruit-laden lote-trees with thorns removed" and "[banana] trees layered [with fruit]" (verses 28-29). By reflecting upon all of these things, we can form a general view of Paradise. Some of its characteristics remind us of things in this world; others are unique blessings and beauties of Paradise that no one has ever seen or known, and that our minds cannot imagine or express. We must be aware that beautiful things and surprises are waiting for believers in Paradise, things and surprises prepared by God's infinite knowledge and beyond our imagination. As Ash-Shura/ Consultation [42] 22 tells us: "They will have whatever they wish for with their Lord. That is the great favour," everything in Paradise, including all of its natural beauties, are brought into being in accordance with a believer's own desire and pleasure. In other words, God allows a believer's imagination a role in forming Paradise's environment as a favour from Him.

In order to attain Paradise, people are tested in this earthly life. True believers show great effort and zeal in order to please God, for they turn to God sincerely, thank God continually, pray to Him, and repent of their sins. As a reward, God offers them the blessings of Paradise. Fruit is perhaps the food most often mentioned in the Quran. In Paradise, believers receive whatever type of fruit they desire. The Quran describes this: "Its shading branches will droop down over them, its ripe fruit hanging ready to be picked." (Al-Insan/ Mankind [76] verse 14) Thus, we understand that fruits of Paradise grow on trees in natural surroundings and that believers can easily pick and eat them. Al-Waqia/ The Inevitable [56] 28-29 mentions "fruit-laden lote-trees with thorns removed" and "[banana] trees layered [with fruit]," meaning that the fruit can be obtained easily due to Paradise's infinite blessings.

Muslim ibn Yasar al-Juhani said: when Umar ibn al-Khattab كَرَّمَاللّٰهُ was asked about the verse "When your Lord took their offspring from the backs of the children of Adam" - al-Qanabi recited the verse - he said: I heard the Messenger of God ﷺ say when he was questioned about it: God created Adam, then passed His right hand over his back, and brought forth from it his offspring, saying: I have these for Paradise and these will do the deeds of those who go to Paradise. He then passed His hand over his back and brought forth from it his offspring, saying: I have created these for Hell, and they will do the deeds of those who go to Hell. A man asked: What is the good of doing anything, Messenger of God? The Messenger of God ﷺ said: When God creates a servant for Paradise, He employs him in doing the deeds of those who will go to Paradise, so that his final action before death is one of the deeds of those who go to Paradise, for which He will bring him into Paradise. But when He creates a servant for Hell, He employs him in doing the deeds of those who will go to Hell, so that his final action before death is one of the deeds of those who go to Hell, for which He will bring him into Hell.

Why did I spend so many words on describing paradise? If that is where we all strive to end up, then let us practise here, as the Quran states: "Say: shall I give you glad tidings of things far better than those? *For the righteous* are Gardens in nearness to their Lord with rivers flowing beneath; Therein is their eternal home; with spouses purified and the good pleasure of God, for in God's sight are (all) His servants." (Al-Imran/ Family of Imran [3] 15). Mehmet S. Aydin in an article on *Qur'anic revelation and the environment* concludes: "We all know that here we are not living in Paradise, but at least traditionally we maintained a sense of analogy which enabled us to entertain a proper conception of Paradise while moulding our earthly environment. How about the generations to come? What will become of them if they are to inherit a morally polluted interior landscape within a seriously polluted natural one?"

Reading the many promises and descriptions of paradise in the Quran, what comes to my mind is 'Be in this world as the Bee' from *Al Fawaid* (a collection of wise sayings) of Ibn Al-Qayyim Al-Jawziyya (1292-1350 CE) wherein is included that it was said by one: "I can't imagine that someone could hear about Paradise and the Hellfire, and yet can still waste an hour without performing any act of obedience to Allah; neither remembrance, prayer, reciting the Quran nor an act of charity or kindness." Someone said to him: I weep profusely. He replied: "That you laugh while confessing your sin is better than you weeping and yet being full of pride because of your deeds. For the deeds of a conceited person will never rise above his head." The person then requested: Please counsel me. So the ascetic replied: "Leave the world to those who crave after it, as they leave the Afterlife to its seekers. And be in this world as the bee: it eats only good, produces only good, and when it rests upon anything it neither ruins it nor deflowers it."

In our gardens in this world, however, it seems we find it an increasingly good idea to tarmac over our outside spaces (the most heartbreaking version I came across was where the outside space of a children's nursery had been turned from a garden which would have lots of plants for the children to wonder at and discover, to being tarmac-ed over. All that was left of nature was a paper flower on the inside of the door stating "this is a flower" – is this how we want our children to know about Creation?). I would suggest there are three main reasons *not* to consider doing this to your outside space: it increases risk of flooding (and as we have seen in for example July 2007 in England this risk is not just theory; the Environment Agency has estimated that up to two thirds of the floods which happened in the summer of 2007 were caused by surface water overwhelming the drainage system), it is expensive and it steals space from the rest of God's Creation. On increased risk of flooding, as Water UK warns: "Put simply, if we tarmac and concrete over more land in river catchments rainfall will not infiltrate, thus reducing the replenishment of underground water supplies. But at the same time rainfall will also runoff more quickly [to sewerage systems not built for our extravagant water use and big run offs, RtV], which means that peak river flows will be increased in times of storm and this will lead to increased flooding". On cost, from a 2003 price list (and with rising oil prices, I understand prices now would be higher) I found out that to cover your outside space (garden or driveway) costs some £40-60/ m2, "kerbs, edgings and any required drainage points are not included, although VAT is", according to one supplier. I believe you can buy an amazing number of seeds and plants for children to grow and enjoy with that money plus enhance neighbourly relations if you share tools.

And with regards to stealing space from other communities (like animals and plants), the Environment Agency suggests: "[p]onds and green spaces will provide habitats for wildlife to flourish, reduce pollution and provide areas for people to enjoy, adding value to your site. Even in the most constrained site you can use green roofs to reduce surface water run-off, or to collect rainwater for flushing toilets or watering gardens." A green roof is a roof of a building that is partially or completely covered with vegetation and soil, or a growing medium, planted over a waterproofing membrane. For ideas about green roofs, check www.greenroofs.com and www.livingroofs.org.

Although I am not encouraging anyone to take any extra flights, with Dubai (UAE) being a popular holiday destination, perhaps check the latest information on the *Quranic Garden* that UNESCO is working on setting up in the Emirate of Sharjah, a garden based on the scientific and aesthetic concepts contained in the Quran. According to news on the project "the elements of this botanical garden will be drawn considering the verses (more than 150) that mention the Gardens of Paradise (*jannat al-firdaws*). God willing, the opportunity of establishing a Qur'anic botanical garden will be extremely useful to achieve important objectives in the fields of environmental conservation, scientific research, education and recreation." A similar garden is planned for Qatar.

Examples of action

27. Abu Huraira reported that God's Messenger ﷺ said: "Hell and Paradise fell into dispute and Hell said: I have been distinguished by the proud and the haughty. And Paradise said: What is the matter with me that the meek and the humble amongst people and the downtrodden and the simple enter me? Thereupon God said to Paradise: You are (the means) of My Mercy whereby I show mercy to those of My servants whom I wish, and He said to Hell: You are (the means) of punishment whereby I punish those of My servants whom l wish. Both of you will be full." Live simply (as Duane Elgin defines it: "living in a way that is outwardly simple and inwardly rich") and please God. A helpful Christian resource: www.simpleliving.net.

28. Yousuf Dadoo (Professor, Arabic and Islamic Studies, University of South Africa) suggests: "Cooperate with all like-minded individuals, organisations and institutions across the religious spectrum for applying sustainable development on the basis of the Quranic principle of mutual cooperation for promoting virtue (Al-Maidah/ The Table Spread [5] 2)". Join Friends of the Earth, Greenpeace, World Wide Fund for Nature (WWF) or the Women's Institute ("From climate

change and reducing food waste to ending violence against women and promoting Fairtrade, our campaigns make a real impact", www.thewi.org.uk); see also article 14 of the Universal Islamic Declaration of Human Rights: "Every person is entitled to participate individually and collectively in the religious, social, cultural and political life of his community and to establish institutions and agencies meant to enjoin what is right (*ma'roof*) and to prevent what is wrong (*munkar*)." An exciting initiative in Germany is *Grün Helme* (Green Helmets), a Muslim-Christian green new variation of the Peace Corps co-founded by Aiman Mazyek, Secretary-General of Central Council of Muslims in Germany www.gruenhelme.de.

29. Imran narrated: I said, "O God's Messenger ﷺ! Why should a doer (people) try to do good deeds?' The Prophet ﷺ said, "Everybody will find easy to do such deeds as will lead him to his destined place for which he has been created." If there is anything you do this week, ponder on Paradise and how you can show you would like to go there, for example by emulating Paradise in our towns and villages: be God's gardener.

30. Muawiya ibn Qurra said, "I was with Maqil al-Muzn when he removed something harmful from the road. Then I saw something and went over to it. He asked. 'What made you do that, nephew?' He replied, 'I saw you do something, so I did it.' He said, 'Nephew, you have done well. I heard the Prophet ﷺ say, "Whoever removes something harmful from the road has a good deed written for him. Anyone who has his good deed

accepted will enter the Garden.'" Or as Abu Barza al-Aslami said: "I said, 'Messenger of God, show me an action by which I will enter the Garden!' He said, 'Remove harmful things from people's path.'". Organise a street clean and have a nicer neighbourhood in this world plus contribute to your record for the next life.

31. Show God we like what paradise looks like and make our cities greener again, for example plant trees in this life, for example via Trees for Cities: an independent charity undertaking tree planting and greening initiatives in urban areas of greatest need and we want to stimulate a greening renaissance in cities around the world. www.treesforcities.org.

32. Turn your outside space (whether some acres or postage stamp size inner city patch) into your reflection of heaven. For some ideas: www.reep.org/resources/islamic-gardens. To know what plants will grow well in your area check the UK Natural History Museum's *Postcode Plants Database*: www.nhm.ac.uk/fff.

PART 2: WORSHIP (*IBADAH*)

Introduction

"I did not create the jinns and the humans except to worship Me alone." (Al-Dhariyat/ The Winds That Scatter [51] 56)

Ibadah is often translated as 'worship'. However, according to Ismail al-Faruqi, the full meaning of '*ibadah*' means "any and all actions entered into for the sake of God, and fulfilment of the general imperative of Islam regarding human life on earth". The foundation of worship is humility and submission. In Islam it has many definitions, but their meaning is the same. Amongst them: "worship is submission to God with utmost humility and love of Him. Worship is obedience to God by complying to that which God has commanded upon the tongues of His Messengers. Worship is divided into that of the heart, the tongue and the limbs." Worship is a collective term for everything which God loves and is pleased with from among the words and actions, such as supplication, prayer and having patience. Almighty God says (in the Quran): "Say: Verily my prayer, my service of sacrifice, my life and my death are all for God the Lord of the Worlds" (Al-An'am/ Livestock 6:162), and the Prophet ﷺ said "God the Exalted said: My servant does not draw near to Me with anything more loved by me than the obligatory actions which I have imposed upon him". As Amherst D. Tyssen (1843-1930 CE) muses in a poem: "Who is the pious Muslim, who? He who believes in God above: Who scans the universe around and o'er its face sees marks abound of matchless wisdom, power, and love."

Testimony of faith (shahada)

"I have submitted my wholeself to God and so have those who follow me..." (Al-Imran/ The Family of Imran [3] 20)

The testimony of faith is simply 'I believe there is no God but God and that Muhammad is his Messenger.' According to Syed Abul Ala Mawdudi (1903-1979 CE) a believer "can never be narrow in outlook" because he "believes in a God Who is the Creator of the heavens and the earth, the Master of the East and the West and Sustainer of the entire universe. After this belief he does not regard anything in the world as a stranger to himself. He looks on everything in the universe as belonging to the same Lord he himself belongs to. His sympathy, love and service are not confined to any particular sphere or group. His vision is enlarged, his intellectual horizon widens, and his outlook becomes as liberal and as boundless as is the Kingdom of God."

One of the conditions of *shahada* is submission and compliance. This implies actual physical enactment with deeds of our testimony. In fact, this is one of the main meanings of the word Islam itself, "the submission to the will and commands of God.", as God commands: "Turn unto Him repentant, and surrender unto Him" (Az-Zumar/ The Troops [39] 54). Another condition is that the Muslim adheres to the *shahada* until he dies. This is must if the *shahada* is to mean anything in the Hereafter, not resting on your laurels of what you may have done in the past. The Prophet ﷺ said, "A man spends a long time doing the deeds of the people of Paradise and then he ends his deeds with the deeds of the people of Hellfire. And a man spends a long time doing the deeds of the people of Hellfire and

124

then he ends his deeds with the deeds of the people of Paradise." In another case, the Prophet ﷺ said, "By the One whom there is no other God, one of you does the actions of Paradise until there is just a handspan between him and Paradise and then the book [preordainment] overtakes him and he does the actions of the people of Hell and he enters into it". And God says in the Quran, "O believers, observe your duty to God with right observance, and die not save as Muslims [surrendering yourselves to God]" (Al-Imran/ The Family of Imran [3] 102).

Muslim Wahb ibn Munabbih (eighth century CE, who lived to the age of ninety) was once asked, "Isn't the statement of 'there is no God but God' the key to Paradise?" He answered, "Yes, but every key has ridges. If you come with the key that has the right ridges, the door will open for you. Yet if you do not have the right ridges the door will not open for you." These 'right ridges' are what will differentiate the person who will benefit from his making of the statement from the one who will not benefit, no matter how many times a day he may have made that statement.

The testimony of faith of submission to God is nicely summarised by Mohammed Alexander Russell Webb (1846-1916 CE) speaking at the 1893 CE World Parliament of Religions in Chicago, USA: "With this spirit of resignation to the will of God is inculcated the idea of individual responsibility, that every man is responsible not to this man or that man, or the other man, but responsible to God for every thought and act of his life. He must pay for every act that he commits; he is rewarded for every thought he thinks. There is no mediator, there is no priesthood, there is no ministry." Along with self-respect this belief also generates in man a sense of modesty and humbleness. A believer never becomes proud, haughty or arrogant. The boisterous pride of power, wealth and worth can have no room in his heart, because he knows that whatever he possesses has been given to him by God, and that God can take away just as He can give. The believer never becomes despondent. He has a firm faith in God Who is Master of all the treasures of the earth and the heavens, Whose grace and bounty have no limit and Whose powers are infinite. This faith imparts to his heart extraordinary consolation, fills it with satisfaction and keeps it filled with hope. Although he may meet with rejection from all sides in this world, faith in and dependence on God never leave him, and on their strength he goes on struggling (*jihad*). Faith is what inspired several faith groups in Birmingham (UK) to work together on environmental work. From a joint declaration in June 2006, to encouraging faith ambassadors (volunteers willing to champion environmental sustainability and in particular CO_2 reduction projects within their faith group or place of worship) to becoming finalist in the Big Green Challenge, a national competition of community projects by NESTA (National Endowment for Science, Technology and the Arts) is very exciting. It is an inspiration to be on the Steering Group. For more information check the Birmingham Friends of the Earth website: http://faithandclimatechange.wordpress.com.

Yahya-En-Nasr (John) Parkinson (1874-1918 CE) has written a nice poem called *The Spirit of God* which includes the following observations: "On the perfume of flowerlets in the dell, on the white sea-foam on the ocean swell, on the shivering lances of silvery light, on the shimmering

sunbeam's arrowy flight, the Spirit of God is nigh."
Someone truly worshipping, by admiring His Creation.

Our testimony that Muhammad ﷺ is the Messenger of
God implies a number of things. At the forefront of these is
that we believe in it. We are declaring that he is a servant of
God and not an object of worship. Another important aspect
of our declaration that Muhammad ﷺ is the Messenger of
God is that we obey him in what he commands of us and
believe what he tells us. God has made obedience to the
Prophet ﷺ a form of obedience to Him (for example
"Whoever obeys the Messenger has obeyed God." (An-
Nisa [4] 80). God has warned us against allowing our love
for anyone or anything to grow more than our love for God
and His Messenger ﷺ. God says: "Say: If it be that your
fathers, your sons, your brothers, your spouses, or your
kindred; the wealth that you have gained; the commerce in
which you fear a decline: or the dwellings in which you
delight - are dearer to you than God, or His Messenger, or
the striving in His cause;- then wait until God brings about
His decision: and God guides not the rebellious." (Al-
Tawbah/ Repentance [9] 24). Let this verse not be
misinterpreted: terrorism is *never* allowed.

Examples of action

33. Can you help Seyyed Hossein Nasr: "If one could only
    bring back the sense of enchantment of the natural
    world in our time in a society dominated by the
    scientism which is a product of modern science!"

34. Prophet Muhammad ﷺ said, "None of you truly
    believes until he loves for his brother what he loves for

himself." Imam Nawawi (1234-1278 CE) commented in his compilation *40 Prophetic Traditions*: "the brotherhood referenced is that of humanity." If we were living in Bangladesh would we like to suffer increasing floods due to climate change mainly caused by people in rich countries? Or increasing droughts in Niger? Help you poor brothers, sisters by watching *Age of Stupid* and taking action.

35. With neighbours or friends set up an EcoTeam. Global Action Plan's (www.globalactionplan.org.uk) EcoTeams programme "helps households to reduce their impact on the environment and to save money. EcoTeams are groups of 6-8 people who meet once a month for approximately 5 months. At each meeting, EcoTeam participants decide together on the environmental actions that they are able and willing to do at home, and share experiences of the actions they have already taken."

36. According to Francis Lamand (President, Islam and the West, Paris, France) to counter some of the myths that surround Islam, we need "concrete partnerships […] the idea of needing to build joint projects rather than just exchanging views, the need to work together rather than simply holding endless talking shops". Why not set up a faith and environment book club or turn a piece of derelict land into a multifaith garden?

37. According to Abdul Malik Mujahid (President, US-based DawaNet), our motives in volunteering can turn our action into worship of our Creator: volunteer for

one of the many environmental charities, for example working on conservation.

38. There are endless means to show God we believe in Oneness of Creation, respecting rest of Creation, of which we are part: add a plant to your office space, and be conscientious when organising an event (see: www.sustainable-development.gov.uk/advice/documents/SustainableEventsGuide.pdf). But remember, do not keep postponing it 'until you have time', because the Prophet ﷺ stated: "God leaves no more excuses for a person once he has given him sixty years to live."

Prayer

"Establish regular prayer, enjoin what is just, and forbid what is wrong; and bear patiently whatever may befall you; for this is true constancy. And do not swell your cheek (with pride) at men, nor walk in insolence on the earth, for God does not love any man proud and boastful. And be moderate in your pace and lower your voice; for the harshest of sounds, indeed, is the braying of the donkey." (Luqman [31] 18-19)

For prayer to be valid you have to be in a state of purity and thus our Prophet ﷺ also reminded Muslims of prayer with the words "There is nothing more dear to God than a servant praying to Him." There are no limits to praying to God and drawing close to Him, which explains why understanding prayer and being dedicated to it benefits everyone. According to Harun Yahya (1956- CE) "[a]s well as verbal prayer, Allah [God] expects His servants to demonstrate how important they consider a prayer that asks for something to be, by their endeavor. This endeavor is called "prayer in action."

Ablution (*wudu*)

"O you who believe! When you prepare for prayer, wash your faces, and your hands (and arms) to the elbows; rub your heads (with water); and (wash) your feet to the ankles. If you are in a state of ceremonial impurity, bathe your whole body. But if you are ill, or on a journey, or one of you comes from offices of nature, or you have had marital relations, and you find no water, then take for yourselves clean sand or earth, and rub therewith your faces and hands, God does not wish to place you in a difficulty, but to make you clean, and to complete His favour to you, that you may be grateful." (Al-Ma'ida/ The Table Spread [5] 6)

Water is essential for the survival of all living beings. The word water occurs 66 times in the Quran. Water fulfils fundamental human needs, being used not only for drinking but also for a wide range of other uses, including food production and cooking, hygiene, sanitation, individual livelihoods, industry, development and performing ablutions. However, of all the water on earth, 97 per cent is salty and two per cent is frozen. Only one per cent is potable. It has been estimated that in order to ensure our basic needs, every individual needs 20 to 50 litres of water free from harmful contaminants each and every day. However, despite water's necessity to life, the reality is that billions of people worldwide are denied access to adequate clean water: a billion people lack access to an adequate supply of water; 2.4 billion people lack access to adequate sanitation; over 2 million people, mostly children, die annually from water-related diseases. Lake Chad has shrunk by 95 per cent since the mid 1960s. And the region's climate has changed during that time, with the monsoon rains which previously replenished the lake now greatly reduced. But in the UK in 2007, 33 per cent strongly agreed or tended to agree that they do not pay much attention to the amount of water they use at home.

According to information included in the book *Water Management in Islam,* edited by Naser I. Faruqui, renewable available water in the Middle East and North Africa region dropped from an average of 3,300 cubic metres per person per year in 1960 to 1,250 m3 per person per year in 1996, and is expected to decline to 725 m3 per person per year by 2025.

The third UN World Water Development Report, published in March 2009, found that global water use has increased three fold over the last 50 years, at twice the rate of population. Agriculture represents almost 70 per cent of this consumption and 40 per cent of agriculture is to grow feed for farmed animals. Households in the UK consumed an average of 150 litres per person each day in 2004, where the Environment Agency thinks this will go up to 200 litres per person per day by 2030; this means a yearly per person use of 54,750 litres. Many millions around the world have only access to 10 litres of water per person per day (slightly more than the amount of an average single toilet flush in the UK); this comes to a yearly per person use of just 3,285 litres.

The problem of water scarcity has been compounded by man-made factors such as pollution, the mismanagement of water resources and increasing demand, particularly in the industrial sector. Mohamed El-Ashry of the World Resources Institute estimates that 65-70 per cent of the water people use throughout the world is lost through evaporation, leaks, and other losses. At the same time, lack of access to water by poor people is being exacerbated by population growth and water privatisation policies that inadequately protect access by poor individuals and communities, including in Indonesia, Latin-America, India and Sri Lanka. In the face of a growing global water crisis, corporations are turning water into a profit-driven commodity. Nowhere is the corporate water-grab more insidious than the exploding corporate control of our drinking water.

It takes 162g of oil and seven litres of water (including power plant cooling water) just to manufacture a one-litre bottle, creating over 100g of greenhouse gas emissions (10 balloons full of CO_2) per empty bottle. Extrapolate this for the 'developed world' (2.4 million tonnes of plastic are used to bottle water each year) and it represents serious oil use for what is essentially a single-use object (and usually a short use at that). To make the 29 billion plastic bottles used annually in the US, the world's biggest consumer of bottled water, requires more than 17 million barrels of oil a year, enough to fuel more than a million cars for a year. Bottled water corporations also use clever marketing and misleading advertising that makes people doubt the safety and quality of their own tap water. Bottled water sellers like to confuse us by suggesting their water is pure and filtered to take out bacteria (like saying there's no strawberry in peanut butter…it is true, but completely irrelevant as normal peanut butter *never* has strawberry…). In March 2004 one and in July 2007 another had to admit one brand of bottled water was actually tap water (sold at a cost 10,000 times tapwater), "Public Water Source", "source P.W.S.". In reality, bottled water is less regulated than public water systems, and studies reveal that bottled water can actually contain harmful bacteria and other contaminants. Public water systems are required to disclose the source and quality of their water and are accountable to the public. Often, water bottlers are not. Furthermore, the corporations threaten local control of water supplies in communities around the world when they aggressively build bottled water plants over community protest. Endocrine disruptors (EDCs) mean confusing *fitra* situation by anything that mimics natural hormones…this could come from synthetic hormone (like in 'the pill'), but also other chemicals, like phlalates (from the plastics 'family'). The European Commission commissioned an independent study by the Fraunhofer Institute entitled *Study on endocrine disrupters in drinking water*. Its final report, published in February 2003 concluded that exposure to EDCs from consumption of drinking water is very unlikely to occur, even if the highest concentration of an individual EDC reported for drinking water is considered for the assessment of effects on humans. Tests carried out on surface water have shown positive results in sensitive bioassays in fish and in bioassays in vitro. However, no such positive results have been found with drinking water. Recent studies using extremely sensitive analytical techniques have been negative. Generally, the nature of these substances means that they are unlikely to remain dissolved in water and water treatment will provide further significant barriers. There is now a body of experimental evidence to support these arguments. Much of the research has been carried out with the cooperation of UK drinking water suppliers and the UK water industry continues to support and carry out research in this field. It has been suggested that substances present in some materials used to transport drinking water may be of concern. There are tight regulatory controls on the materials that can be used in contact with drinking water and all research on this topic to date is reassuring.

God's Messenger ﷺ appeared while Saad was taking the ablutions. When he saw that Saad was using a lot of water, he intervened saying: 'What is this? You are wasting water." Saad replied asking: "Can there be wastefulness while taking the ablutions?" To which God's Messenger ﷺ replied: "Yes, even if you take them on the bank of a rushing river." Extravagance is to use water without any benefit, like washing the parts more than three times. And according to Salih Al-Fawzan in his *Summary of Islamic Jurisprudence* mentions that "excessiveness in pouring water, which is considered wastefulness, leads to other illegal, detestable consequences, such as: … excessiveness in worship: ablution is an act of worship, and if any act of worship is performed excessively, it becomes void".

Muhammad Al-Bukhari (810-870 CE, key hadeeth compiler) says that: "[t]he scholars do not like one to use water beyond what the Prophet ﷺ used for ablution." While interpreting this *hadeeth*, scholars have also pointed out that it does not refer only to using less water while taking the ablutions, but to a basic principle of Islam. They have emphasized the following points in connection with it: God's Messenger ﷺ is stating an important prohibition; the prohibition concerns something for which no effort was exerted in obtaining it, nor money spent, but is free: the water of a flowing river; moreover, the excessive use of water in this case causes no deficiency to nature, nor does it cause pollution, nor spoil the ecological balance; it causes no harm to living beings. Lastly (but not least), the matter in question, that is, taking the ablutions, is not some trivial matter; it is a necessary condition for the obligatory prayers. If then, despite all the above, it is 'detestable' (*makruh*) to use excessive water from a river while taking the ablutions and it was prohibited by the Prophet ﷺ, how much stronger is the proscription on being wasteful and extravagant in some matter in which the above conditions are not applicable? That is, if wastefulness is in something that required the expending of effort, expense, or at least time; if it caused deficiency to or pollution of nature, thus spoiling the ecological balance; if it harmed living beings; if it violated the rights of forthcoming generations to live in a healthy environment; if it was arbitrary and meaningless, and merely for enjoyment; if it was contrary to the basic aim; then what would the situation be?

The Quran and *Sunna* stipulating that water is the basis of life lays a number of obligations and responsibilities on Muslims (for this reason the *Majallah*, or Ottoman civil code, included 92 articles on the subject of water management): the conserving of existent water supplies in the best possible way; the prevention of any activity that might lead to the pollution of water sources or spoil the purity and characteristics of the water; never adopting an extravagant and irresponsible attitude in the consumption of water; rational and regular utilisation of water and water sources. In the UK we use four times more water than our great-grand parents at the beginning of the twentieth century. The amount has tripled in the last 30 years alone. While the average house in England (UK) has on average 35,000 litres of water falling on its roof each year, most of us pay (in UK in sewage part of water bill) to have that water pumped away, cleaned, then pumped back to our homes as potable water, where a third of it is flushed straight down the toilet or used to water plants and gardens (which actually prefer rain water). Supplying water to the average home creates about 80kg of carbon dioxide per person per year at the pumping stations. If we all did our own rainwater harvesting we could immediately close 5 power stations and save 4 per cent of UK's entire energy use. For some £2-3,000 it is possible to have a decent quality rainwater harvesting system installed, which would save some 50 per cent off water and sewerage bill (and if you really want to know: payback time is around 10 years, though funny how nobody asks this question when buying a car....). I remember a holiday in South-Africa during a drought. Though we stayed at a luxury hotel, we still had to be careful with water. The cleanest would take a shower with the bath plug in, the next would use the bath water and after all were finished, the bath water was used to flush the toilet.

How much water did the Prophet ﷺ use then? Humran (the freed slave of Uthman bin Affan) narrated: "I saw Uthman bin Affan asking (for a tumbler of water) to perform ablution (and when it was brought) he poured water from it over his hands and washed them thrice and then put his right hand in the water container and rinsed his mouth and washed his nose by putting water in it and then blowing it out. Then he washed his face thrice and (then) forearms up to the elbows thrice, then passed his wet hands over his head and then washed each foot thrice." After that Uthman said, "I saw the Prophet performing ablution like this of mine, and he said, 'If anyone performs ablution like that of mine and offers a two unit (*rakat*) prayer during which he does not think of anything else (not related to the present prayer) then his past sins will be forgiven.'

Amr bin Yahya (on the authority of his father) narrated: "My uncle used to perform ablution extravagantly and once he asked Abdullah bin Zaid to tell him how he had seen the Prophet ﷺ performing ablution. He asked for an earthenware pot containing water, and poured water from it on his hands and washed them thrice, and then put his hand in the earthen-ware pot and rinsed his mouth and washed his nose by putting water in it and then blowing it Out thrice with one handful of water; he again put his hand in the water and took a handful of water and washed his face thrice, then washed his hands up to the elbows twice, and took water with his hand, and passed it over his head from front to back and then from back to front, and then washed his feet (up to the ankles) and said, "I saw the Prophet performing ablution in that way." Anas also narrated: "the Prophet ﷺ used to take a bath with one *Sa'* or up to five mudds (1 *sa'*= 4 *mudds*) of water and used to perform ablution with one mudd of water." However, Abu Dawood narrated that the Prophet ﷺ said: "There will be a people amongst this ummah who will transgress in their supplication and ablution."

And if there is no water: the reverence towards soil is also demonstrated in the ritual of *tayammum*, or "dry *wudu*" which permits the use of dust in the performance of ritual purification before prayer when water is not available. Lastly, it is interesting to note that Jordan, a country which is ruled relatively secular compared to Iran or Saudi Arabia, and which has significant religious minorities, uses Islamic sources along with secular slogans to promote water conservation by the population.

Examples of action

39. Make *wudu* like the Prophet ﷺ did, as Anas narrated: "the Prophet ﷺ used to perform *ghusl* (the complete bathing) with a *sa* of water or 3 to 5 *mudd* (each 4 *mudd* equals one *sa* [or 2.01 litre]). He also used to make ablution with one *mudd* [0.51 litre] of water." Ubaidullah ibn Abu Yazid narrated that a man asked Ibn Abbas, "How much water is sufficient for *wudu*?" He answered, "One *mudd*." "And how much is sufficient for *ghusl*?" He said, "One *sa*." The man said, "That is not sufficient for me." "Ibn Abbas said, "No? It was sufficient for one better than you, the Messenger of God ﷺ."

40. Remember, from now on make *wudu* like the Prophet ﷺ did: the Prophet ﷺ, as Abdullah ibn Mughaffal narrated that he heard him say, "there will be people from my nation who will transgress in making supplications and in purifying themselves."

41. And on the topic of water use: Anas bin Malik: narrated "whenever God's Messenger ﷺ went to answer the call of nature, I along with another boy used to accompany him with a tumbler full of water." (Hisham commented, "So that he might wash his private parts with it.)". I note the containers provided in the mosque or Muslim places today are often more like two litres.

42. Put or arrange a reminder in all places where ablutions are made on how much (little!) water the Prophet ﷺ used and turn the tap off, because, as Fahd ibn Abdir Rahman ash-Shuwaib (Al-Qur'an was-Sunnah Society of North-America) states, "If you consider this [above] *hadeeth* well, O my Muslim Brother, you would feel ashamed of what some people do these days - one of them opening the water tap and making *wudoo* and sometimes talking to his companion whilst the water is running out - what an excess in wastefulness! So he who does that should fear Allaah [God] and remember this *hadeeth* and keep it in mind and follow the Sunnah with regard to using the water sparingly and not being wasteful - and here the true following of the Prophet ﷺ is made clear and the true Muslim's belief. It is from the *Sunnah* for the Muslim who wishes to make *wudoo* to have with him a container large enough for a *mudd* of water - in order to force himself to return to the following of the *Sunnah*."

43. Turn the tap off while you are brushing your teeth. Doing this can save some five litres per minute. And regularly check for leaking taps: a slow dripping tap can easily waste six litres of water per day.

44. Get a water butt (or two) to collect rainwater for the garden, for (house) plants and to wash the car. From floods in the UK in the summer of 2007 we should learn that even houses which were not affected by the flood directly, had their water cut off due to the need to protect the main power station. This meant more people were directly affected: would they have had one or more water butts, they would have had continued access to water (even if this was for all purposes except drinking).

45. If you have the means to invest: get a rainwater harvesting system (check for example UK Rainwater Harvesting Association; www.ukrha.org; for the US: www.rainharvesting.com; and for Australia: www.rainharvesting.com.au).

Bathing (*ghusl*)

"O you who believe! Approach not prayers with a mind befogged, until you can understand all that you say- nor in a state of ceremonial impurity (except when travelling on the road), until after washing your whole body. If you are ill, or on a journey, or one of you comes from offices of nature, or you have had marital relations, and you find no water, then take for yourselves clean sand or earth, and rub therewith your faces and hands. For God does blot out sins and forgive again and again." (An-Nisa/ The Women [4] 43)

Climate change will have an increasingly significant impact on the availability of water in several regions of the world. This will happen as a result of the melting of glaciers on the one hand and changed patterns of rainfall on the other. In those regions where agriculture is dependent entirely on rainfall, reduced levels of rainfall would only add to already increasing stresses in the availability of water for agriculture as well as human consumption, already challenged by increased erosion. The UN International Governmental Panel on Climate Change (a scientific intergovernmental body established to provide decision-makers and others interested in climate change with an objective source of information about climate change) in November 2007 confirmed some disastrous consequences of climate change, unless humanity changes its ways and adapts drastically.

And as sea levels rise, caused by melting poles, they threaten to contaminate groundwater, affecting drinking water and agriculture in coastal zones. Increased evaporation will reduce the effectiveness of reservoirs. Increased extreme weather means more water falls on hardened ground unable to absorb it - leading to flash floods instead of a replenishment of soil moisture or groundwater levels. In some areas, shrinking glaciers threaten the water supply. Higher temperatures will also increase the demand for water for cooling purposes.

Several verses of the Quran deal with the hydrological cycle and the fundamental role water plays in sustaining life on earth ("We made from water every living thing" is mentioned at least three times in the Quran). In referring to the fertility of the soil, to the unique properties of fresh and sea water, to the course of rivers and the presence underground of springs and aquifers, and most significantly to the aquatic origin of life, the Quran places water at the top of all the natural phenomena on earth. The miracle of water is emphasized in a particular verse where God, addressing those who may doubt the truth of resurrection, first gives the example of the growth of the foetus within the mother's womb, leading to the birth of a human being. The verse then concludes: "If you are still in doubt as to resurrection, consider this: you can see the earth dry and lifeless and suddenly when we send down waters upon it, it stirs and swells and puts forth every kind of lovely plant!" (Al-Hajj/ The Pilgrimage [22] 5)

Anas relates that when the Prophet ﷺ made ablutions, he would use a quantity of water that could fill cupped hands (*mudd*), and when he took a full bath, he would use four times that much (*sa*). Aisha رضي الله عنها narrated that: "The Prophet ﷺ and I used to take a bath from a single pot called *Faraq*." And Abu Salama رضي الله عنه narrated: "Aisha's brother and I went to Aisha and he asked her about the bath of the Prophet ﷺ. She brought a pot containing about a *sa* of water and took a bath and poured it over her head and at what time there was a screen between her and us."

Yahya related to me from Malik from Hisham ibn Urwa from his father from Aisha رضي الله عنها, that whenever the Messenger of God ﷺ, did *ghusl* for major ritual impurity, he would begin by washing his hands, and then do *wudu* as for prayer. He would then put his fingers in the water and rub the roots of his hair with them. Then he would pour as much water as two hands can hold on to his head three times, and over the entire surface of his skin. And Yahya related to me from Malik from Ibn Shihab from Urwa ibn az-Zubayr from Aisha رضي الله عنها, *Umm Al-Muminin* (mother of the believers), that the Messenger of God ﷺ used to do *ghusl* for major ritual impurity from a vessel which contained a faraq (3 *sa*).

Examples of action

46. Anas narrated that the Prophet ﷺ used to take a bath with one *sa* or up to five *mudds* (1 *sa*= 4 *mudds*) of water and used to perform ablution with one *mudd* of water. One *mudd* is about half a litre of water; one *sa'* is about two litres of water. People often think they cannot do with less, but when put on a water meter, average use goes down by 10-15 per cent, so most of us can do with less, plus remember all those generations before us who used so much less and survived and all those generations after us who will have no choice but to use less.

47. Abu Jafar narrated: "While I and my father were with Jabir bin Abdullah, some people asked him about taking a bath. He replied, "A *sa* of water is sufficient for you." A man said, "A *sa* is not sufficient for me." Jabir said, "A *sa* was sufficient for one who had more hair than you and was better than you (meaning the Prophet ﷺ)." And then Jabir (put on) his garment and led the prayer." Take a shower instead of a bath.

48. In Malik's *Muwatta* it states: Yahya related to me from Malik from Nafi that Abdullah ibn Umar رضى الله عنه used to say "There is no harm in doing *ghusl* with water that has been used by one's wife as long as she is not menstruating or in a state of major ritual impurity (*junub*)." Reuse water whenever possible.

49. Learn about the different causes of water pollution and how to avoid them, for example via www.water-pollution.org.uk . We may think that things like being water wise are small things, but as Ghailan narrated that Anas رضي الله عنه said: "You people do (bad) deeds (commit sins) which seem in your eyes as tiny (minute) than hair while we used to consider those (very deeds) during the life-time of the Prophet ﷺ as destructive sins."

Prayer

"If My servants ask you about Me, I am near. I answer the call of the caller when he calls on Me. They should therefore respond to Me and believe in Me so that hopefully they will be rightly guided." (Al-Baqarah/ The Cow [2] 186)

> *1. In the Name of God, Most Gracious, Most Merciful.*
> *2. Praise be to God, the Lord of All the Worlds;*
> *3. The Most Gracious, Most Merciful.*
> *4. Master of the Day of Judgment.*
> *5. You alone we worship and from You alone we seek help.*
> *6. Guide us to the straight way,*
> *7. The way of those on whom you have bestowed Your grace, not the way of those who earn Your anger, nor of those who go astray.*

The above Quran chapter is called The Opening (*Al-Fatiha*). The Prophet ﷺ called it 'The Opening of the Book.' The reason for this is that it is the first chapter that one reads when one opens the Quran, though it was not the first chapter to be revealed. The Prophet ﷺ also called it 'The Mother of the Quran' (*Umm al-Quran*). The Prophet ﷺ said: "The Mother of the Book: they are the Seven Oft -Repeated Verses and the Glorious Recital." The reason for this – and God knows best – is that it contains within it the general meaning of the Quran. It embraces all the principles and major themes that the Quran addresses. In his daily prayers, a Muslim asks God: "Guide us to the Straight Path." ("The way of those on whom you have bestowed Your grace, not the way of those who earn Your anger, nor of those who go astray", verses 6-7 of the first chapter of the Quran) It has been prescribed for us by none other than our Creator who, in His infinite wisdom, has commanded us to repeat it in every unit of prayer that we offer. It is a verse of the opening chapter of the Quran, and our prayers are not valid if we fail to recite this chapter therein.

There are four aspects to this guidance that we are asking for: the first is for us to be blessed with the ability to arrive at knowledge of what is good and how to attain it and knowledge of what is evil and how to avoid it. Allah has blessed us with our five senses and our faculties of reason so we can learn and come to know these things. The first meaning that the verse conveys is a request: our request to be made firm and constant on the 'straight path' with all that it entails. The essential factors upon which we need constancy are the five pillars of Islam, the six pillars of faith, our ethical principles, and the basics of what is lawful and prohibited that are clearly expressed in the Quran and *sunnah* and that are matters of consensus among the Muslims since the earliest days. The second meaning that the verse conveys is our request to attain an increase in guidance. God says: "God increases the guidance of those who are guided." Knowledge is not to be sought as an academic exercise. It is sought as a matter of faith and then to be implemented.

One day the Prophet ﷺ swore an oath to do one thing but then did another. From this we derive the following principle of Islamic law: when a person believes something to be correct so much so that he swears by it but then realises that something else is better – either because circumstances have changed or because new evidence has presented itself – then he should expiate for his oath and do what is better. The second Caliph, Umar bin al-Khattab ﷺ, wrote to Abu Musa al-Ashari wherein he said: "Do not let a verdict that you gave yesterday prevent you from following the truth today if you review the matter and are guided to what is more correct. The truth is timeless, and going back to the truth is better than persisting in falsehood."

One meaning that the verse "Guide us to the Straight Path" conveys, is that of seeking guidance to the devotion and worship that we should exhibit in every circumstance and that of being guided from what is already good and wholesome to what is even better. God says: "Those who listen to the word and follow the best of it". The Prophet ﷺ said: "In this world, women and good scents have been made dear to me, but dearest of all to me is prayer." And Jabir ibn Abdullah narrated that God's Messenger ﷺ said: "The key to Paradise is prayer and the key to prayer is cleanliness."

Examples of action

50. Be extra alert during your prayers; become aware of elements of Creation you recite in your prayers (one eighth of verses refer to God's signs). *"Then when the prayer is finished, spread through the earth and seek God's bounty."* (Al-Jumua/ The Congregation [62] 10). In prayer we recite parts of the Quran to remind us of other ways of prayer (taking care of Creation).

51. After your prayers make *dua* (supplication) for endangered creatures. According to the World Conservation Union (IUCN) 2008 *Red List of Threatened Species,* about 38 per cent of the 44,838 species listed (which is only a tiny percentage of existing species) are designated as "threatened" and 7 per cent are "critically endangered.", up from 16,118 in 2006. The total number of extinct species in 2006 had reached 785 and a further 65 are only found in captivity or in cultivation. Make *dua* for these plants and animals, including the ones in your own neighbourhood and garden. Make *dua* that God guides you and your family in your actions to care for other creatures (communities like us) as God intends. You can pray for threatened plants and animals by name by going to the IUCN's Global Species Assessment Photo Gallery at www.iucnredlist.org.

52. Reflect on importance of prayer, and that though saying daily prayers is one of the five most important obligations on Muslims, the Prophet ﷺ and his fellow travellers used to delay even saying their prayers until they had first given their riding and pack animals fodder

and had attended to their needs: "When we stopped at a halt, we did not say our prayers until we had taken the burdens off our camels' backs and attended to their needs."

53. The Prophet ﷺ said: "Do not be conceited (thinking that your sins will be forgiven because of your prayer [alone])." So put your prayers into action as T.E. Lawrence (a.k.a. Lawrence of Arabia) suggests: "The first duty of every Moslem was to study the Koran, the sacred book of Islam, and incidentally the greatest Arab literary monument." Notice the number of references to nature ('sign' in nature and 'verse' in Quran are both *ayah*).

54. When praying in the mosque, go walking as the Prophet said ﷺ "And if they knew what lies in walking (to the mosque) in the noon heat, they would race each other to it."

Friday prayer (*jummah*)

"O you who believe! when the call is made for prayer on Friday, then hasten to the remembrance of God and leave off trading; that is better for you, if you know." (Al-Jumua/ The Congregation [62] 9)

The average number and percentage of trips people make by walking or cycling has declined. In 1952 in the UK, 27 per cent of journeys were made by car, by 2007 this was 84 per cent. As Muslims this should concern us as Abu Abs narrated: "I heard the Prophet ﷺ saying, "Anyone whose feet are covered with dust in God's cause, shall be saved by God from the Hellfire." And Abu Musa reported God's

Messenger ﷺ as saying: The most eminent among human beings (as a recipient of) reward (is one) who lives farthest away, and who has to walk the farthest distance, and he who waits for the prayer to observe it along with the Imam, his reward is greater than one who prays (alone) and then goes to sleep. In the narration of Abu Kuraib the words are: "(He waits) till he prays along with the Imam in congregation."

Jabir bin Abdullah narrated: Our houses were situated far away from the mosque; we, therefore, decided to sell our houses so that we may be able to come near the mosque. The Messenger of God ﷺ forbade us (to do so) and said: There is for every step (towards the mosque) a degree (of reward) for you.

Abu Huraira رضي الله عنه reported: the Messenger of God ﷺ said: He who purified himself in his house, and then he *walked* to one of the houses of God for the sake of performing an obligatory act out of the obligatory acts of God, both his steps (would be significant) as one of them would obliterate his sin and the second one would raise his status. And Yahya related to me from Malik from Zayd ibn Aslam from Ata ibn Yasar from Abdullah as-Sanabihi that the Messenger of God ﷺ, said, "A trusting slave does *wudu* and as he rinses his mouth the wrong actions leave it. As he cleans his nose the wrong actions leave it. As he washes his face, the wrong actions leave it, even from underneath his eyelashes. As he washes his hands the wrong actions leave them, even from underneath his fingernails. As he wipes his head the wrong actions leave it, even from his ears. And as he washes his feet the wrong actions leave them, even from underneath the toenails of both his feet." He added, "Then his *walking* to the mosque and his prayer are an extra reward for him."

Thabit reported that he was with Anas in a corner above one of his rooms. He said, "We heard the call to prayer and he came down and I came down as well. He took short steps and said, 'I was with Zayd ibn Thabit and I walked with him in this fashion. He said, "Do you know why I did it to you? The Prophet ﷺ, walked in this manner and he said, 'Do you know why I walked with you?' I replied, 'God and His Messenger know best.' He said, 'So that there would be a greater number of steps in search of the prayer."

But what when it rains or the weather is bad you may ask? We then still have no reason to go by car: Abdullah bin Harith reported that Ibn Abbas commanded the *muezzin* (caller to prayer) to summon the people to prayer on Friday and make announcement to say prayer in their houses when it was rainy, and the rest of the *hadeeth* is the same (except this) that he said: 'I do not like you should walk in muddy slippery place'. And Nafi said; "Ibn Umar gave a call for prayer in Dzajnan on a cold night, then said, 'Say prayers in your abodes'; and he informed us that the Messenger of God ﷺ, used to order a *muezzin*, on a cold or rainy night and during journey, to give a call for prayer, then say, on finishing it, 'Beware! Say prayers in (your) abodes'.

Examples of action

55. Walk to *Jummah*: Aws ibn Aws ath-Thaqafi narrated: "I heard the Messenger of God ﷺ say: "If anyone makes (his wife) wash and he washes himself on Friday, goes

out early (for Friday prayer), attends the sermon from the beginning, walking, not riding, takes his seat near the imam, listens attentively, and does not indulge in idle talk, he will get the reward of a year's fasting and praying at night for every step he takes." Consider doing other (short) journeys on foot as well (see also under transport).

56. Sahl bin Sad narrated: "We used to be very happy on Friday as an old lady used to cut some roots of the *silq* [Arabic word for the leaves known as chard, Swiss chard, or silverbeet], which we used to plant on the banks of our small water streams, and cook them in a pot of hers, adding to them, some grains of barley." (Yaqub, the sub-narrator said, "I think the narrator mentioned that the food did not contain fat or melted fat taken from meat.") When we offered the Friday prayer we would go to her and she would serve us with the dish. So, we used to be happy on Fridays because of that. We used not to take our meals or the midday nap except after the *Jummah* prayer (that is Friday prayer).

Eid

"He is the One who rendered the sun radiant, and the moon a light, and He designed its phases that you may learn to count the years and to calculate. God did not create all this, except for a specific purpose. He explains the revelations for people who know." (Yunus/ Jonah [10] 5)

Muslims celebrate two *Eids* (festivals): *Eid Al-Fitr* and *Eid Al-Adha*, timed according to the Hijri calendar. *Eid Al-Fitr* ('to break the fast') is celebrated at the end of the month of Ramadan, or month of fasting; *Eid Al-Adha* refers to the commemoration of Prophet Ibrahim's ﷺ (Abraham's) willingness to sacrifice his son – note though that in Islam, we believe God did not actually ask Abraham to sacrifice his son, but Abraham had a dream in which he thought God had asked him this and he was willing to oblige, see Al-Saffat/ Those Who Set The Ranks [37] 102).

Apparently it is better to hold *Eid* prayers in an open place or ground if there is no obstacle like rain or bad weather. The Prophet ﷺ only once performed *Eid* prayers in the mosque due to rain. One Eid I thought the day was going to be on a Tuesday I believe, so made an appointment for something else on the Monday before. At the last moment the mosque I planned to go to for *Eid* prayers changed its *Eid* day to Monday. When I arrived on the mosque grounds after my appointment, I noticed the grounds were full of plastic bags (I later heard, making it even worse, that these had been given out by the mosque, with the idea to put their shoes in them). I almost wanted to cry: all these people had gone to the mosque with their best intentions, had done their *Eid* prayers but were going to cause the deaths of so many animals for hundreds of years to come (some species mistake the bags for food and choke on them and because plastic does not biodegrade for such a long time several animals can die from the same bag), plus blight the views of my neighbourhood. Or as the Worldwide Fund for Nature (WWF) puts it "plastic ain't fantastic": a post-mortem performed on a turtle found dead off the Scottish coast revealed it had ingested 18 kilogrammes of plastic bags, the equivalent of 291 bags. Also, according to research by the United Nations Environment Programme (UNEP) published in June 2006 over 46,000 pieces of plastic litter are floating *on every square mile* of ocean today. In the Central Pacific, there are up to 6 pounds of litter to every pound of plankton.

Examples of action

57. Give walking to the mosque on *Eid* a try. Said Ibn Jubayr said: "Three things are *Sunnah* on *Eid*: to walk (to the prayer-place), to take a bath, and to eat before coming out [if it is *Eid al-Fitr*]." As with the *Jummah*, on returning home from the *Eid* prayer, it is recommended to take a different route than that which was taken to the prayer. This seems to only make sense if one goes walking so one can meet different people on the way (not hiding in a car box).

58. Islam urges us to enjoy life with every lawful means of enjoyment, especially on *Eid* days: take the family to a nearby park and enjoy God's 'second book' ('book' of Creation, complementing the Quran). For those not near to us, send them an e-card instead of a paper one: save cash and support Creation (watch your paper use in general: the average Briton uses over 200kg of paper a year, the average American almost 300kg – and remember paper comes from trees, so every time you are about to print or buy wrapping paper, think: is this worth destroying trees for? Not using or reusing is free. This is why I chose a publisher with a strong environmental policy and prints on demand.)

59. Prophet Mohammad ﷺ said: "Exchange gifts in order to foster love." Instead of buying material gifts for friends and family, give them a homemade voucher (for example to babysit, do the shopping, do some DIY) or

take them out (for example to a museum, meal out, a toys or books library – if no toys library exists in your area, set one up: what an *Eid* gift to the community. See the website of the National Association of Toy & Leisure Libraries for advice: www.natll.org.uk).

60. Bring your own bag to the mosque to put your shoes in, and take it back home after prayers for next reuse of the bag. Encourage the mosque to suggest this to worshippers via Friday prayer before *Eid* instead of handing out plastic bags.

61. According to Abdelaziz bin Abdullah al-Sheikh (Mufti of Saudi Arabia): "The sacrifice of an animal is not an obligation for Muslims, but it is a tradition [a *sunnah*]. Those who have the means to sacrifice an animal can do it. For those who do not, it is not obligatory". The sheikh said this in 2001 at the occasion of foot and mouth disease outbreak. And Mohammed Farid Wagdi (1875– 1940 CE) in his *Wagdi's Encyclopaedia* states in an article on sacrifice that there might come a day when Muslims shall have to substitute the rite of animal sacrifice with other methods of giving alms.

Earth is my mosque

"For what cause should I not serve Him Who has created me, and unto Whom you will be brought back?" (Yaseen/ Yaseen [36] 22)

Jabir bin Abdullah narrated that the Messenger of God said: "I have been given five things which were not given to any of the Prophets before me. These are: […] 2. The earth has been made a place of prostration for me, and a place to perform *tayammum*. Thus, my followers can pray wherever (that is, in any lawful place) they like, when the time of prayer is due. [...]". The Prophet ﷺ also said: "The earth has been created for me as a mosque and as a means of purification; therefore, if prayer overtakes any person of my community, he should say his prayers (wherever he is)" So Islam teaches us the whole earth is made like a mosque. What did he ﷺ want to tell us? He ﷺ meant that this is a sacred place, a holy place, so you should not act in a disrespectful way toward it. You should not abuse anything on the face of the earth. According to Adi Setia (Assistant Professor of History and Philosophy of Science, Department of General Studies, International Islamic University Malaysia) this means that "hence the ethics applicable to the mosque are also applicable to the earth." Wail Abdel-Mutaal Shihab (Deputy Managing Editor, IslamOnline Shariah Department; graduate of Al-Azhar University), states: "Transferring such environmentally sound principles [from the mosque] to the larger world can instil love and care for the planet in the hearts of people. People will learn to abstain from polluting the surrounding environment. They will work on securing a clean and healthy atmosphere for all. Air, rivers, seas, oceans, animals, plants, and all creatures will be protected."

The Prophet ﷺ refers to praying anywhere; could we pray on our current streets? I remember one day going for a walk in my lunch break. The streets were all but deserted. It was one of those non-descript grey days in early spring. All of a sudden I noticed a homeless man walking some 30- 40 metres ahead of me. The reason I noticed him: I saw him picking up some trash (I cannot remember exactly what it was) from the middle of the pavement. Immediately several thoughts came to my mind … this man, neglected by society, *living* on the street, actually felt some kind of ownership over the area of Creation he was walking on? Or did he have genuine good manners and would he have done it, homeless or not? And how come his action struck me so much? Is it because it has become such an uncommon sight to see someone clear up the street (besides the City Council workers)? Note that if 'earth' did not really mean *all* earth, then there would be no need for explicit, limited and detailed exceptions: graveyards; churches and synagogues (those with statues or sculptures); dunghills, slaughterhouses, middle of the roads, resting places of the camels near watering holes, bathrooms and on the roof of the 'house of God' (prayer in the *Kabah*, the black cube inside the *Haram* in Makkah).

In 1991 Hesam Addin Abdul Salam Joma, studying at the University of Pennsylvania in the US, wrote a dissertation entitled *The Earth as a mosque: Integration of the traditional Islamic environmental planning ethic with agricultural and water development policies in Saudi Arabia*. In it he suggests that Saudi Arabia take a holistic Islamic approach and the Islamic values of justice, moderation and equilibrium in tackling development, with an integration of Islamic environmental planning principles. As religion knows no national borders, I suggest his approach could be replicated all over the Muslim world, God willing.

Examples of action

62. Think about whether you would be able to pray anywhere in your community, and if not, organise a

street cleaning. According to Zahloul El-Naggar (Professor of Geology and member, Supreme Council for Islamic Affairs, Cairo, Egypt), the word *tuhur* as included in the *hadeeth* 'cleanliness (*tuhur*) is half of faith', "refers to *'taharah'* (purification) of one's body, clothes, shoes, home, roads, water streams, utensils, food and drink and all that man uses in his everyday life. It also refers to the purification of the heart, *nafs* (oneself) and all that is related to a Muslim in his life concerning his family, society and the whole world. This applies to any Muslim, whether a man or a woman, a child, a teenager or a youth." In Islam, physical, moral and spiritual cleanliness form an indivisible whole. Muslims should neglect neither the cleanliness of their surroundings, houses, the roads they use, and parks and gardens, nor any sort of moral and spiritual cleanliness.

63. Encourage, support and help your mosque to 'go green'. For example, Chicago's Mosque Foundation in the US has partnered with a local faith-based environmental organisation, *Faith in Place*, to champion the environmental causes within the Chicago and American Muslim community. Several community-based initiatives are being discussed and implemented, including making the new mosque building more energy efficient, by switching to renewable solar energy for heated water, using LED bulbs and lights, improving insulation, encouraging the consumption of humanly raised, of course halal animals, and organic fruits and vegetables raised on farms which do not harm the soil and the earth. Their inspiration comes from the belief that, as M. Zaher Sahloul (President, Mosque

Foundation, US) puts it: "We can't preach what we don't practice. Our faith is a faith of action, not a faith of rituals and superstition. Unless we embody our core values, and act on them, we will continue to daydream and chatter about the glorious past."

64. At next elections, vote for a candidate that will most enhance (in deeds, not just words) our environment, facilitate green environment to be able to pray anywhere. If there is no suitable candidate: be one, or at least become member of the party. As G.F. Haddad states: "involvement in politics in order to effect change is by far a lesser evil than defeatist isolationism and in fact is a duty for it is _the_ most effective way to "change something wrong by hand or by word..." - as the Prophet ﷺ ordered."

Purifying Social Tax (zakat) and charity (sadaqah)

"You are those who are called to spend in the way of God, yet among you there are some who hoard. And as for him who hoards, he hoards only from his soul. And God is the Rich, and you are the poor. And if you turn away He will exchange you for some other folk, and they will not be the likes of you." (Muhammad [47] 38)

In the Quran there are five words used for charity: *zakat* (obligatory charity, above wealth threshold), *sadaqah* (charity), *khairat* (good deeds), *ihsan* (kindness and consideration), *infaq fi sabil Allah* (spending for the sake of God).

Abu Huraira narrated ﷺ : "Each person's every joint must perform a charity every day the sun comes up: to act justly between two people is a charity; to help a man with his mount, lifting him onto it or hoisting up his belongings onto it is a charity: a good word is a charity, every step you take to prayers is a charity and *removing a harmful thing from the road is a charity*." And while doing the latter, think of Yahya-en-Nasr (John) Parkinson's (1874-1918 CE) poem *Creativity* starting with: "What a wonderful world we live in, with its stars and its planets and suns; we are part of the changeable cosmos, our life through the core of it runs."

Al-Nisaai reported that the Prophet ﷺ said "Stinginess and faith never exist together in the heart of the believer." The Prophet ﷺ also described the serious nature of stinginess and its consequences: "Beware of stinginess, for those who came before you were destroyed because of stinginess. It commanded them to be miserly, so they were miserly; it commanded them to cut family ties, so they cut them; and it commanded them to be immoral, so they were immoral."

According to Al-Tirmidhi the Prophet ﷺ said: "Every nation has its *fitna* (trial or temptation), and the *fitna* of my *ummah* is wealth." Eagerness to acquire wealth is more damaging to a person's religion than the wolf who attacks the sheepfold. This is what the Prophet ﷺ meant when he said: "Two hungry wolves sent against the sheep do not do more damage to them than a man's eagerness for wealth and standing does to his religion." For this reason the Prophet ﷺ urged Muslims to take just what is sufficient, without hoping for more, which could distract him from remembering God. The Messenger of God ﷺ said: "All that you need of wealth is a servant and a means of transportation to go out for the sake of God." The Prophet ﷺ issued a warning to those who want to accumulate wealth, except for those who give in charity: "Woe to those who want to accumulate wealth, except for the one who says with his wealth, 'Here! Here! Here!' (that is, giving it away) to one on his right, one on his left, one in front of him and one behind him,"– meaning all forms of charity.

At the same time, having no wealth does not mean someone cannot give charity because 'even a smile is charity'. According to Egypt-based Philanthropy for Development (www.philanthropyfordevelopment.org), "Volunteerism is a *sadaqa* given on health, thus if one possesses no money, volunteerism is the *sadaqa* that he/ she gives to serve the community with what she/ he possesses." In her report *Role of the Mosque* published by the Muslim Parliament, Ruqaiyyah Waris Maqsood (a prolific author amongst others, especially in the field of social issues) suggests to include a "'Who can offer what?' community projects' inventory in the mosque to "Try to get all community members to volunteer some sort of service or activity", including those who are willing and able to support others, for example the elderly, with their gardening.

An-Nawawi holds that if someone is able to earn a suitable living and wants to occupy himself by studying some of the religious sciences but finds that his work will not allow him to do so, then he may be given *zakat* since seeking knowledge (including environmental issues) is considered a collective Muslim duty. As for the individual who is not seeking knowledge, *zakat* is not permissible for him if he is able to earn his living even though he resides at a school. An-Nawawi says: "As for one who is engaged in supererogatory worship (*nawafil*) or for one who occupies himself in *nawafil* with no time to pursue his own livelihood, he may not receive *zakat*. This is because the benefit of his worship is confined only to him, contrary to the one who seeks knowledge."

A report from the New Philanthropy Capital (NPC) *The Green Philanthropy* found the 100 largest UK charitable trusts allocate just 2 per cent of their £1.1bn annual funding into environmental charities and less than 5 per cent of the £8bn of private donations in the UK go to environmental causes. The NPC described these figures as "puzzling and woefully inadequate", warning that "we ignore environmental problems at our peril". It concludes that "there's a tremendous public conscience about poverty, but there isn't an analogous one for the environment", which is of serious concern as "[d]eforestation and over-fishing not only destroy natural resources, but threaten livelihoods and cause poverty". The report says that 1.3 billion people depend on fish, forests and agriculture for employment. Tropical deforestation also causes 20 per cent of global CO_2 admissions. Or as former UN Secretary-General Kofi Annan states: "All our efforts to defeat poverty and pursue sustainable development will be in vain if environmental degradation and natural resources depletion continue unabated".

Examples of action

65. Abu Dharr said, "The Prophet ﷺ told me 'Do not consider anything correct insignificant, even meeting your brother with a happy face." Consider how you can implement 'reduce, reuse, recyle'. Do it for God and be rewarded. When donating to charity, do consider if they can do something positive with it: the Association of Charity Shops stated that £4.5m a year is wasted on sorting, recycling and storing unsuitable donations - money that could otherwise be used to help charities fund the work of their beneficiaries.

66. Instead of wasting money on surplus goods (saving resources and transport) give surplus items away as charity to the poor (give them what is right, not what is left). Thank God for what you have and remember to make sure you do not cause harm when using His gifts is showing gratefulness to God. As Abu Dhar narrated: "Once I went out at night and found God's Messenger walking all alone accompanied by nobody, and I thought that perhaps he disliked that someone should accompany him. So I walked in the shade, away from the moonlight, but the Prophet looked behind and saw me and said, "Who is that?" I replied, "Abu Dhar, let God get me sacrificed for you!" He said, "O Abu Dhar, come here!" So I accompanied him for a while and then he said, "The rich are in fact the poor (little rewarded) on the Day of Resurrection except him whom God gives wealth which he gives (in charity) to his right, left, front and back, and does good deeds with it."

67. Plant a tree: the Prophet ﷺ said: "whosoever plants a tree, or grows crops, and a man, bird or an animal or a beast of prey eat its fruits, it is a charity for him" Additional benefit: researchers say giving leads to a healthier, happier life.

68. The Prophet ﷺ encouraged the faithful to be engaged in charitable deeds every single day. He ﷺ is reported to have said, "Everyday that the sun shines each one of you ought to do some charitable deeds."; He ﷺ also said, "There is reward for you in acts of compassion rendered to every creature with a throbbing heart (or liver)." On this, there are good grounds for co-operation between environmental activists and Muslims who care about social issues, as Rahat Kurd (member of the Ottawa Chapter of the Canadian Council of Muslim Women) shares: "Increased understanding of these basic principles of a way of life that literally means "Peace" might help the cause of environmental activists seeking "greener" policies from Muslim-run organizations, communities, and on the international level, the governments of Muslim countries."

69. Support end of world poverty by supporting the environment. Do an internship or voluntary work with the Islamic Foundation for Ecology and Environmental Sciences (IFEES, www.ifees.org.uk), or other such organisation. Or enable someone to do it.

70. Abu Dharr is reported as saying, "Your putting some of the water from your bucket in your brother's bucket is *sadaqa*; your removing stones, thorns and bones from

people's path is *sadaqa*; your guiding a man in a place where there are no guides is *sadaqa*."

Fasting

"Observing the fasting is prescribed for you as it was prescribed for those before you, that you may become pious." (Al-Baqarah/ The Cow [2] 183)

Fasting is divided into two kinds: the obligatory fast, and any non-obligatory fast. The obligatory fast is categorised as three kinds: (1) fasting the month of Ramadan; (2) fasting to expiate for religious offences; (3) fasting to fulfil a vow. Of the three, fasting the month of Ramadan is the most important. The elements of fasting are two: to worship God by abstaining from fastbreakers, combined with intention.

Key to this notion of a God-fearing life is the idea of *tazim* - reverence; veneration; respect. In this age of irreverence, Ramadan is a call to renew our reverence and love of God by venerating the divine commands and respecting their limits (our free will, for which we have to account on Day of Judgment). In the UK, we could be more respectful with each person generating half a tonne on average of domestic waste per year. Between 1990 and 2005, GDP grew in real terms by 43 per cent. GDP increased steadily from the early 1990s, with a 17 per cent rise between 1999 and 2005. GDP per head increased by 36 per cent between 1990 and 2005 and 14 per cent from 1999 to 2005. But with all this 'progress' as Muzammal Hussain, initiator of London Islamic Network for the Environment (LINE, www.lineonweb.org.uk, serving as example for MINE and ShINE – Midlands and Sheffield Islamic Network for the

Environment) muses: "Is nature backwards, or are we? [...] As society succeeds in producing ever more complex products, its failure to deal wisely with what we no longer use, becomes increasingly problematic. Nature, it appears is far ahead. For unlike in 'modern' human societies, nature recycles everything it produces."

Fasting is one of the best acts of worship. It is mandated by God to purify the soul along with the practice of good deeds. Thus the faster ought to be aware of acts or behaviours that may spoil his fast so that he or she will attain the highest benefit physically and spiritually. Fasting is a state of mind that transcends the physical restraint. We like to fast, as it pleases God...other good deeds, *like planting a tree*, are rewarded at least 10 times: Yahya related to me from Malik from Abu Zinad from al-Araj from Abu Hurayra that the Messenger of God ﷺ said, "By the One in Whose hand my self is, the smell of the breath of a man fasting is better with God than the scent of musk.' He leaves his desires and his food and drink for My sake. Fasting is for Me and I reward it. Every good action is rewarded by ten times its kind, up to seven hundred times, except fasting, which is for Me, and I reward it.' "

The virtues of fasting are great indeed: God has chosen fasting for Himself, and He will reward it and multiply the reward without measure, as we learn from the *hadeeth*: "Except for fasting which is only for My sake, and I will reward him for it." If a person's stomach is hungry, this will keep many of his other faculties from feeling hunger or desires; but if his stomach is satisfied, his tongue, eye, hand and private parts will start to feel hungry. Fasting leads to the defeat of Devil; it controls desires and protects one's faculties. When the fasting person feels the pangs of hunger, he experiences how the poor feel, so he has compassion towards them and gives them something to ward off their hunger. Hearing about them is not the same as sharing their suffering, just as a rider does not understand the hardship of walking unless he gets down and walks. Fasting trains the will to avoid desires and keep away from sin; it helps a person to overcome his own nature and to wean himself away from his habits. It also trains a person to get used to being organised and punctual, which will solve the problem that many people have of being disorganised, if only they realised. The person who is fasting should avoid all kinds of forbidden (*haram*) actions, such as backbiting, obscenity and lies, otherwise his reward may all be lost. According to Ibn Maajah the Prophet 🕌 said: "It may be that a fasting person gets nothing from his fast except hunger."

Examples of action

71. Hold an Earth fast. The late David Brower (Founder of Earth Island Institute) said in 2000, "Many environmentalists hail new efficient and 'green' energy sources, while forgetting that our greatest untapped source of energy is still the energy we can conserve by not using so much of it. Earth Day Energy Fast is the kind of idea that we need right now to put 'conservation' back in the conservation movement. To all those who are concerned about climate change, air pollution, species extinction, and the other costs to the earth of making energy, it's time to take action. Give the Earth a break it can feel by going on an Earth Day Energy Fast." - www.earthdayenergyfast.org: Find out

how many barrels of oil or equivalent you have leaking out of your house, then see what you can do stop the spill. There is now also a *Fasting for the Planet*, initiated by the London Islamic Network for the Environment (LINE) and St Ethelburga's, which "aims to facilitate two kinds of movements. A movement towards, and a movement away from. Through participating, people will be expressing an intention to move away from submission to: i) corporate domination; ii) consumerism; iii) the dominant, interest-based and fictitious monetary-system; iv) a dependence on fossil fuels. Simultaneously, by fasting participants hope to i) strengthen their inner resources, with an associated intention to move towards: ii) simplicity, sharing and community building; iii) economic systems that are nurturing to life, soul and community; iv) non-polluting energy, and sustainable use of the earth's resources.", www.fastfortheplanet.net.

72. Take the Green Ribbon Pledge. While the red ribbon stands for AIDS awareness, the pink ribbon for breastcancer awareness, the green ribbon stands not only for environmental awareness but also means the person wearing it has taken the pledge to conserve. Join people worldwide who have taken the green ribbon pledge to conserve energy for a secure future. There are hundreds of things you can do every day to reduce energy consumption. The result will be that you have saved energy and money, increased national security, improved our air and water quality, lessened threats posed by global warming, and benefited the health of all humans. Take the green ribbon pledge and follow it. Be

a part of the world movement and do what you can to conserve energy, www.greenribbonpledge.org.

73. Fulfil your needs, but hold a regular fast on your wants, because as English author G.K. Chesterton (1874- 1936 CE) states: "there are two ways to have enough. One is to have more. The other is to need less."

Ramadan (month of fasting)

"Ramadan is the (month) in which was sent down the Quran, as a guide to mankind, also clear (Signs) for guidance and judgment (between right and wrong). So every one of you who is present (at his home) during that month should spend it in fasting, but if any one is ill, or on a journey, the prescribed period (Should be made up) by days later. God intends every facility for you; He does not want to put to difficulties. (He wants you) to complete the prescribed period, and to glorify Him in that He has guided you; and perchance you shall be grateful." (Al-Baqarah/ The Cow [2] 185)

I read an interesting comment in an online sermon (*khutba*) by Muhammad Alshareef (founder, Al-Maghrib Institute, USA and Canada): "How many years have we been fasting Ramadan? Ten, 15 or 40 years? Are we 10, 15 or 40 times better? Or, does it seem like we have arrived back at the drawing board every time Ramadan comes around? All acts of worship are for our own benefit! If we don't do it, harm befalls us, which is the way life was programmed."

Hadeeths are evidence that the most important thing in the eyes of God is not merely physically restraining from the obvious food and drink, but the total commitment of the servant's body and soul to the letter and spirit of fasting. The curfew of the body and mind during the state of fasting enables the person who has fasted in the true spirit of Ramadan to have the necessary requirements to withstand the turbulence of life for the next eleven months. One of the most important things fasting affords the observer is helping him control or change his or her habits, the reason being human life is an embodiment of acquired habits. Fasting helps in conditioning the heart, the soul, and the body on the virtues of patience, tenacity, and firmness in the face of adversity. Patience is the pinnacle of self-mastery, discipline and spiritual agility. Patience is to turn the phrase "I can't" into "I can." It is to say, the difficult is easy. In Birmingham (UK) for some years now we have been organising an organic *iftar* (breaking of the fast) a ladies-only bring-a-vegetarian-dish (to be inclusive) where we in a relaxed atmosphere – the local Zawiya is most kind to host this - reflect on our food, share our green initiatives and provide light entertainment (for example Ulfah Arts reading poems on Creation).

Yahya related to me from Malik from his paternal uncle Abu Suhayl ibn Malik from his father that Abu Hurayra said, "When Ramadan comes the *gates of the Garden are opened* and the gates of the Fire are locked, and the satans are chained." And Abu Hurayrah ﷺ said: "The Messenger of God ﷺ said, 'There has come to you Ramadan, a blessed month. God has made it obligatory on you to fast (this month). During it the gates of Paradise are opened and the gates of Hell are locked, and the devils are chained up. In it there is a night that is better than a thousand months, and whoever is deprived of its goodness is deprived indeed.'"

Examples of action

74. The Messenger of God ﷺ said: "Ramadan has come to you - a month of blessing, in which God covers you with blessing, for He sends down mercy, decreases sins and answers prayers. In it, God looks at your competition (in good deeds), and boasts about you to His angels. So show God goodness from yourselves, for the unfortunate one is he who is deprived in (this month) of the mercy of God, the Mighty, the Exalted." For example, have a consumption fast (essentials are excluded) during Ramadan, like a number of American Muslims did in 2007 because, as they mention in their *Ramadan Compact*, "much as overeating can sicken the body, over-consumption can sicken the earth. Case in point, the climate crisis." For more information and inspiration, see: http://ramadancompact.blogspot.com.

75. Or hold an energy fast-a-thon (see http://fastathon.org for tips and suggestions on how to organise it). Or a carbon fast as a wake-up call to consumption and an opportunity to rethink the way our lifestyles impact people living in poverty.

76. To help buildings (house, mosque etc) 'join' you in the energy fast (and thus save costs), do an ecoaudit and insulate. Check www.ecocongregation.org and available grants.

77. Another idea is making a list of small actions, one for every day of Ramadan, including changing a lightbulb

to an energy efficient one, saying no to bottled water (drink tap), from checking your house for draughts (stop energy waste), to praying for people living in poverty and affected by climate change. Do it with friends and family to support and learn from one another. For ideas, check Every Action Counts, www.everyactioncounts.org.uk.

Pilgrimage (Hajj)

"And proclaim unto mankind the Pilgrimage (the Hajj). They will come unto you on foot and also on every lean camel; they will come from every deep ravine that they may witness things that are of benefit to them, and mention the name of God on appointed days over the beast of cattle that He has bestowed upon them." (Al-Hajj/ The Pilgrimage [22] 27-29)

According to the Saudi Arabian Ministry of Hajj, the word '*hajj*' literally means 'to set out for a place'. For a Muslim, that place is the city of Makkah. There are three obligatory acts of the pilgrimage: intention (*niyyah*) of pilgrimage, the call to God's service (*talbiyyah* – English translation: "At your service, O Lord, at Your service. There is no associate with You. The Praise and blessing are Yours, as well as the sovereignty - with You there is no associate."), and wearing the pilgrim's garment (*ihram*). As this is not a scholarly work (and I am not a scholar), I will not go into details of these acts. The act of wearing the pilgrimage garb, however, is more than the mere assumption of specified clothing: *ihram* refers to a state of consecration which means one has 'forbidden' oneself the usual worldly concerns, pursuits and pleasures in order to be purely available for the sacred: reflecting on the Creator, our role in this life and Creation mainly.

In 1927, an estimated 300 to 350 thousand did the *hajj*, half of them from outside Saudi Arabia. In 1972, there were a total of just over 1 million *hajjis*. The *hajj* in 1429 AH (in December 2008) was done by 2.5 million pilgrims, including 1.7 million non-Saudis, but excluding a significant number of pilgrims without permits. This is the Saudi Arabian equivalent of more than 25 concurrent Football World Cups or 30 simultaneous Super Bowls. The number of non-Saudi pilgrims almost doubled from 1996 – 2008 (from 1 to almost 1.8 million). And then there are the *umrah* ('lesser pilgrimage') pilgrims. The Saudi Ministry of Hajj expects the number of *Umrah* pilgrims for the 1429 AH Umrah season to rise to 3.5 million, an increase of nearly half a million on the previous year's figures).

According to Fadhlalla Haeri "[p]rayer […] if not offered in sincere supplication, can be reduced to a simple cry for material help, and if giving becomes self-gratifying, it enhances the ego rather than reduces it. If fasting be performed simply as abstention from food, its benefit may only be dietary, and if *the pilgrimage loses its spiritual and social content, it becomes simply a form of uncomfortable folkloric pageantry*." (my emphasis) An example for whom the *hajj* was probably quite uncomfortable, but definitely not folkloric pageantry, was Chechen Dzhanar-Aliyev Magomed-Ali who cycled from Urus-Martan, a small village in Chechnya (Russian Federation), to Makkah…and back, a trip of 12,000 kilometres which he did in ten weeks at the age of 63. Harun al-Rashid (763 – 809 CE), the fifth Caliph, and his wife Zubayda performed the *hajj* on foot from Baghdad (Iraq). Inspired by what they saw on their way, Zubayda sponsored and promoted public works in the name of Islam, in particular wells and water reservoirs referred to as *Zubayda's Way*.

Abu Hurairah ﵁ reported that the Prophet ﷺ was once asked: "What is the best deed?" He replied: "To have faith in God and His Messenger." The enquirer asked: "What next?" The Prophet ﷺ said: "To strive in the cause of God." "What is the next best thing?" He replied: "Hajj Mabrur (a faultless Hajj that is free of sin and is graced with Divine acceptance and pleasure)." Al-Hasan said: "It means that a person after performance of Hajj should desire and be inclined to the life of the Hereafter rather than the material pleasures of this world."

Carsten Niebuhr (a German in the service of the king of Denmark, the sole survivor of a group of five who travelled through Egypt and the Arabian Peninsula from 1761 to 1763 CE) muses in his book *Travels through Arabia and Other Countries in the East* (English version first published in Edinburgh in 1792): "Every Mussulman, it is well known, is obliged, once in his life, to visit Mecca, and perform acts of devotion in the sacred places. If this law were strictly observed, the concourse of pilgrims would be immense; nor could the city contain such crowds from every country in which the Mahometan religion has been introduced." Though I agree with his sentiments, nowadays it seems less of a question of all poor Muslims from around the world going but materially better off people going numerous times "because they can afford to". I was fortunate in going on *hajj* in early 2005, but felt distracted and disturbed by the number of people who would ask (before, during and after), even as an introductory question "and, how many times have you been?" It seemed that for an increasing number of people who could afford it, *hajj* was no longer 'the journey of a lifetime' in which to reconnect with our Creator and reflect on Creation, but a yearly or at least regular 'ritual'. This is perhaps most vividly illustrated by the following: the Saudi Telecommunications Company (STC) proudly announced that it had raised its "capacity to more than 1.352 million telecom lines in Arafat" and that it was "passing more than 230 million calls and 300 million message in 3 the days". As a joke mentioned on *Islam From Inside* mentions "The Kaaba is the hub of the Muslim world, now it will also be a telecommunications hub for the Muslim world." – so as an article by the World Shia Federation asks, "are you a haji or a tourist"? In the latter case you may be interested in Abraj Al Bait (www.abrajalbait.com), the largest retail space in Makkah, one of "the most luxurious and high tech retail developments" on the site adjacent to the King Abdul Aziz gate of the holy mosque.

Better to remember the following, from a Friday sermon in Oxford (UK) in January 2006 (week of the *hajj*) as posted on the website of the Muslim Educational Centre of Oxford (www.meco.org.uk): "We pray that they will not be returning to resume their usual lifestyles but will imbibe and incorporate the real benefits of the *hajj*, and not by wallowing in the social prestige accorded to them now that they are *hajjis* (those who have completed the pilgrimage). They need to be aware of the spiritual path that can elevate them to them becoming genuine believers and truly righteous. The *hajj* is therefore the ultimate expression of reconciling the vertical with the horizontal aspects of life, of combining the eternal with the earthly planes, of uniting the material and the mystical, of joining the theological with the temporal. If the returning pilgrims do this, then the real purpose and true mission of the hajj would be realised."

It has been reported from Abul Hassan Ridha رَضِىَاللهُعَنْهُ that on reaching the *Rukn-ul-Yamaani* (south west corner of the *Kabah*), one should raise hands in supplication and say: "O God! O Controller of health and its Provider, One who grants it, One who bestows it as a reward or as a grace on me *and all creation*, O Merciful in this world and the Hereafter, shower Muhammad and his progeny with Your blessings, grant me health, lasting and complete and thankfulness for it, in this world and in the Hereafter, by Your mercy, O Most Merciful of the merciful."

In 2006 - 2007 alone, Australia exported 1,43 million live sheep to Saudi Arabia (of 4.1 million which are shipped from Australia alone to the Middle-East each year, 75,000 of which die, due to change in their diet, stress and/ or disease), in ships taking some three weeks to arrive and three sheep sharing a single square metre of space. Ever since I heard about this, I was very disturbed about this. Fortunately, I managed to find some clarity on this. Mohamed Sayed Tantawy (Grand Sheikh, Al Ahzar University in Egypt) in April 2008 issued a *fatwa* about the long distance transportation of animals and slaughter: "We hereby say that the call of Islam is to be lenient with the animal and to treat it with mercy, among which is transporting the animal. Such transportation must be carried out by a comfortable mean that guarantees its safety, prohibits its torture, threatening its life or afflicting it with diseases that are contagious to the human being or third party. This is deduced for the Prophetic Saying of the Prophet ﷺ "Any good deed rendered in a hardship is like an almsgiving and his ﷺ saying: "A woman entered hell fire for detaining a cat which she had neither fed nor left to eat the leftovers of the land." I wonder, why is it necessary anyways to transport so many animals live halfway across the globe when I understand 80 per cent of the slaughterhouses in Australia are certified halal and during *hajj* people do not get close to the animals: the hajj-goers buy a ticket, certifying an animal will be ritually killed in their name. The Saudi Project for Utilisation of Hajj Meat also mentions: "Shari'ah permits the Muslim to slaughter his offering by proxy given to any trusted person or entity, whether this offering is *Hady*, *Fidyah*, *Sadaqah* or *Udhiyah*. The person or entity receiving the proxy should undertake performance of all that which is required to discharge his responsibility in accordance with the principles of *Shari'ah*."

Anyways, when in Saudi Arabia for *hajj* (or *umrah*) try to visit the King Abdullah International Gardens (www.kaig.net, due to open in 2010 CE) just outside Riyadh, a most appropriate place as apparently the name Riyadh is derived from plural of the Arabic word *rawdha*, meaning a place of gardens and trees. The Gardens will consist of two giant crescent-shaped enclosures (five times the size of the Eden Project in UK's Cornwall, covering an area of 24 acres), with different indoor gardens each representing a different era in botanical time, starting with the Devonian period (when some of the first plants evolved

400 million years ago), then the Carboniferous garden (tropical wetland swamp forest of about 300 million years ago), then other periods including the Jurassic era (some 206 million to 142 million years ago), the Cretaceous era (142 million to 65 million years ago, the time of the dinosaurs), the Cenozoic era (65 million to the present) and the Pliocene era (3.5 million to 1.2 million years ago). Any known species that have become extinct since their origin will be represented by models painted a ghostly grey. A final garden, the one I would be most keen to see is called the *Garden of Choices*, which will attempt to explain what may happen to the Earth in the future as a result of the different possible scenarios resulting from human activity. Visitors can follow two paths: a 'do nothing' path leading to a dead-end, while the other path widens out into a range of botanical possibilities. The project's designers have promised to make it as eco-friendly as possible, for example by using renewable energy (including solar energy) and recycling water. To be honest, I had not expected this kind of project in a country where the minister in charge of the environment is also the Minister for Defence and Aviation.

Examples of action

78.   According to Muhammad Naasir-ud-Deen Al-Albani (1914 - 1999 CE): "the mere wish and intention to perform *Hajj* is not sufficient as that has been with him since leaving his own land - rather he must perform by word and action what will cause him to be *muhrim* [pilgrim]." For example he reminds us we are allowed to "Smelling sweet smelling plants" (though unfortunately I cannot remember seeing any left). Now

that planes have been invented it is not necessary to fly in, stay in air-conditioned hotels and be back in a few days. Ahmad Thomson went on *hajj* in 1977 over land and wrote two books about this: *The Difficult Journey* and *The Way Back*.

79. I understand all schools of thought in Islam agree that it is unlawful to cut or pull out plants or vegetation (even thornbushes) growing within the area designated as the Sacred Precinct in Makkah, except for what is grown by man, and a species called the odoriferous brush. The Prophet ﷺ stated: "There is no one who makes *talbiyyah* [call to God's service] except that whatever is on his right and left - trees and stones also make *talbiyyah* until the earth resounds from here and here - meaning - on his right and left." When on *hajj*, ponder about that.

80. Ibn Abbas narrated: "I proceeded along with the Prophet on the day of Arafat (9th *Dhul-Hijja*). The Prophet heard a great hue and cry and the beating of camels behind him. So he beckoned to the people with his lash, "O people! Be quiet. Hastening is not a sign of righteousness." If we are less in a hurry – not just during *hajj* – we can enjoy our surroundings more, have an interest in improving them…

81. And upon return, as Ali Shariati asked in his book *Hajj*: "Oh *Hajj* - where are you going now? Back home to your life and to your world? Are you returning from Hajj the same way you came? Never! Never!" As according to David Clingingsmith, lead author of *Estimating the Impact of the Hajj: Religion and*

178

Tolerance in Islam's Global Gathering (April 2008) "Hajjis show increased belief in peace, and in equality and harmony among adherents of different religions", returning *hajjis* should get inspired by opportunities in working together with those of other faiths in preserving Creation as collected by the Alliance for Religions and Conservation (ARC, www.arcworld.org).

82. As Shelina Zahra Janmohamed (of www.spirit21.co.uk fame) comments: "If we believe that by sitting at home and engaging in armchair protests that we can make an impact, then we are deluded. Muttering *astaghfirullahs* [God forgive them] whilst propped on a comfortable cushion with no connection to the outside world cannot create change. The *hajj* gives us that very evidence - you have to be right in the centre of things to make an impact." Get involved in your community, either by joining an existing group or set one up. You could look at getting a grant or award, for example http://itsyourcommunity.co.uk

PART 3: TRANSACTIONS (*MUAMALAT*)

Introduction

"O you who believe! Stand out firmly for God, as witnesses to fair dealing, and let not the hatred of others to you make you swerve to wrong and depart from Justice. Be just: that is next to piety: and fear God. For God is well-acquainted with all that you do." (Al-Maidah/ The Table Spread [5] 9)

It is not enough to have faith and worship in the traditional way, such as praying: whenever faith is evoked in the Quran, an injunction to react immediately always follows and charitable acts are especially encouraged. So, for example, "Those who believed *and* who did good deeds" (Al-Asr/ The Declining Day [103] 3) or "For those who believe *and* do good deeds is every blessedness and a beautiful place of final return" (Ar-Rad/ The Thunder [13] 29). In our transactions as a society we can sometimes have a strange set of priorities: at a weapons fair (Defense Systems and Equipment International, DSEi) it is not the weapon buyers that get arrested, but demonstrators for peace; a climate camp near an airport (from where an increasing number of flights pollute our shared and fragile earth) does not trigger a cap on flights but an injunction against the peaceful protesters who want to save the planet (do not get me wrong, I am all for arrests of those who do criminal damage, are intent on terrorist acts etcetera). And talking about peace: according to the Worldwatch Institute in 2006 world military budgets (paid from our taxes) stood at $1,232 billion, 228 times as much as was spent on UN peacekeeping.

According to Mintel, a market research company, the estimated spending power of Muslims in the UK is £20.5 billion. There are more than 5,000 Muslim millionaires in the UK, with combined assets worth more than £3.6 billion. So we can buy so many things, but "what is the point of having a good house, if you don't have a decent planet to put it on" as US author and philosopher Henry David Thoreau (1817-1862 CE) said. So better to think like Mohammad Marmaduke Pickthall (1875-1936 CE, translator of the Quran into English): "Everything in the world is yours, until and unless you try to grab it and keep it for yourself alone."

Shopping

"But when they see some bargain or some amusement, they disperse headlong to it, and leave you standing. Say: "The (blessing) from the Presence of God is better than any amusement or bargain! and God is the Best to provide (for all needs)."(Al-Jumua/ The Congregation [62] 11) "...But spend not wastefully (your wealth) in the manner of a spendthrift. Verily spendthrifts are brothers of the devils..."
(Al-Isra/ The Night Journey [17] 26-27)

Often people feel helpless in the face of global issues such as environmental destruction and poor countries' exploitation, but ethical consumerism can be a driving force for change and what I like about Islam: you are only responsible for your own deeds (or lack of them) and as Umar al-Farooq ﺭﺿﻲﺍﻟﻠﻪﻋﻨﻪ reminds us "Call yourselves to account before you are called to account". When going out shopping we may not immediately think we can change the world, but consider every purchase an expression of your ethics, supporting ethical/ green companies, avoiding companies that are not in line with your ethics, Islam's principles. At a talk on *Islam and Environment* I was invited to give at a church, one of the questions related to the time involved in making the right choice when in the shops. I did agree that with so many options on offer (a full aisle of options of this, a full aisle of options of that), it can be a challenge. However, the response that came to my mind is: when we have an exam ahead of us (be it driving exam, or school exam), we do not just pray we will do fine and that the examiner will be in a good mood, because we all know this is a recipe for disaster, to fail the exam miserably. So we study hard, we revise and go over things time and time again. Well, from what I understand of Islam, Day of Judgment is the exam of exams, so besides our prayers, we should live and breathe our faith at all times, putting in our best effort. To make things manageable, I try to do research one thing at a time and then stick to that decision, including kitemarks, such as Fairtrade and Soil Association (for organic). Also, I try to buy my basics in bulk (saves money, packaging and frequency of shopping) from trusted, ethical sources such as Traidcraft (www.traidcraftshop.co.uk, *fighting poverty through trade*), Goodness Direct (www.goodnessdirect.co.uk, *making healthy shopping easy*) or Ethical Superstore (www.ethicalsuperstore.com). I reuse jars to keep manageable quantities at hand for daily use.

To avoid becoming paralysed by too much choice and overwhelmed by number of decisions, I made and regularly update a list of things to look at and I then focus on one thing on the list a month (or more if I have time, but one is the minimum). A main guideline I use when buying something: do I know what I am buying (I mean, can I understand at least basically the list of ingredients or does it require the knowledge of someone with a double PhD in Chemistry)? When at risk of buying something unnecessarily or without thinking, I try to remember what Muhammad Asad (1900 – 1992 CE, born Leopold Weiss, author of *The Road to Mecca*) stated when commenting on [17] 27: "Squandering implies an utter lack of gratitude for the gift of Sustenance bestowed by God upon man".

Over 260 million new pairs of shoes are bought each year in the UK. The garment industry in the UK alone is worth £36 billion a year. Much of the clothing we wear is made of cotton. Cotton is the world's most important non-food agricultural commodity, yet, according to the Environmental Justice Foundation (EJF), it is responsible for the release of $2 billion of chemical pesticides each year, within which at least $819 million are considered toxic enough to be classified as hazardous by the World Health Organisation (WHO). According to the EJF's report *The deadly chemicals in cotton* published in 2007, cotton accounts for 16 per cent of global insecticide releases – more than any other single crop. Almost one kilogram of hazardous pesticides is applied for every hectare under cotton. Between 1 and 3 per cent of agricultural workers worldwide suffer from acute pesticide poisoning with at least one million requiring hospitalisation each year, according to a report prepared jointly for the FAO, UNEP and WHO. These figures equate to between 25 million and 77 million agricultural workers worldwide. According to the WHO 20,000 people die every year from pesticide poisoning.

I have a recurring dream, of which the last scene often pops up in my mind when considering buying something. In summary it goes a bit like this: it is the Day of Judgement and I am waiting in the queue to have my hearing and account for myself. When it is my turn, all of a sudden the rest of the queue disappears and it is replaced by a pile of rubbish, MY rubbish, everything I have *ever* bought and then thrown away. I feel disgusted about the size of the dump....

According to a report *Global Entertainment and Media Outlook: 2006-2010* issued by global accounting firm PricewaterhouseCoopers, worldwide advertising spending in 2005 was $385 billion (some 20 million more than the GDP of Switzerland, Worldbank 2005). The accounting firm's report projected worldwide advertisement spending to exceed half-a-trillion dollars by 2010. In its *Global Entertainment and Media Outlook: 2007-2011*, it has stated that by 2011 it expects that worldwide advertisement spending could even reach $2 trillion (similar to the GDP of the UK). Why mention this? Because it is good to be aware of this pressure put on us when shopping. Though "Muslims are offended by creating a want rather than addressing a need, by psychological manipulation", we are human and if advertising would not work, it would not represent a whole percent of world GDP. Also note an example of research on specific marketing to Muslims: "Islam is the religion of a vast and growing number of consumers around the world. There is evidence to suggest that religious beliefs can impact consumer behavior and response to advertising messages. [...] Recommendations are provided for international advertisers developing messages for Muslim consumer segments", as included in *Journal for Euromarketing* in 2002. Or as Batool Al-Toma observed in *Meeting Point*, the newsletter of the UK New Muslims Project, how "crafty entrepreneurs within our own community" are wanting to 'Islamicise' everything for the sake of selling us goods from 'Islamic' fizzy drinks, 'Islamic' toothpaste to even 'Islamic' windows which "for the growing numbers of disillusioned old cynics are no more 'Islamic' than what is generally available on the open market". In November 2007 Iran and Malaysia even announced the joint production of an "Islamic car". No it will not be pollution free to support Creation: it will have a special compartment to keep a Quran (what is wrong with the glove compartment?), a hijab and it will have a *Qibla* (direction to pray) indicator.

According to a JWT survey, British Muslims are significantly more positive towards brands and branding that the general population. The report suggests that brands that take the trouble to establish solid connections with Muslims can expect greater loyalty than they can from other British consumers. Fifty-eight per cent of the Muslim respondents said they feel that brands make life "more interesting", compared to 20 per cent of the general sample. And while only a quarter of the general sample said they make a point of knowing which brands are popular, 63 per cent of Muslims said they do so – and this climbs to 71 per cent amongst those aged 18 to 29. And according to the "biggest lifestyle study of Muslim women undertaken in the UK" by Sisters Magazine and Ummah Foods, the average

UK Muslim woman "shops in Primark, TK Maxx and Topshop" (UK high street discount retailers). A report published in September 2008 *Spotlighting Europe's Muslim consumers*, includes the quote: "Since Muslims are the fastest growing consumer segment in the world, any company that is not considering how to serve them is missing a significant opportunity to affect both its top- and bottom-line growth". Be ready to resist.

In this respect I might mention that I am part of a panel that every so often gets asked to participate in a "new product concept study". I think of it as my free training (I actually even get £4 per study, for 15 minutes internet work) on what not to buy and what to watch out for to make sure I get what *I* want, not what supplier wants me to buy. As launching a product can be quite an expensive exercise, the aim of these surveys is to test how best to market any product. Questions normally include whether I believe I would *need* such a product or whether I would *want* it; whether the product has "a premium looking package" or even whether "package makes it *look* like a good quality and healthy product" (my emphasis). It also often includes a question on whether such new product idea would replace something I use now, or whether I would buy it in addition to my current products. Most products are hopelessly over-packaged or filled with unhealthy colourings etc, so I use my chance for feedback as part of my green struggle (*jihad*) strategy to always complain about polluting and unhealthy sides of products and suggesting that "my alternatives" are always organic, fair trade items. By the way, when you can now buy 'organic' (which is then often sold at a premium by canny supermarkets), the methods used are "as old as the hills" and should more rightly be called the 'traditional way'.

Most things we buy, we ultimately want to get rid of again. Currently the vast majority of our waste ends up in landfill, a 'hole in the ground'. In recognition of the increasing quantities of waste that are being disposed of to landfill (some 85 per cent of municipal waste) the UK Government has, from October 1996, imposed a tax on certain types of waste deposited in landfill (encourage local authorities and businesses to switch to more environmentally friendly and sustainable methods of waste disposal). And from 2010 there will be a £150 fine for every tonne of rubbish sent to a landfill that passes the limit set in the EU Landfill Directive. This amount will somehow have to make it to our tax bill, so less waste will save us money in our tax bill.

While many people intuitively think that reusable nappies (diapers in the US) are better for the environment, disposable nappies account for some 95 per cent of the market and around 2.5 billion disposable nappies are sold in the UK each year (apparently the average baby will get through 5,840 nappies). This leads to 2-3 per cent of our household waste being estimated to be disposable nappies, or approximately 400,000 tonnes of waste each year. Though a study funded by the Environment Agency published in 2005 suggested that disposable and washable nappies were environmentally similar, it has been widely criticised (for example by the Women's Environmental Network). The study mentions that "to compare the nappies fairly, the study considered the environmental impacts associated with an average child wearing nappies during the first two and a half years of its life." What the summary does not mention is that the washable nappies option included washing 80 per cent of the nappies in special washing sessions for the nappies and in a third of the cases wash at 90 degrees, assumes buying 47.5 (a half?!) nappies (and with 6.1 changes a day this would mean washing less than once a week), mentions that 10 per cent of the nappies would be ironed (who would do that?). Also: gone are the days of soaking and boiling terries, folding and pins.

Technology has caught up here as everywhere and low temperature washes of shaped nappies with poppers or Velcro in new, soft and absorbent fabrics are the norm. Plus, you save £500 over nappy lifetime of first child and even more so with further children. In October 2008, the Environment Agency realised this as well and published an update to its 2005 report where it concluded: "[c]ombining three of the beneficial scenarios (washing nappies in a fuller load, outdoor line drying all of the time, and reusing nappies on a second child) would lower the global warming impact by 40 per cent from the baseline scenario, or some 200kg of carbon dioxide equivalents over the two and a half years, equal to driving a car approximately 1,000 km." Note also disposable nappies can take 500 years to decompose (it is good to have access to good literature from 500 years ago, but their waste? – I pity our successors) and it takes a cup of crude oil to produce the plastic for just one disposable nappy and, in the UK alone, seven million trees are felled each year to produce wood pulp for disposable nappies. Babies survived until the 70s with cotton nappies. Why cannot we all still use them now? They produce 60 times less solid waste than disposables. And, last but not least, I read that girls take 5 months and boys take 7 months longer to become 'potty-trained' when using disposables. Why? Because in disposables the children are so dry (due to super-soaking chemicals) that they are less keen to be distracted from their play to become independent. In 1950 (when all children wore cloth nappies), 90 per cent of them were toilet (potty) trained by 18 months; in the 1980s, about 50 per cent of children wore cloth nappies, while the other 50 per cent wore disposable nappies and only about 50 per cent of the children were toilet trained by the age of 18 months. Today, almost 90-95 per cent of children wear disposable nappies and only about 10 per cent of children are toilet trained by the age of 18 months (the average age for potty training is now about 30 months – costing 12 months more too).

Buying ethical products sends support directly to progressive companies working to improve the status quo, while at the same time depriving others that abuse for profit. For example, when you buy an eco-washing-up liquid you are giving its manufacturer the funds it needs to invest in clean technology and advertise its products to a wider market. At the same time, you are no longer buying your old liquid, so its manufacturer loses business and will perhaps change its ways. Another attraction of ethical buying is its convenience. After all, everyone needs to go shopping or to consume resources in one way or another. As an ethical consumer, every time you buy something you can make a difference. The benefits to society of buying ethically are potentially far-reaching. It encourages innovative products and companies while discouraging others that ignore the social and environmental consequences of their actions. It empowers the consumer, giving you a say in how the products you buy are made, and how the company that makes them conducts its business. It can and has made a difference in the past.

As 'the first American Muslim' Mohammed Alexander Russell Webb (1846- 1916 CE) observes: "In the household of the true Mussulman there is no vain show, no labored attempt to follow servilely the fashions, including furniture and ornaments, in vogue in London and Paris. Plainness and frugality are apparent everywhere, the idea being that it is far better to cultivate the spiritual side of our nature than to waste our time and money trying to keep up appearances that we hope will cause our neighbors to think that we have more money than we really have and are more aesthetic in our tastes than we really are."

So in conclusion, when shopping, "ask yourself, what did they do 50 years ago before plastic was around. The answer is usually there. Recognize that disposable is a word made up by businessmen whose only criteria is that you will throw an item away and buy another one [costing money and Creation, RtV]. Finally, acknowledge that just because it's the way everyone does it, doesn't mean it's good. Examine your lifestyle, investigate the consequences of your actions, and ask yourself "Is this something I really want to be a part of"?" Dave Chameides, the author of this quote, thus decided to test himself: http://365daysoftrash.blogspot.com.

Examples of actions

83. When buying clothes, go for quality, not quantity. As the Messenger of God ﷺ said: "Listen, listen! Wearing old clothes is a part of faith, wearing old

clothes is a part of faith." Or as Hisham said, "I asked Aisha, 'What did the Prophet ﷺ, do in his house?' She replied, 'He did what one of you would do in his house. He mended sandals and patched garments and sewed." So reduce, reuse and then recycle (who says you cannot wear 'last year's fashion' any more?).

84. Remember to keep your shopping in check, as according to Abu Huraira ﷺ, the Prophet ﷺ said, "Let the slave of *Dinar* and *Dirham*, of *Quatifa* and *Khamisa* (that is, money and luxurious clothes) perish for he is pleased if these things are given to him, and if not, he is displeased!" Abundance of a resource does not justify its wastage, as the Prophet ﷺ advised Muslims not to waste water even when near a river for ablution. If you have no use for something anymore, but it still has life, freecycle (recycle for free by giving it away) it, like sisters in Canada have done: the *Ottawa Islamic Community Closet*, founded by Noor Limame, is "a sisters only group that trades their own personal belongings in order to help one another for absolutely no profit at all".

85. The less you buy, the less you need to be out there earning money to afford it, the more time you have for the more important things in life, like spending time with family and doing charitable actions. Try www.downshiftingweek.com (pick any week… and then keep going!). Or "Do it yourself! When your friends say, "You know you can buy one of those..." do you say, "Yeah, so?" - www.make-stuff.com

86. Instead of buying new books, check www.greenmetropolis.com to buy second hand books if in the UK or in the US try www.paperbackswap.com: "Mail a book. Get a book. Any book you request is yours to keep, share or swap. No late fees. No processing charges. No hidden charges. Every time you mail a book to another member, you can request one for yourself from over 2.5 Million.", or BookMooch (http://bookmooch.com) "lets you give away books you no longer need in exchange for books you really want." All have sections on books on religion and environment.

87. For other shopping needs, consider www.ethicalconsumer.org or www.ethicalsuperstore.com (good for bulk buys, alone or with a friend) and look out for fair-trade and organic as according to the Fairtrade Foundation: "[a]ll Fairtrade certified producers are required to comply with the international Fairtrade environmental standard as part of the requirements of certification. The standard requires producers to ensure that they protect the natural environment and make environmental protection a part of farm management. Producers are also encouraged to minimize the use of energy, especially energy from non-renewable sources." For a cheap and green makeover, organise a swap event with your friends or as Islamic circle social (any useable leftovers are given to charity).

88. When shopping for the baby, try washable nappies: www.realnappycampaign.com (for UK) or www.realdiaperassociation.org (for US), swap clothes with friends or buy them from a charity shop. An article on the ethics of climate change uses the subtitle 'Pay

Now or Pay More Later?' where 'later' probably refers to the children, remember that.

89. Go plastic bag free or, even better, help make your borough or city plastic bag free…several countries have done it, Modbury in South Devon in UK needs copycats (www.plasticbagfree.com). In 2002, the Republic of Ireland became the first country in the world to charge for plastic bags - a policy which cut usage by 90 per cent almost overnight (so we do not really *need* plastic bags after all then?). To help my resolve in not using plastic bags, I normally carry a cotton string bag in my handbag for unexpected buys and when setting out to shop, I take a backpack made from hemp (the good cousin, not the naughty one).

90. When you have finished using what you have bought, recycle as much as possible, as the World Assembly of Muslim Youth WAMY states: "Islam […] supports the maximum use of recycling, and today this can include the recycling of organic kitchen waste (into compost), glass, paper, cardboard, metal, oil, cloth, books, building and furniture materials, batteries, TV and computer components, and even some plastics. The more this is done, the more likely it would be that our water, air and soil would be safe and healthy for humans and all living things." For example, the average UK family uses some 500 glass bottles and jars annually. Though it will never decompose if it ends up in landfill, recycling just one glass bottle would save enough energy to power a computer for 25 minutes. To know what you can recycle and how, check

www.recyclenow.com. It also has information on home composting.

Toiletries

"O Children of Adam! Wear your beautiful apparel at every time and place of prayer: eat and drink: But waste not by excess, for God loves not the wasters." (Al-Araf/ The Heights [7] 31)

Using perfume is encouraged in Islam for both men and women, though for women not for use in public. The perfumes of the days of the Prophet ﷺ can, however, not be compared with the vast majority of perfumes on the market today. Modern perfumes can include animal ingredients, which are usually extracted from live animals in a painful way, such as ambergris (lumps of oxidized fatty compounds, whose precursors were secreted and expelled by the sperm whale. Ambergris is commonly referred to as 'amber' in perfumery and should not be confused with yellow amber, which is used in jewellery); castoreum (obtained from the odorous sacs of the North American beaver); civet (also called civet musk, this is obtained from the odorous sacs of the civets, animals related to the mongoose).

What would Prophet Muhammad ﷺ have thought of using live animals for our pleasure in this way, risking animals for our pleasure? Let us remember he was a big animal lover as becomes clear from for example the following: Prophet Mohammed ﷺ loved cats. It was normal for his cat to purr and come close to him. He always made sure that there was food and water for the cat. He also petted and loved his cat. This cat was one day taking a nap next to the Prophet Mohammed ﷺ and it cuddled next to Prophet's body in such a way that it was sleeping on a part of his gown. The Prophet ﷺ woke up by the call of prayer from the mosque and saw the cat in deep slumber on his gown. In order not to disturb the cat's sleep, the Prophet ﷺ cut off that part of the gown with scissors on which the cat rested. He ﷺ then went to pray in the mosque. At this point people may think of the *hadeeth* that angels do not enter the house with a dog in it. I wonder though, is this due to the dog (as often assumed) or the owner, not allowing the dog a natural (*fitra*) life; that is, with fellow dogs as they are social animals? For as Khaled Abou El Fadl, (Professor of Islamic Law, UCLA, US) states, how can God "create animals with these natural tendencies and then condemn them as thoroughly reprehensible?"

Synthetic alternatives are not always the answer: there is scientific evidence (for example as published by the US Government's National Institute for Health) that some common ingredients, like certain synthetic musks, can disrupt the balance of hormones in the human body (endocrine disruption) and even cause cancer. Or birth defects, as a study published in November 2008 by Imperial College London showed, warning pregnant women to avoid the use of make-up containing phthalates (a family of chemicals that are produced in the millions of tons annually worldwide). Independent laboratory tests published in 2002 found phthalates in more than 70 per cent of health and beauty products tested and sold in the US – including popular brands of shampoo, deodorant, hair mousse, face lotion and every single fragrance tested. Concerns about the health impacts of phthalates continue to mount, with research from 2005 linking high phthalate levels with feminised genitals in baby boys. A US government-funded study by Dr Swan (Professor of obstetrics and gynaecology) showed that the higher the levels of phthalates in the mother during pregnancy, the more likely the researchers were to find the baby boys to have incomplete genital development. Most worryingly, the changes occurred at phthalate levels that have been measured in about a quarter of women in the US. The worldwide fragrances and perfumes market is projected to reach $33.6 billion in 2012 (more than the G8 Gleneagles pledge of $27.12 billion in 2007 nominal terms - for increased level of annual aid flow to Africa by 2010, of which only $4 billion was programmed to by the end of 2007), with the perfume market for the premium brands in the Emirates alone estimated to be worth $270 million.

Too many toiletries, for example disinfectants, contain formaldehyde (a carcinogenic or cancer causer, as confirmed by the US Environmental Protection Agency, EPA, and the International Agency for Research on Cancer, IARC). Another synthetic chemical, triclosan is found in soaps, deodorants, toothpastes, shaving creams, mouth washes, and cleaning supplies and is infused in an increasing number of consumer products, such as kitchen utensils, toys, bedding, socks, and trash bags, sometimes as the proprietary microban treatment. Researchers found that triclocarban (a 'cousin' of triclosan) disrupts reproductive hormone activity, and triclosan interferes a type of cell signalling that occurs in brain, heart and other cells. The use of triclosan in household products also introduces the chemical to surface waters where it can form dioxins. Two concerns that have been raised regarding the widespread environmental distribution of triclosan and triclocarban are promotion of bacterial resistance, and hormone disruption in vertebrates (meaning they get confused about their gender and 'forget' to do their normal duties, thus impacting their numbers in further generations). This is especially worrying as research published in March 2008 by the US Department of Health showed that 75 per cent of people tested had significant measurable quantities of triclosan in their urine. The best news is (which should come as little surprise as the Prophet ﷺ said: "There is no affliction that God has created, except that God also has created its treatment.") that research has confirmed that using an antibacterial soap was no more effective in preventing infectious illness than plain soap.

And as for fragranced consumer products (such as air fresheners, laundry supplies, personal care products, and cleaners), results from a recent regulatory analysis, coupled with a chemical analysis of six best-selling products in the US (three air fresheners and three laundry supplies) by Prof. Steinemann, provide some worrying findings. First, no law in the US requires disclosure of all chemical ingredients in consumer products or in fragrances (and it seems this also goes for other countries including the UK it is also all but impossible to find ingredients of fragranced consumer products). Second, in the six tested products, nearly 100 volatile organic compounds (VOCs) were identified, but none of the VOCs were listed on any product label. Most worryingly, of the identified VOCs, ten are regulated as toxic or hazardous under US laws.

Considering a 2007 study by a chemist suggests British women absorb an average of five pounds of cosmetics a year through their skin and mouths, some moderation would not only be good for our health, but also Creation and wallet. I noticed the author of this study got criticised for having a vested interest in highlighting danger of mainstream cosmetics as he has since set up an organic cosmetics business, BeingOrganic.com – out of "frustration" with inability to find suitable products (did you know products labelled as 'natural' are not generally restricted in the ingredients they can use?). The truth is: he set up his business as a result of his findings, not vice versa. Plus, how often is the argument of vested interest used when cosmetics companies claim that cosmetics are safe?

"In one of the most dramatic failures of regulation since the introduction of asbestos", Friends of the Earth US and Australia have found that "corporations around the world are rapidly introducing thousands of tons of nanomaterials into the environment and onto the faces and hands of millions of people, despite the growing body of evidence indicating that nanomaterials can be toxic to humans and the environment." According to their report issued in May 2006 "[p]reliminary scientific research has shown that many types of nanoparticles can be toxic to human tissue and cell cultures, resulting in increased oxidative stress, inflammatory cytokine production, DNA mutation and even cell death".

What do you think the following is: "Water, Sodium Laureth Sulfate (SLS), Disodium Cocamphodiacetate, PEG-30 Glyceryl Cocoate, PEG-200 Hydrogenated Glyceryl Palmate, PEG-7 Glyceryl Cocoate, Disodium

Ricinoleamido MEA-Sulfosuccinate, Fragrance, Sodium Laureth-8 Sulfate, Disodium EDTA, Polyquaternium-10, Sodium Methylparaben, Sodium Oleth Sulfate, DMDM Hydantoin, Magnesium Laureth Sulfate, Magnesium Laureth-8 Sulfate, Magnesium Oleth Sulfate, Apricot Extract, Propylene Glycol Dicaprylate, Propylene Glycol Dicaprate, D&C Yellow #10 Lake". Answer: a premium branded product targeted at those with sensitive skins ('kids extra gentle'). But peer-reviewed journals and governments have found that some of its main ingredients are a significant irritant, especially SLS: industrial uses of SLS include garage floor cleaners, engine degreasers, and car wash soaps.

Over time I had been reading all kinds of scary information about what impacts we have on nature and its different species due to what we pour down the sink. So one day I took the plunge and bought toothpaste with only natural ingredients. At times I felt I was putting the health of my teeth on the line to save some unknown small sea creature and I had to get used to the absence of foaming with my new toothpaste. I remember reactions from friends along the line of 'how can you brush your teeth with plant gel?'. Well, I have to admit it did take some time to get used to the idea (especially after the years of brainwashing by the media), but then again I would rather use ingredients I have some vague idea of what they are than a concoction of "sodium hexametaphosphate, titanium dioxide, propylene glycol, sodium lauryl sulfate or dicalcium phosphate dihydrate" (whatever they may be), common ingredients in most 'mainstream' toothpastes. Best of all, though the toothpaste itself is more expensive, ever since I switched, my dentist (who I had not told of my switch) does not suggest to do a chemical plaque removal any more, saving me more than I spend extra on the toothpaste.

Examples of actions

91. Use natural cosmetics and toiletries, as God means them to be (unfortunately the term 'organic' is barely regulated when it comes to toiletries and cleaning products, as opposed to in the food arena). Check the Halal Food and Cosmetics Consultancy (HFCC, www.halalconsultancy.co.uk), and more generally the ingredients: www.cosmeticsdatabase.com ; for more positive alternatives: US Organic Consumers Association www.organicconsumers.org/bodycare/index.cfm. They cost a bit more (in money), but save you in exposure to chemicals, diseases and, God willing, consequences on Day of Judgment for polluting environment. Use olive oil as body oil instead of chemical mix as Abu Usayd رضي الله عنه says: "The Prophet ﷺ said: 'Use olive oil in eating and for rubbing (on the body), for it is from a blessed tree'". Preliminary research suggests olive oil protects against cancer.

92. Industrialised countries have only paid about US$163 million towards helping the Least Developed Countries (LDCs) adapt to global warming - less than what Canadians spent on hair conditioner in 2006, according to a report by the UK-based development agency, Oxfam. Worse still, less than US$10 million of this had been dispensed by December 2007, the UN Development Programme's Human Development

Report 2007-2008 pointed out. Previous generations survived perfectly fine without hair conditioner: avoid the polluting chemicals and increase your charity.

93. The average woman uses 20 different beauty products. Save cash and support Creation, try trimming this quantity and make your own for others. Or go the full hog as Haleh Afshar (Visiting Professor of Islamic Law, Faculté Internationale de Droit Comparé at Strasbourg, France), suggests to ban all (chemical) cosmetics, because "[i]n fact beauty products of all kinds can fail us again and again and don't seem to result in any kind of change. These are experiments that we do everyday and yet we still believe in them. It's a problem." If you do want to use toiletries, check the ingredients and be safe ('perfume' is a concoction of synthetic fragrance which could contain over 100 chemicals), for example on the website of Women's Environmental Network (WEN, www.wen.org.uk), especially the 'Careful Beauty' online checklist. Organic toiletries are more expensive, but personally save me more in migraines, cancer risk and environmental damage.

Cleaning
"Remember He covered you with a sort of drowsiness, to give you calm as from Himself, and he caused rain to descend on you from heaven, to clean you therewith, to remove from you the stain of Satan, to strengthen your hearts, and to plant your feet firmly therewith." (Al-Anfal/ Booty [8] 11)

According to UK Government information more than £1 billion is spent in the UK alone on cleaning products each

202

year. But with many modern cleaning products having a negative impact on the environment, is this too high a price (on top of health risks also mentioned above) to pay for our sparkling homes? Choosing and using cleaning products with care can make a difference. Note that there is hardly any regulation of claims of 'green' or 'Earth friendly' products in the marketplace. Manufacturers can essentially print anything they want on their products, and there is no requirement that such claims reflect reality. When this is done purposefully to increase sales, this is usually referred to as 'greenwashing'. In the UK for example there is a washing up liquid sold under one of the big supermarkets' own brands (not mentioning name as I would not like to be sued, plus I am sure I did not come across the unique and only product sold as such). It just mentions 'naturally effective' but if you want to find out the actual ingredients, it is not enough to just go to the manufacturers website, you need to do it with the product in hand as after clicking around for a while you realise you need to put in the products' barcode. If the product was truly green and the manufacturer was proud of that, then why make it so extremely difficult to verify/ confirm this? Naturally effective…. Yes, that is what those chemicals are: aggressive cleaners, but good for your health or the environment?

For the same reason as changing toothpaste (some of what we pour down the drain mimics hormones and is known to alter some species' behaviour, fooling them into thinking they are female when in fact they are male, thus forgetting to do their male duties and disturbing their reproduction, or worse: actually makes some species change gender…), I changed my washing up liquid and washing machine powder to more environmentally friendly alternative. I noticed absolutely no difference in how clean my clothes and dishes were getting, but did notice an immediate improvement to my hands' eczema-like symptoms, saving me much money in hand creams, thus more than compensating for the increased costs of washing liquid and washing machine powder (I have also tried so-called eco-balls instead of washing powder, which is useful when clothes are only lightly soiled).

Another thought on this topic: I notice that many cleaning products have serious warnings in their 'small print' (such as "Do not use near fire, flame, or pilot light." or "keep away from children") plus one or more 'toxic' signs. Of course we do not want to live in filthy houses, but the more I read about the impact of bleach etc, the more I wonder why go for such chemical cocktails? Many will have 'lemon scent' but never been near a lemon. If we want lemon, why not just use lemon? According to research funded by ChemTrust "[a]lthough it is clear that many factors play a role in breast cancer, a contribution of environmental chemicals cannot be dismissed." This is because the steep increase of the number of people affected by breast cancer cannot be explained by genetic (which explains about one in twenty) and lifestyle factors alone. In the UK a woman now has a one in nine chance to be diagnosed with breast cancer.

On the subject of cleanliness in the kitchen I had another brainwave. When we have prepared something in the kitchen, it is common to do like you are suggested to do by the advertisements…a quick spray and then clean up as you would not want any tomato juice on the carrots. But when I checked the label of the worktop 'cleaner'…so what would I rather do…leave the tomato juice to mix with the carrots, use a sponge with a bit of water and then dry with a tea towel, or have my carrots soaked in chemical residues from the 'cleaner'? I now use a natural and environmentally friendly one (Ecover or Bio-D).

Abu Huraira narrated that God's Messenger ﷺ said, "We (Muslims) are the last (people to come in the world) but (will be) the foremost (on the Day of Resurrection)." The same narrator told that the Prophet ﷺ had said, "You should not pass urine in stagnant water which is not flowing then (you may need to) wash in it." Wastes and exhausts, resulting from man's daily and ordinary activities or from industrial activities and uses of modern and advanced technology, should similarly be carefully disposed of or eliminated, in order to protect the environment against corruption and distortion and to protect man from the effects of these harmful impacts on the environment, its beauty and vitality, and to ensure the protection of other environmental parameters. The accumulation of waste is largely a result of our wastefulness; whereas Islam's prohibition of wastefulness requires the reuse of goods and recycling of materials and waste products in so far as is possible, instead of their disposal as trash.

The values underlying these prohibitions should be understood as applicable to the pollution of critical resources and habitats in general. Wastes, exhausts, and similar pollutants should be treated at their sources, with the best feasible means of treatment, taking care in their disposal to avoid adverse side effects that lead to similar or greater damage or injury. The juristic principle in this connection is "Damage shall not be eliminated by means of similar or greater damage." This is also true of the harmful effects of cleansing and other toxic or harmful materials used in homes, factories, farms, and other public or private premises. It is absolutely necessary to take all possible measures to avoid and prevent their harmful effects before they occur, and to eliminate or remove such effects if they do occur in order to protect man and his natural and social environment. Indeed, if the damage resulting from these materials proves greater than their benefits, they should be prohibited. In this case, we should look for effective and harmless or less harmful alternatives. And as a reminder as to the lengths the Prophet ﷺ would go to avoid harm, even emotional harm: he ﷺ told to put bird eggs back in the nest after seeing the mother bird distressed.

Examples of actions

94. Several Muslim majority areas that I know are dirty, but this has nothing to do with Islam, as the Prophet ﷺ taught us "Cleanse your courtyards" This is 'free exercise' (save on the gym and get in shape). An inspiring example is that of a woman in Aceh (Indonesia) who lost everything in the *tsunami*. Within months, she had set up a traditional Indonesian homegarden characterised by spatial plant stacking, water conservation and nutrient recycling, all achieved with no external assistance. In a space measuring just 3x5 metres, some 30 crops were discovered.

95. When Abu Musa was sent to Basra as the new governor, he addressed the people saying: "I was sent to you by Umar Ibn Al-Khattab in order to teach you the Book of your Lord [that is, the Quran], the *Sunnah* [of your Prophet ﷺ], and to clean your streets." How clean is your street? I hear 'but, that's the Council's job' or 'Muslims live in poor areas'. That is often true, but like at home: even if someone is 'in charge' of the cleaning, do you drop any rubbish all over the place? If people displaced after an earthquake can have a clean 'street' with flowers in between the tents (I have seen this with my own eyes in Bam, Iran), then all can do it. Again, skip your gym and organise a street clean. To get in the mood, view *Clean Medina*, issued by IFEES (www.ifees.org.uk).

96. Beware of claims, as the US Environmental Protection Agency (EPA) stated in May 2008 when fining a company: "We're seeing far too many unregistered products that assert unsubstantiated antimicrobial properties" (and which might be dangerous, for health and nature). Check the ingredients of products for carcinogens (cancer triggers): volatile organic compounds (VOCs), such as formaldehyde (found in plywood and particle board and especially bad for asthmatics), benzene, and trichloroethylene, all known irritants and potential carcinogens and methylene chloride (converts to carbon monoxide in the body). For furniture, try an auction (my desk is from eBay) or a swap with friends (my sofa started life as the top half of a bunk bed).

97. As we now spend the majority of our time (up to 90 per cent) indoors, indoor air quality is of more concern for our health, consequences of which can manifest themselves quickly or after years. A study by the US Environmental Protection Agency (EPA) in 1987 found indoor pollution levels up to ten times higher than those outdoors - even in locations with significant outdoor air pollution sources, such as petrochemical plants. These levels can only have become worse with our significantly increased use of sprays, toilet blocks and artificial scents. Save cash and support Creation and stop buying these chemical concoctions. For a nice smell inside take an orange and press it full of cloves (nice activity to do with friends or children), open the windows or, as the Prophet ﷺ said: "Burn incense in your homes with frankincense and thyme" (make sure it is natural/ organic to avoid chemicals).

98. *"Cleanliness is half of faith"*, but does not need to be expensive. Save cash and support Creation: lemon, vinegar and salt are all you normally need (no need for expensive, 'fancy' products) for keeping things clean. To bring a fresh shine to wooden furniture, re-oil with a bit of oil (for example olive oil). NASA (as part of making space travelling possible) has found that houseplants are the most effective indoor air cleaners, so no need anymore to buy expensive and toxic air 'fresheners'. The scientist behind this research, Dr Wolverton, published his simplified information in a book *How to grow fresh air, 50 houseplants that purify your home or office..*

Banking, Saving and Investment

"O you who believe! When you deal with each other, in transactions involving future obligations in a fixed period of time, reduce them to writing. Let a scribe write down faithfully as between the parties: let not the scribe refuse to write: as God Has taught him, so let him write. Let him who incurs the liability dictate, but let him fear His Lord God, and not diminish aught of what he owes. If a party liable is mentally deficient, or weak, or unable himself to dictate, let his guardian dictate faithfully, and get two witnesses, out of your own men, and if there are not two men, then a man and two women, such as you choose, for witnesses, so that if one of them errs, the other can remind her. The witnesses should not refuse when they are called on (for evidence). Disdain not to reduce to writing (your contract) for a future period, whether it be small or big: it is more just in the sight of God, more suitable as evidence, and more convenient to prevent doubts among yourselves but if it be a transaction which you carry out on the spot among yourselves, there is no blame on you if you reduce it not to writing. But take witness whenever you make a commercial contract; and let neither scribe nor witness suffer harm. If you do (such harm), it would be wickedness in you. So fear God; for it is Good that teaches you. And God is well acquainted with all things." (Al-Baqarah/ The Cow [2] 282)

You can in your intentions and actions try to be the best Muslim you can, but what about your money? Banks and buildings societies and the policies they pursue have an impact on the community around us and globally. Their impact has two dimensions: the way they operate (for example internal operations, what customers they take) and the types of companies they help finance. Consequently, the money that you deposit in a bank or building society could be used to support activities that you support, or object to. According to research done by internet bank Smile, however, married Britons are still more likely to divorce than to change their bank account provider.

An urgent reason to look into what your bank is doing with your money, is the impact on the environment and poverty in many other countries. For example, Global Coal Management PLC (GMC), a UK-listed company, is looking to operate an open pit mine through its Bangladesh-based subsidiary Asia Energy that would extract 15 million tonnes of coal per year from Phulbari, a key rice producing area that contributes to the food basket of Bangladesh. The necessary investment funds for this project, $300 million, are part-provided by UK banks. It is being sold as a great investment: a report for the company claims that Bangladesh "will receive benefits worth $21 billion over the 30 years of the mine's lifetime. Of this, $7.8 billion will come as a direct benefit and $13.7 billion, as indirect or multiplier benefits. The mine itself and the coal-fired plant for production of electricity will contribute one per cent per annum to the GDP of the country." However, it would displace 130,000 people (ten whole villages), which, as Nima Banik (lecturer, Phulbari Women's Degree College) puts it: "No matter wherever we are put, if we get evicted from our homes, we will lose our traditions, social organization and businesses. These losses are beyond compensation." And as Anu Muhammad's (Professor) adds: "It is Bangladesh where the coal has been found; and a foreign company will become its owner. There is no proper way to measure the actual benefit of Bangladesh and the price it would have to pay for it. What becomes clear is Bangladesh will have to buy its own coal from the company at an international price." It would also destroy thousands of acres of agricultural land, accelerate desertification, and mining experts warn that the final hollow, after 30 years of digging and other activities, will contain toxic substances. This will indirectly affect some 100 villages for many generations. But GCM shareholders can rest assured as GCM's vision is to "maximise shareholder value". So, a good investment, for whom?

And the above is not the only example unfortunately, but common. Another example is in Thailand where Muslim villagers in Chana District (Southern Thailand) are trying to stay on their communal land against the Trans Thai-Malaysian Pipeline and Industrial Project (for more on this and more check *The Corner House*, which "support democratic and community movements for environmental and social justice", www.thecornerhouse.org.uk). According to research published by amongst others Friends of the Earth Scotland, in the two years prior to April 2008, British banks were involved in over $108 billion of lending to companies involved in the coal sector alone. The Royal Bank of Scotland (RBS), Barclays and HSBC financed coal mining companies operating in Bangladesh, Kazakhstan and Indonesia and new coal power stations from the US to Australia.

Growing increasingly uncomfortable with what I read about what my bank invested my money (no matter how small it was) in, but wary of inconvenience of bank change, in the end I thought to myself: what would be worse, having some potential inconvenience in the administrative hiccups in changing banks or explaining myself on Day of Judgment about what my money had been used for? So I went to the Co-operative Bank (the only high street bank in the UK with an ethical policy, as I did not want to lose access to ATM/ hole-in-the-wall) and asked them what I needed to do to change to them. Afterwards I wish I had done it much earlier: all it turned out I had to do was fill in some forms with my personal and account details and signing that I authorised my new bank to do all the paperwork to get my money from my old bank into my new bank including all the direct debits and standing orders. In no time I was sorted.

Friends of the Earth Netherlands (*Milieudefensie*) research done under the campaign *Not With My Money* found that transferring 10,000 EUR (or around £7,000 in 2007) in savings from a Dutch high-street bank to sustainable banking specialists, Triodos Bank, "results in as much reduction of greenhouse gas emissions as not driving your car for six months." (1,400 kg CO2). I have not found exact figures for other countries, but considering the global nature of banking I would be surprised if figures for other countries would differ widely.

In 2002 the then UK Chancellor Gordon Brown launched the Charity Bank (www.charitybank.org), the UK's first registered charity which is also a bank. Regulated (like other financial service providers) by the Financial Services Authority (FSA), the Charity Bank's sole business is to accept deposits in order to make affordable loans for charitable purposes. Individuals can open a savings account in the knowledge that their money is earning a social as well as a financial return. The Bank's origins are with the Charities Aid Foundation (CAF). In 1996 it seeded a loan fund, Investors in Society, which provided affordable credit to 200 charities. It used the experience to build the Charity Bank, an enterprise with the capacity to grow and provide social benefits to a much wider community.

By investing in renewable and sustainable technologies you also support creating 'green jobs', a new, more sustainable 'Industrial Revolution'. Research suggests that climate change could be a £30 billion opportunity for British business. One of the people that has taken advantage of the opportunities of wind energy is Unsal Hassan, co-founder of Garrad Hassan (www.garradhassan.com).

Examples of actions

99. Change your bank to a more environmentally friendly, ethical one and be sure that what your money is up to will, God willing, not undo your good deeds on Day of Judgment. UK consumer watchdog *Which?* reported in August 2007 that the "'[b]ig four' banks trail on customer satisfaction", so you should be helped more nicely as well. On investment products, I would personally also avoid certain 'Islamic' investment products, such as *Dow Jones Islamic Market Oil & Gas Index* which seem detrimental to Creation.

100.   Fulfil your needs, but not all your (financial) wants as the Prophet ﷺ said: "wealth is (like) green and sweet (fruit), and whoever takes it without greed, God will bless it for him, but whoever takes it with greed, God will not bless it for him, and he will be like the one

who eats but is never satisfied." Become a 'smiles millionaire' instead or "Forget the FTSE [UK stock market]: invest in Cabbages!" as a BBC report mentioned after visiting a community supported agriculture project (www.soilassociation.org/csa, CSA).

101.   The Prophet ﷺ said: "By God, I am not afraid that you will become poor, but I am afraid that worldly wealth will be given to you in abundance as it was given to those (nations) before you, and you will start competing each other for it as the previous nations competed for it, and then it will divert you (from good) as it diverted them." When investing in a company or investment fund, look at the 'triple bottom line', not just the economic return, but also its social and environmental impact. Letting your 'money talk' does contribute to banks' choices: in March 2008 Shell had to shelve Sakhalin II (the world's largest integrated oil and gas project, located on and off-shore of Sakhalin Island in the Russian Far East, which had been plagued by environmental problems, including threats to the critically endangered Western Gray Whales, damage to wild salmon spawning grounds, and negative impacts to indigenous and fishing cultures) as they could not secure enough funding. It may mean less money in this world, but a much better record on Day of Judgement, God willing.

Pensions
"Those who believe and do good works, for them is pardon and a rich provision" (Al-Hajj/ The Pilgrimage [22] 50)

The origins of the ethical investment in the west can be found in the temperance movement from the 1900s whose traditional concerns were alcohol, gambling and tobacco. For many the first introduction to ethical investment came as a response to the human rights abuses in South Africa under apartheid. Other, often connected issues are armaments (production and sales) and the 'Third World'. Likewise pornography, animal testing, intensive farming and fur have been longstanding issues for the UK ethical investor in particular.

The ethical market (pension and otherwise) was just over £6 billion at the end of 2005. Although this is of course a nice size, it unfortunately still clearly pales when you know that the UK pension system has approximately £1.9 trillion pension assets under management and in the US in 2005 retirement assets amounted to $14.5 trillion.

It is up to individual to take action about where his/ her money is invested. For example if you work for a Local Authority in the UK, the Campaign Against Arms Trade (CAAT) has found that at least 75 of the 99 local authority pension funds have investments in BAE Systems, one of the world's largest arms companies (and arms are not only bad for peace, they are also very environmentally unfriendly).

Examples of actions

102.   Since 3 July 2000 all company pension schemes in the UK are forced to declare their ethical policy. Do you know what your pension fund's *Statement of Investment Principles* (SIP) states? Ring your pensions department and ask them to let you have a copy of the SIP. Under

the Pensions Act 1995, you have a right to see the SIP at any time. If you are not 100 per cent sure, contact your Pension Scheme's Trustees to increase the pressure in relation to social and environmental issues. Be aware that most pension funds will have very non-committal criteria relating to 'positive investment' or 'engagement to encourage better practice'. This wording can be used to great effect, but can also be used to allow a 'business as usual' investment philosophy, where no companies are excluded or no real 'engagement' takes place. What is critical is that Trustees are asked questions that relate both to social and environmental issues *and* to a potential financial risk to your pension fund. There is little point in raising pure moral issues, as the Trustees are under no obligation to respond to such queries (though if they would not be open to answering such queries, perhaps that is answer enough?). Trustees are required by law to respond, in writing, to any queries relating to their SIP or to potential financial risk relating to the Scheme's investments. For more information: www.ethicalinvestors.co.uk/pension.htm

103.   Give your pension a good review to see if they are in line with your beliefs and values. Check for example: www.ethicalinvestment.org.uk and Ethical Investment Research Services (www.eiris.org)

104.   Do not wait until pension age ("now busy studying", "now busy raising kids" – none of us can surely be more busy than the Prophet ﷺ was?) to do your bit for Creation: according to Abu Huraira the Prophet ﷺ said "God will not accept the excuse of any person

whose instant of death is delayed till he is sixty years of age."

Gifts

"Who is there that will offer to God a good gift so He will double it for him, and he shall have an excellent reward."
(Al-Hadid/ The Iron [57] 11)

Companies and organisations sometimes give away gifts, something complementary to help the recipient remember the giver next time they need a service or delike.

Want to have a warm glow? Using brain-imaging technology, a team of researchers from the University of Oregon found that giving to charity triggers the same "warm glow" that people experience when they satiate their hunger or socialise with friends.

Also we have much pressure to give gifts at any occasion or large gifts, but follow the way of the Prophet ﷺ: as the Messenger of God ﷺ said, "O trusting women, none of you must consider even a roasted sheep's trotter too small to give to her neighbour."

Examples of actions

105.   Instead of things that recipients may possibly throw away, how about offering your time? As *Green Muslims in the District* (Washington DC, USA) summarise it: "Give of your time and experience before you have to turn to your wallet. A bottle of lotion or a new tool never strengthened a community the same way good companionship did!"

106. Or how about giving your gift to someone more in need of something? You can also suggest this if you have something to celebrate coming up (for example a wedding) and you want to avoid the headache of unwanted presents by sharing your joy, for example via Good Gifts (www.goodgifts.org) The Good Gifts Catalogue is the brainchild of the Charities Advisory Trust, a registered charity, with over 25 years experience. For more information, visit www.charitiesadvisorytrust.org.uk.

107. If you do want to give something physical, how about a home grown plant or some home grown flowers? Abu Huraira reported God's Messenger ﷺ as saying: "He who is presented with a flower should not reject it, for it is light to carry and pleasant in smell." For "Islamic ethical gifts" (where I believe 'Islamic' covers 'ethical') check The Fig and The Olive (www.thefigandtheolive.com), set up in 2008.

108. What about making a gift list for God: a pledge? Islamic Networks Group (ING, www.ing.org), based in the US, has a nice example: "ING employees and speakers pledge to take at least 10 and as many of the following [20] steps as they can to do their part for the environment. They also pledge to learn more about the issue of global warming and educate friends and family members."

Utilities

"Waste not by excess: for God loves not the wasters." (Al-Anaam/ Livestock [6] 141 and Al-Araf/ The Heights [7] 31)

Housing is responsible for around 30 per cent of the UK's total energy consumption. A typical UK household spends around half of its utility bills on heating space. In an un-insulated home, around a third of this heat is lost through the walls. Without loft insulation you could be losing as much as 15 per cent of your heating through your roof, the same percentage is lost in draughts. Wall insulation can reduce heat loss by up to 40 per cent through cavity walls and up to 60 per cent through solid walls. Cavity wall insulation and loft insulation – as a friend once summarised it: giving your property a woolly jumper – are the least visible, most cost effective and energy efficient measures (every square metre of cavity wall insulation will save more than a tonne of CO_2 over the average life of the building and in an uninsulated home, £1 in every £3 spent on heating is wasted). Contrary to perhaps popular myth, on average only around 10 per cent of the heat from housing is lost through windows and doors, because comparing inch with inch indeed more is lost via windows, but because most properties have far more wall and ceiling/ roof than windows, it contributes less to the total heat loss. Installing standard double-glazing could reduce this by half (the bit the double-glazing window people overemphasize), but putting up heavy curtains (those with black out lining for example) can also make a significant impact, for a fraction of the price, as can installing so-called secondary glazing (I have seen several examples where the double-glazing was of such poor quality, especially uPVC fittings, that they had secondary glazing added).

You just want your gas and electricity, how can you make a difference there? One is the same as the other, right? Here I will only discuss energy, as water matters are tackled under *wudu* and *ghusl*. I was shocked when I read on the website of the International Energy Agency that the average global efficiency of fossil-fuelled power generation has remained stagnant for decades at 35 to 37 per cent. Put another way, two-thirds of the fuel that is burned to produce power is lost - vented as 'waste' heat, before it even reaches us. The good news is that the G8 leaders in June 2007 agreed to "adopt instruments and measures to significantly increase the share of combined heat and power (CHP) in the generation of electricity". CHP (also known as cogeneration) is an attractive and proven technology that can significantly improve power plant efficiency. And I believe we should look at much more decentralised power generation, not just to avoid the *makruh* (Islamically detestable) amounts of energy waste in the centralised stations, but also as part of climate change mitigation (as floods in July 2007 have shown, where only due to huge collective efforts, and with less than an inch to spare, were not another 500,000 people not cut off from their supplies on top of the 350,000 who were – for up to 17 days).

When I did a radio interview on BBC WM one day I was warned to put my sunglasses on when going to the part of the building where you go to answer the call of nature, as the lights would be so bright there. I was indeed thankful for the warning (though it was an early Sunday morning interview in winter, and had cycled in grey sky weather, so I did not have my sunglasses on me). As soon as I walked into the room with cubicles I thought 'I wish I knew where the switch is, and could siphon off the saved electricity costs to the poor in Africa, or perhaps just spend it more wisely within the BBC on increased background research for their programmes'. But alas, not in my hands. Let me share also what I have carefully checked for myself and for you: it is a myth that switching costs more energy than to leave lights on; it was only true until the fifties if you were switching a light off for less than two minutes.

I used to get my electricity (I have no gas connection) from your average mainstream supplier. When I realised they had a 'green tariff' I switched to that (just one phone call was all it took, no extra costs). One of the items on my 'an action a month'-list was to change to a green supplier. I later did find a power supplier (Ecotricity) which pro-actively supports increase of sustainable power provision at the same price as other providers, so I changed to them (again, one phone call was all it took). So now I am "fighting climate change with my electricity bill" as they say.

With increased awareness about climate change matters (and global demand for oil continuing to rise faster, with the International Energy Agency (IEA) report estimating that it will rise by an average of 2.2 million barrels of oil a day in 2008, compared to 1.5 million barrels per day in 2007), the nuclear lobby is gearing up again, presenting it as "the CO2 free alternative". However, when I hear this, I immediately think: how does the uranium get here (main deposits are in Australia, Kazakhstan, Sudan)? Also with nuclear power having been used for decades, still no sustainable solution has been found for the highly radioactive waste (and at this tense security time I would not want any terrorist getting hold of it). Or as new research by the Oxford Research Group (July 2007) concludes "[f]or the nuclear weapons proliferation and nuclear terrorism risks to be worth taking, nuclear must be able to achieve energy security and a reduction in global CO_2 emissions more effectively, efficiently, economically and quickly than any other energy source. There is little evidence to support the claim that it can, whereas the evidence for doubting nuclear power's efficacy is clear." One of the side-effects of nuclear power, argues Mark Z. Jacobson (Professor of civil and environmental engineering, Stanford University, US) in his article on *Review of solutions to global warming, air pollution, and energy security* in December 2008, is also an increased risk of nuclear war: "Because the production of nuclear weapons material is occurring only in countries that have developed civilian nuclear energy programs, the risk of a limited nuclear exchange between countries or the detonation of a nuclear device by terrorists has increased due to the dissemination of nuclear energy facilities worldwide." Thirdly, a major study (researchers looked at 17 study papers that covered 136 nuclear sites in seven countries) presented in the European Journal of Cancer Care has confirmed long held suspicions that children and young people who live near a nuclear plant are far more likely to develop leukaemia: incidence rates of leukaemia increased by 21 per cent in children aged up to nine years, and by 10 per cent in young people aged up to 25 years. Is our greed for energy more important than our children's health? And last but not least, Islamically, according to Usama Hasan (trained in Theoretical Physics at Cambridge and traditional Islamic sciences) "if it is true (as put forward in a recent report by an environmentalist group) that Britain does not need nuclear power and that it can meet all its remaining energy needs via renewable energy

222

and reducing energy waste, then the principles of *Shari'ah* would dictate that we avoid nuclear power, given the risks of contamination, nuclear waste, nuclear accidents, etc."

In our developed (over-developed?) countries we are used to thinking big, and grand installations (all dependent on 'the grid' which provides us with energy from major power stations). I prefer an approach like that of Muhammad Yunus, Nobel Peace Prize winner and founder of Grameen Shakti (meaning 'rural power', a subsidiary of his Grameen Bank; www.gshakti.org) which promotes, develops and popularises renewable energy technologies in remote, rural areas of Bangladesh. Nearly 70 percent of homes in the country have no electricity and rely on kerosene for lighting, which is smoky and a fire risk. In November 2007, when cyclone Sidr struck Bangladesh, solar was a lifeline: solar mobile phones warned people of the cyclone's approach, and the majority of solar installations survived its impact. An extra benefit of the programme is that it provides highly prized 'green jobs' for poor, rural women who are trained as technicians. Another renewable energy source, according to American educator Stanwood Cobb (1881– 1982 CE) "the windmill, as far as can be ascertained, actually originated with the Muslims. The first windmill known to history was built around 640 AD [CE] by order of the Caliph Omar. A few centuries later an Arab geographer reported that the windmill was used widely in Persia to pump water for irrigation. From Persia and Afghanistan the windmill spread throughout the Islamic world. It ground wheat, crushed sugar-cane and pumped water. Later it came into use in Europe by way of Morocco and Spain." What now?

Examples of action

109.   As mentioned in a Friends of the Earth (UK) *tip of the day*: "[t]onnes of greenhouse gases are pumped into the atmosphere every year by appliances left on standby in the UK (and representing 8 per cent of the electricity used in our homes). The energy used is equivalent to powering around 600,000 homes every year, and is a significant contribution to UK emissions of climate changing gases. How many appliances around your home are on standby? Switch them off when not in use (check it will not reset the memory) - and unplug chargers once appliances are charged up ("the revolutionary eco-gadget" according to eco-auditor Donnachadh McCarthy, as the greenest and cheapest energy is the energy not used: "Just think how much money you could save!") or as Jabir narrated that the Prophet ﷺ said: "Put out lamps when you go to bed", shut the doors, close waterskins and cover water and food containers." In a 'green streets' competition, families achieved an average energy use reduction of 25 per cent (thus 25 per cent reduction in energy bills), with only limited amounts of money and focus on behavioural changes.

110.   Find out where your supplier gets its power from: www.electricityinfo.org, and thus what types of electricity generation you are supporting. For an overview of green (renewable) alternatives: www.greenelectricity.org. Change your electricity supply to a more environmentally friendly one, such as Ecotricity (www.ecotricity.co.uk) or Good Energy (www.goodenergy.co.uk). It often does not even cost

more. There is much scope for improvement: according to recent figures from UK energy regulator Ofgem as out of the 26 million homes supplied with electricity, just 350,000 are signed up to a green or renewable tariff. For support on what is best deal in your area: http://green.energyhelpline.com/energy. New Ofgem guidelines launched in June 2007 state: "all green tariffs would be awarded a rating ranging from 1-5 stars."

111.   Get involved in the promotion of renewable energy use, for example encourage increased use of solar power and make use of the wind that God gives us for free every day and is not polluting. Become a member of the World Renewable Energy Network (WREN, www.wrenuk.co.uk), chaired by Ali Sayigh. Or the sun and its energy, for example Solar Energy International, a US non-profit organisation whose mission is to help others use renewable energy and environmental building technologies through education: www.solarenergy.org, or www.trec-uk.org.uk, the Trans-Mediterranean Renewable Energy Cooperation (TREC), an initiative of the Club of Rome, an international network of scientists and engineers developing a collaboration amongst countries in Europe, the Middle East and North Africa to take advantage of the truly enormous quantities of energy falling as sunlight on the world's deserts - and wind energy in those regions too. If you hear promotion of nuclear again, think of the *fatwa* by Nahdlatul Ulama (NU), the country's largest Islamic group in Indonesia: "We concluded that its [nuclear plant] downsides

outweigh potential benefits from the plant. It threatens the survival of human beings in the area".

112. Check your utility metres regularly and see where/ how you can save cash and support Creation. For example, turn down your thermostat by just a degree and slash 10 per cent off the energy used in heating in your home, and thus save money at the same time. When buying electrical items do not just check purchase price, but also running costs (because energy costs are going up, but our houses are also more and more filled with power hungry gadgets). A helpful website for this (besides questioning seller about this) is Sust-It, which aims "to make us all more energy efficient by providing consumer information on the most energy efficient products on the market." (www.sust-it.net).

113. Insulate your home. See www.sustainable-energyacademy.org.uk which has a number of examples from around the UK of homes which have been improved to reduce their CO_2 emissions by 60 per cent or more (thus saving much money on heating the home). Loft insulation can be a DIY job, but cavity wall insulation and other work not so (www.ciga.co.uk).

114. For more energy saving tips, check www.energysavers.gov (for the US) or www.energysavingtrust.org.uk (for the UK). The Energy Saving Trust offers free, impartial and independent advice on energy use and how to make savings on your gas and electricity bills. For general green home advice, check: www.greenhomeguide.com.

Need more advice on where to start? Call the Green Doctor, set up by Groundwork, who "work to improve the environmental performance of homes by offering specialist and personalised advice and support while conducting energy use audits". They "are also able to direct householders towards subsidised grants and services." (www.groundwork.org.uk). If you know it all, why not set up as a local adviser and help others?

Charitable endowments (waqf)

"O you who believe! Call to witness between you, when death draws nigh to one of you, at the time of making the will two just persons from among you, or two others from among others than you" (Al-Maidah/ The Table Set [5] 106)

According to Habib Ahmed in his book *Role of Zakah and Awqaf in Poverty Alleviation* "the objective of waqf may be for the society at large, including the provision of religious services, socio-economic relief to the needy, poor, education, *environmental*, scientific and other purposes" (my emphasis). And "there can be *awqaf* for the poor, *awqaf* for education, *awqaf* for health care, *awqaf* to *preserve forests*, *awqaf* for helping newly wed women, *awqaf* to *feed birds or to maintain cats* etc". His research finds that most of the *awqaf*, however, are religious in nature and that "the social objectives are not being realised".

According to Iyad Abumoghli (Senior Environment and Knowledge Management Adviser, United Nations Development Programme, UNDP) "Islam encourages individual Muslims to participate in the conservation and sustainable development of natural resources through various gifts, inheritance, and loans. The most important institution of Islamic law in this regard is the charitable endowment (*waqf*), which constitutes the major avenue for private contribution to the public good. The *waqf* may take the form of a land trust dedicated in perpetuity to charitable purposes such as agricultural and range research, wildlife propagation and habitat development, a village woodlot, or a public cistern, well, or garden; or it may take the form of a fund or endowment for the financing of such projects."

It is related that when the Caliph Umar ibn al-Khattab ﷺ acquired land in Khaybar, he went to consult the Prophet ﷺ and said, "O Messenger of God, I have acquired land in Khaybar; never have I received property dearer to me than this; so what do you command me to do with it?" And the Prophet ﷺ, replied, "If you wish you may make it an endowment and give its produce as charity." His son, Ibn Umar, remarked that "Umar gave it in charity, declaring that it must not be sold or gifted or inherited, and that its yield would be devoted to the poor, to kinsfolk, to the freeing of slaves, for the cause of God, for travellers, and for guests." The governing authorities may set provisions and standards for such *waqf* lands and funds, and for the qualifications of their managers, so that the benevolent objectives of such projects may be effectively fulfilled.

The reward accruing from seven things continue to reach the person concerned even if he is in his grave: knowledge he has taught, *water he has provided for the public benefit, any well he has dug, any tree he has planted*, a mosque he has built, recitations of the Quran bequeathed to him, and children who pray for him after his death. In Kuwait, for example, in its efforts to conserve its biological diversity, the *Al-Waqf Fund for Preservation of the Environment* requested the Kuwait Institute for Scientific Research (KISR) to develop a Master Plan for establishment of a botanical garden in the country. And in South Africa, Awqaf SA has set up a special charitable endowment fund to plant trees, grow food, and provide water in poor and needy communities on a sustainable basis.

Examples of action

115. If there is any action you want to focus on this week: include something green in your will, as Imam Ali ibn Abu Talib (600 - 661CE), cousin and son-in-law of the Prophet ﷺ did, as is clear from this extract of his will: "I further order that young date-palm of the estate not to be cut until it is fully afforested with date-palm and take up the shape of a well-developed palm-orchard". For examples of what to do now: save threatened habitats worldwide (www.worldlandtrust.org); donate to the National Trust: www.nationaltrust.org.uk (UK); www.nationaltrust.org (US); or support the International Conservation Union and take out a *waqf* for water: www.iucn.org/places/wescana/programs/water/

116. Do in your city what Chicago (US) Muslims have done in theirs: donate a garden. Conceived by Talat Othman, a Chicago businessman, funded by the community, Ahmed Rehab (Executive Director, Council on American - Islamic Relations [CAIR] Chicago

Office) stated at the opening of the garden: "First, it fulfils a key Islamic value and that is care for our environment; second, it sets a great precedent for mainstream Muslim philanthropy, a breakaway from traditional philanthropy that only benefits Muslims; third, it cultivates a sense of belonging to this great city among members of the Muslim community, and a sense of appreciation for the Muslim community among members of the general public."

117.   Soumy Ana has written several teaching resources on ecology and Islam which are available for free on the internet as *waqf* (which means author has herself decided to give up rights to the work for the benefit of the community; this is not what I sometimes see that whole copyrighted works are copy-pasted fully elsewhere without the author's permission 'for the sake of God', that is not *waqf*, but theft in my view): www.ummah.com/islam/taqwapalace/soumy_ana.html

118.   What enduring action will you do? Salah ad-Din (Saladin, 1138-1193 CE) established a tomb for Imam Al-Shafi in 1176 CE and he established the coffin that tops the tomb in 1178 CE. It was made of Indian teak wood and divided into meticulously embellished geometrical patterns. As for the dome, it was established by his son Al-Kamel in 1211 CE. Over the dome beside the crescent, there is a brass ship that contains wheat to feed birds.

Leisure
"Always keep in mind that your time and energy is not to be wasted in useless, unproductive and frivolous matters.

So do not indulge in evil, vain talk of any sort, that is to say, do not speak, listen or do anything that is naught, of no account, unprofitable, nonsense, foolish, ineffectual, vain, futile, frivolous, unhealthy, unpleasant, abominable, offensive to the mind, detestable, repugnant, hideous, unwholesome, impairing, hurtful, harmful, or injurious, or anything that could bar you from being and remaining mindful of the Quranic teachings" (Al-Muminum/ The Believers [23] 3 and [41] 26]

The Messenger of God ﷺ said, "There are two blessings which many people lose: (They are) health and free time for doing righteous deeds." According to Ibn Butlan's (died in 1038 CE) *Taqwim As-Sihha* (Protection of Health; translated into Latin in 1531 CE as *Tacuinum Sanitatis*), there are six things that are necessary to any human for the daily conservation of his health, with its corrections and operations: "The first care of health is the preparation of the air, which affects the heart. The second is the regulation of food and drink. The third is the regulation of movement and rest. The fourth is the restraint of the body from sleep and from much watching. The fifth is the regulation of the relaxation and constriction of the humours. The sixth is regulation of the person to moderate joy, anger, fear and anxiety."

On 31 January 2008, Abdulaziz Othman Altwaijri (Director General of the Islamic Educational, Scientific and Cultural Organisation, ISESCO), said that "today's world is faced with several environmental problems such as global warming, ozone depletion, water scarcity, and deforestation, whose effect is so harmful to the ecosystem, asserting that these problems are among the new century's most serious issues, hence the need for the international community - governments and civil society organisations and institutions - to take effective action to respond to them."

Research has shown that people in the US, and it would be similar for other western countries, have approximately five hours more free time per week than they had 30 years ago. Thanks to modernity we perform less housework, we have fewer children, and we are retiring earlier. But we are busier than ever before. Although we have more free time, a large proportion of that time is spent watching television, and the remainder of our 'free' time is spent in leisure obligations. These leisure obligations take the place of traditional sources of meaning in our life such as religious traditions, community, etc. Leisure is now a means to an end not undertaken for its own sake. Our leisure obligations are for a purpose – fitness, socialising, or fulfilling expectations.

A more recent leisure activity is 'retail therapy' (shopping to get rid of stress, or that is the excuse). How about instead of buying more 'stuff' (which has cost so much energy to make, to get to us and usually sooner rather than later ends in the bin), why not save cash, planet and donate blood in your leisure time? Each day the National Blood Service (NBS) collects about 7,000 blood donations to maintain supplies to hospitals in England and Wales, though on average just 200 of these donations are from ethnic minority donors. This is similar with tissue donations, which means people of ethnic minority background are thus likely to spend much longer waiting for a suitable donor match to treat leukaemia and other similar potentially fatal illnesses. To encourage more blood donations from these underrepresented donor groups, the National Blood Service launched a *Circle of Life* campaign in October 2007, supported by leaders of faith groups (where ethnic minorities are often overrepresented). Supporting the campaign, Shahid Raza, (President of World Islamic Mission of Europe and Founder of British Muslim Forum) stated: "In Islam blood donation is not only permissible but it is considered as an act of charity, and kindness. Helping someone to save his/ her life or alleviating their suffering by donating blood brings enormous reward by God. As an Imam and director of Imam's and Mosques Council UK, I wish to participate in any campaign in respect of creating and enhancing the awareness of the benefits of blood donation." I guess he was clearly thinking of "Whoever saves the life of a single person, it is as if he has saved the life of all (of humanity)" (Al-Maidah/ The Table Spread [5] 32).

Usamah Khayyaat says: "Brethren in faith! Free time is also a blessing that Allah bestows upon His servants. So if Allah blesses someone with free time and he does not show the gratitude for this blessing through deeds that can elevate him, bring prosperity to his society or strengthen his nation but instead of that, spends it in fun and pastime and sinful words and deeds thereby wasting that precious time, such a person is in a serious and irrevocable loss. It is in the light of this that the Prophetic admonition came thus, "Seize the opportunity of five things before five things come to you: Your life before your death, your health before your illness, your free time before your time of occupation, your youthfulness before your old age and your time of wealth before your time of poverty.""

Several people over the years have asked me 'how come I get done so much?' or something along those lines. It took me quite some time to find the answer, but I think I have now found a major reason: I do not have a TV. According to the UK Government Office for National Statistics, in 2005 people in the UK spent an average 157 minutes (or more than 2.5 hours) *a day* watching TV and videos. Figures for the US are much higher and for other Western countries lower, but still very significant. Though I do not think I achieve anything extraordinary, I am convinced that so many other activities are much more useful than just sitting in front of a box. Of course there are interesting and valuable programmes on offer, but so there are interesting books, friends, etc. to learn from, to enjoy the company of. Not long ago I learned so much doing a weekly hour-long radio show on local community radio: instead of being spoon fed what the TV people wanted me to see, or even National Geographic channel, I had the best excuse I needed to approach strangers to educate me all about saving a local meadow, need for environmental justice for cotton pickers and the ins and outs of a church's inventive recycling scheme (to name but a few). TV is now so much seen as part of basic piece of furniture that the way many people arrange the furniture even is for all to have a good view of the TV. And it is so much seen as a bare necessity that when I was living in Belgium and during a discussion I mentioned that I did not have a TV, those around me were about to start a collection to get me one (assuming reason I did not have one could only be due to financial reasons).

Besides time, not having a TV saves significant amounts of money and pollution. A colour TV licence in the UK for 2009 costs £139.50 a year (black and white £47) and the average TV used 160kW in 2005, adding some £18-33 to the utility bill (depending on electricity provider and whether it is part of your first or last kWs used). In terms of carbon emissions, the Energy Saving Trust says old-style TVs produce 100kg of CO_2 per year, while larger, plasma screens (there are no small plasma TVs yet) will pump out 400kg. If you do want to have a TV, thus bear in mind that the new large flat screen TVs can cost up to three times as much to run as traditional TVs. According to the Energy Saving Trust these can add up to £90 to a typical household electricity bill every year (for that amount you can sponsor an orphan for some 3 months in many poor countries). And when buying a new one, do not throw out your old one: two million TV sets are discarded every year in the UK, most of which end up in landfill sites. Though, as I once read on a blog (Groovy Green) "I don't think when you are 80 and looking back on your life you'll wish you had spent more time watching TV." Or think of the following remark by journalist Nazmul Islam Chowdhury in Dhaka (Bangladesh) while reporting on floods that had submerged half the country: "Watching television for a year in the UK emits the same amount of CO_2 as an average person in Bangladesh emits in total annually, but it is here that the impact of those excessive western emissions is being felt."

We spend only eight minutes a day doing sport and outdoor activity, and according to Public Health Minister Dawn Primarolo in July 2007 "Three out of ten boys and four out of ten girls are not achieving the recommended physical activity levels." (while healthy habit should be 5 times 30 minutes a week). But it seems we would rather go down the route of pill-popping: Peter Weissberg (Medical Director, British Heart Foundation) stated: "We wouldn't have to consider this if we had a population who didn't smoke, who exercised regularly, who really took care of their cardiovascular health. But the fact of the matter is, we choose to live differently and we can offset the risk by being on a statin."

According to the UK Ministry of Health, physically active people have 20–30 per cent reduced risk of premature death and up to 50 per cent reduced risk of major chronic disease such as coronary heart disease, stroke, diabetes and cancer. However, six out of ten men and seven out of ten women are not active enough to benefit their health. In the last 25 years, the distance people walk or cycle has fallen by a quarter. In April 2004 the UK Chief Medical Officer issued recommendations for active living throughout the life course: children and young people should achieve a total of at least 60 minutes of moderate intensity physical activity each day. At least twice a week this should include activities to improve bone health (activities that produce high physical stresses on the bones), muscle strength and flexibility. For general health benefit, adults should achieve a total of at least 30 minutes a day of moderate intensity physical activity on five or more days of the week. The recommended levels of activity can be achieved either by doing all the daily activity in one session, or through several shorter bouts of activity of 10 minutes or more. The activity can be lifestyle activity or structured exercise or sport, or a combination of these. However, an ICM survey commissioned by Play England for 2007 Playday shows that though 71 per cent of adults played outside in the street or area close to their homes every day when they were children, only 21 per cent of children play outside today. Both children and adults considered traffic to be the main factor that stops children and young people playing or spending time in the streets or areas near their homes, with nearly 1 in 4 children and 35 per cent of adults listing it as one of their top three barriers to street play.

On numerous occasions when walking or cycling past a local gym, I notice people arriving and departing in heavy sports cars. It seems sometimes when we analyse our lives and we notice a shortage of exercise we add 'doing exercise' (as in 'going to the gym') to our 'to do'-list. However, it seems somewhat unsustainable (for wallet, Creation and schedule) to drive to the gym (with accompanying petrol costs, thus CO_2), pay for the gym entrance, work out on machines including stationary bike (the average treadmill alone uses around 1500 watts per hour), then drive back home. Replacing our many short car journeys by going by cycle or walking would save us petrol, CO_2 emissions, gym membership and our health. I do appreciate the British roads are not perceived as the safest as a cyclist, but how are we going to make them safer: by adding an extra car to the traffic or by making space for more cyclists by taking a car off the road? I would not be surprised if such question is included in our accountability time on Day of Judgment. Or as an article about Ashram Acres (see under *khilafah*) mentioned "Why run around a gym like a rodent on a wheel if your exertions can actually deliver your dinner - if the calories you expend actually produce the calories you consequently eat?"

According to the latest figures from the Association of British Travel Agents, the number of UK residents travelling abroad continued to rise by 1 per cent in the first months of 2007 with the total holidays taken in 2007 expected to hover around the 44 million mark. But after the above, do not worry: I am not saying all are only allowed to go on a *Green Roof Safari* (though it does sound interesting to do at some point, offering "a unique opportunity to learn about a diverse array of green roof projects in Germany and Switzerland", www.greenroofsafari.com), just encouraging myself and all to be aware of the impacts of our actions, both in this world and for our record on Day of Judgment.

Holidays are a fairly modern 'invention'. If we really need them, is it not more a case for re-evaluating our life? Are we living 'too fast' (a symptom being increase in 'fast food' etc)? What does this tell us about our aim, as Muslims, of full submission to God instead of the here, now and instant? If we are thinking of holidays in the sense of 'keeping the kids busy during school breaks, then again we should be clear what we expose ourselves and our families to and with what aim, because as Imam Al-Qayyim's *Wise Sayings* include: "Wasting time is far more disastrous than death; for wasting time cuts you off from (the good pleasures of) God and the (good life) Hereafter, whereas death cuts you off from this life and its inhabitants".

Marmaduke Pickthall once stated: "When I knew at length that I was going to leave Syria, I was seized with a desire to buy all kinds of notions of the country to show to my people at home - a very foolish way of spending money, I am now aware, for such things lose significance when taken from their proper setting."

It is easy to go on a day out to for example Edinburgh with 225,000 other demonstrators to add your voice to rally to *MakePovertyHistory* when the G8 leaders were meeting there in 2005, but I would suggest it is even much more powerful if we started by fully walking our own talk and truly be "part of the solution" as Tourism Concern puts it instead of just asking others to change. Even if, as Abdullah Quilliam puts it, "It is far easier to ask for what is impossible than to do that which is possible."

As research by Tourism Concern has found, due to the way the holiday industry is currently organised "the communities that provide the natural and cultural resources for our holidays get little in return but suffer the social and environmental degradation that follows." A positive exception is Basata in Egypt, where I was fortunate to once go on a holiday. Basata (www.basata.com) is an eco-lodge meaning 'simplicity' in Arabic and is based in the South Sinai. The South Sinai is considered one of the most beautiful tourist spots in the world. It possesses some of the world's unique coral reefs, marine life and ecosystems and is home to a unique Bedouin population of some 15,000 (though these nomadic peoples are often denied their rights in the pursuit of development at break neck speeds). It attracts thousands of tourists that are vital to Egypt's economy. However, it is fast deteriorating on account of its mounting garbage problem. In recent years, the South Sinai has undergone major developments (for example Hurghada and Sharm El-Sheikh). These have largely resulted in massive construction projects, influx of people (tourists and workers in hotels) and the supporting service sector activities. Most hotels and other centres handle the transportation of their own waste, which in practice means they dump it in the sea: out of sight, out of mind.

The founder of Basata, Sharif El-Ghamrawy, is also the brain behind *Hemaya* (Arabic for 'protection'), a community-based organisation established in 1997 by a group of concerned individuals with the following main objectives: creating environmental awareness among the local community, workers and tourists; preserving endangered species; conserving and managing natural resources; protecting the cultural heritage of the Bedouins as well as assisting them in raising their standard of living. By including the local population and enabling them to benefit from development it supports their survival and that of the fragile Sinai environment, as I read in one of the articles about the Sinai from a local inhabitant "As a Bedouin, the most important thing is to keep the land as clean as it was before". Or as the Hurghada Environmental Protection and Conservation Association (HEPCA) puts it: "The spectacular coral reefs and fascinating marine life of the Red Sea are one of the main attractions for the 8 million visitors coming to Egypt each year. [...] Without proper environmental and logistical planning, and interventions to promote sustainable development, the corals and marine life of the Red Sea will die... affecting not only the environment, but hundreds of thousands of livelihoods, ultimately causing the degradation of the entire tourism industry along the Red Sea coast of Egypt." Or as Sharif El-Ghamrawy says in response to queries why he does not go for a much more lucrative resort: "I would rather give my children a livelihood than a bag of money". There are so many other examples where the options, in balance and harmony between man and nature, include "with us you can sleep in the desert under a billion stars or in a hotel with 3" (Nyazi, Jordan, www.nyazi.com.jo) or "only here can you trek through the last remaining primeval forest in Europe" (GreenVisions, Bosnia and Herzegovina, www.greenvisions.ba).

Or for something of benefit to others as well, consider doing a volunteering work holiday at a farm to reconnect with the rest of Creation. Willowbrook Farm (www.willowbrookorganic.org) for example is a Muslim family run farm on the edge of Oxford (UK) set within the environmentally sensitive Cherwell Valley flood plain. The farm is organically managed (Soil Association accredited) and they are committed to the environmental sustainability and natural biodiversity of the land within its boundaries. They are also committed to maintaining high standards of animal welfare and to promoting local food for local markets. They believe the future of British farming lies in reconnecting farmers and consumers to the land and therefore also support educational and other initiatives aimed at raising environmental awareness particularly concerning farming issues. They "always welcome people to come and get involved in our environmental activities on the farm". Activities range from tree planting to willow weaving and bird hide building. Volunteering on a farm, as World-Wide Opportunities on Organic Farms (WWOOF) puts it, "enable town-dwellers to experience living and helping on a farm", or reconnect to Creation.

Examples of action

119.   If we want to seek knowledge (often cited reason for TV) and stay fit (our body has a right over us), then Abd al-Qadir Al-Jilani (1077- 1166 CE) has some advice: "Walk in search of knowledge and knowledgeable persons until no further walking is possible. Keep walking until your legs become unable to walk, sit down with your outward, then with your inward, then with your heart and then with your essence. When you become totally exhausted, outwardly and inwardly and have to sit, nearness of God and attainment to God will come to you." Another option is to read, for example *One Thousand Roads to Mecca*, a collection of more than 20 accounts of the Hajj spanning ten centuries giving readers a sense of how the hajj has changed over time, edited by American convert Michael Wolfe.

120.   Related by Ibn-Abbas, the Prophet ﷺ said, "Grab five things before five others: your youth before your decrepitude, your health before your illness, your wealth before your poverty, your leisure before your work, and your life before your death." Enjoy an extraordinary holiday and attend a climate camp (for example: www.climatecamp.org.uk). Come, as the organisers say "armed… but only with peer-reviewed science" or for in the US, offer a workshop on 'Islam and environment' at a regional camp (www.climateconvergence.org).

121.   Or: "Lose no time to do good deeds before you are caught up by one of seven calamities awaiting you: a starvation which may impair your wisdom; a prosperity

which may mislead you; an ailment which may damage your health; an old age which may harm your senses; a sudden death; the Dajjal (Antichrist); or Doomsday, which is indeed the hardest and most bitter." Heed Dr Abdulaziz Othman Altwaijri's suggestion and support a flourishing civil society: in your street, your neighbourhood, city or even country.

122. Fatima ﷂ, the Prophet's ﷺ daughter, said that when her father saw her still lying in bed one morning, he told her, "My daughter, get up and witness your Lord's bounty, and do not be among the indifferent; God distributes daily bread between the break of dawn and sunrise." Instead of Alton Towers theme park, take the young ones (and yourself) to a place like Centre for Alternative Technology (CAT, www.cat.org.uk) in Wales.

123. Replace your gym membership with 'green gym' for a conservation charity (for example British Trust for Conservation Volunteers, BTCV, www.btcv.org.uk New Zealand Trust for Conservation Volunteers, www.conservationvolunteers.org.nz or any other national trust in your area).

124. Not that going to the doctor falls under leisure, but you can give your old magazines a new lease of life by taking them to your local doctor's surgery (or Blood Bank) for others to read.

125. When going on holiday, as I read somewhere: "[t]ake nothing but memories, kill nothing but time, and leave nothing but footprints." (proverb native Indians)

Or when diving: "Take nothing with you, leave bubbles behind you" And to enjoy your holiday from the moment you leave home (and save CO2), take journeys by train, starting at www.seat61.com, whose founder does not fly because he "simply prefer[s] a more civilised, comfortable, interesting, adventurous, romantic, scenic, historic, exciting and environmentally-friendly way to travel."

126. Abu Umamah narrated that a man said: "Messenger of God, allow tourism for me." The Prophet ﷺ said: "The tourism of my people is striving in the path of God, the Exalted." Consider going on a positively work-filled holiday and reconnect to the land, check World-Wide Opportunities on Organic Farms WWOOF (www.wwoof.org), options include Western China – the end of the Silk Road -, and Morocco); or contact a farm like Willowbrook Farm directly (www.willowbrookorganic.org).

127. For more tips on how to enjoy a greener holiday, check GreenPassport (an initiative of the International Task Force on Sustainable Tourism Development, www.unep.fr/greenpassport), or GreenTraveller (www.greentraveller.co.uk); or for a useful starting point for the US, check Green Hotels (www.greenhotels.com).

128. Take up Abdullah Quilliam's advice: "Your time and your mind is your garden and your field; let them lie fallow and you will get a good crop of weeds, cultivate them both and you will have a rich harvest of flowers, fruit, and good grain."

PART 4: MORAL CHARACTER (*AKHLAQ*)

Introduction

"O mankind! We have created you male and female, and have made you nations and tribes that you may know one another. Lo! the noblest of you, in the sight of God, is the best in conduct. Lo! God is Knower, Aware." (Al-Hujurat/ Inner Apartments [49] 13)

Islam as a way of life also prescribes a very effective moral system: whatever leads to the welfare of the individual or the society is morally good in Islam and whatever is injurious is morally bad. Islam attaches so much importance to the love of God and love of man that it warns against too much formalism, an example of which I found in the book *The year of living biblically* by A.J. Jacobs: "I was so busy obsessing over the rules [...] that I didn't have time to think."

According to Ziaddin Sardar, "[t]he roots of our ecological crises are axiomatic: they lie in our belief and value structures which shape our relationship with nature, with each other and the lifestyles we lead.", though Abu Hurayra reported that the Prophet ﷺ said, "Wealth does not mean having a lot of property. Wealth means having self-contentment." According to Yasir Qadhi in a *khutba* (sermon) said: "Having good *akhlaq* is a sign of one's strong *eman* [faith]. *Akhlaq* is that it is a sign of the perfection of one's *eman*. This is a very important point that should not be trivialized. A person who does not have good *akhlaq* does not have strong *eman*. It is that simple." Also, as the Prophet ﷺ told us: "The heaviest aspect, the heaviest matter [that will help a believer] that will be in the *mizan* (balance), on the scales on the Day of Judgment, is good moral character."

According to Sayyid Tarik Bin Shabib Al-Said (Patron, Environment Society of Oman) "[w]e are careless with our environment because we can be and because it's easy, but mainly because we don't think ahead; yet we have the capacity to think ahead. It is our job to nurture this ability...the rest will follow." And indeed to nurture this ability is the objective of the Africa Muslim Environment Network (AMEN), a continent that already now feels the consequences of our carelessness with our environment: "to restore the traditional role of the mosque as the *Ummah* centre for spiritual, social and economic fulfilment, and our intention and to do by assisting community development through sustainable use of the environment. We want to do this because we believe that this is the way forward for our Muslim communities in Africa to take action and responsibility for their future, and the earth's future." AMEN was formed in 2006 after several leading Muslims in Africa expressed the need for their communities to address the two critical issues of poverty and environmental degradation in Africa.

According to American convert Nuh Ha Mim Keller "it is of the *sunna* [way of the Prophet ﷺ] to be afraid for one's past, one's state at death, for calamities, and for treachery and disgrace. It is of the *sunna* to be patient and steadfast in worship, in blessings, in tribulations, and in divine punishments in one's body, reputation, family, or money. It is of the *sunna* to have firm patience in avoiding sins, and to make up for one's past misdeeds." And "it is of the *sunna* to intend worship and obedience to Allah by one's intention, deeds, words, and one's every movement and rest".

In 1982, I was an eight-nine year old attending a British school in Argentina. And then the two countries went to war. It being a school in Argentina, in the morning I was taught Spanish, maths and "*las Malvinas* [the name the Argentines give to two small islands outside the coast of Argentina] *son Argentinas*". It being a British school, in the afternoon I was taught English, science and "the Falklands [the name the British give to the islands] are British". Though not becoming much wiser to whom the islands really did belong (or why it mattered that they were linked to one country or other), one of the important lessons I did learn was that people in power and authority can say contradictory things so it is best to do your own homework, have your own moral compass. Though at times I have swayed off the road significantly, I think Islam has significantly strengthened my steps onto the straight path.

According to an article on the moral system in Islam on Islam101 (www.islam101.com), in verse 117 of Chapter Al-Baqarah/ The Cow in the Quran we are given a beautiful description of the righteous and God-conscious man in these verses. He should obey salutary regulations, but he should fix his gaze on the love of God and the love of his fellow men. We are given four heads: our faith should be true and sincere; we must be prepared to show it in deeds of charity to our fellow-men; we must be good citizens, supporting social organisations, and our own individual soul must be firm and unshaken in all circumstances. This is the standard by which a particular mode of conduct is judged and classified as good or bad. This standard of judgment provides the nucleus around which the whole moral conduct should revolve. Before laying down any moral injunctions Islam seeks to firmly implant in man's heart the conviction that his dealings are with God who sees him at all times and in all places; that he may hide himself from the whole world but not from Him; that he may deceive everyone but cannot deceive God; that he can flee from the clutches of anyone else but not from God. Thus, by setting God's pleasure as the objective of man's life, Islam has furnished the highest possible standard of morality. This is bound to provide limitless avenues for the moral evolution of humanity.

According to Richard Louv, author of *Last child in the woods, saving our children from nature deficit syndrome*, "healing the broken bond between our young and nature is in our self-interest, not only because aesthetics or justice demand it, but also because our mental, physical, and spiritual health depend upon it." For example in the UK alone 31 million prescriptions for Prozac were issued in 2006, including 631,000 for children, with a total cost of mental ill-health being estimated at £77 billion a year. Though of course I would not want to suggest that all mental ill health is due to being out of our *fitra* situation, away from nature, Mind, the UK mental charity does call for a new green agenda for mental health, following growing evidence in support of an accessible, cost-effective and natural addition to existing treatment options - ecotherapy.

Akhlaq means 'behaviour' or 'conduct'. To have good *akhlaq* is very important but at the same time it is very difficult. The Prophet ﷺ has explained: "I have been sent to complete the nobility of your character." This means that out of all the tasks which God sent the Prophet ﷺ to us for, one of the most important was to teach us perfect conduct. To gain the best conduct can be compared to climbing out of a deep, dark cave. Imagine trying to climb out from a cave as deep as the world. In the cave, our eyes are useless, we cannot see anything. We have to feel our way with our hands. As we climb higher, we begin to see the light, and our eyes start to open. In the same way, when we try to improve our character, we take one step at a time, higher and higher. The higher we get the closer we get to the light of God, and the better our conduct becomes. Once we get out of the cave, we are surrounded by light and we can see for miles and miles. We can see the sky and the sun. When we reach the top of our character, our soul is surrounded by God's light, and it can see through all the darkness that the world tries to attract us with. It can see the path towards God. It is hard work to reach that stage, but it is one of the tests in life, and the only way that we will become true followers of the Prophet ﷺ. In the Quran, God mentions: "I am the Light of Heaven and Earth and I shall guide those whom I wish." (An-Nur/ The Light [24] 35-36). This light is found in those houses where God's praise is offered day and night. The people of these houses are such that nothing tears them away from the remembrance of God and it is these people whom God will guide onto the right path. Light is there to guide us in the dark. What God is explaining to us is that He will guide us with His light, and will help us to climb out of the cave.

How can we improve our conduct? By trying to be good at all times, whether this is at home, or in the mosque, at school or with our friends. Whenever we do something wrong we should ask God for forgiveness. We must also try our best not to repeat the same mistake again.

As British convert Idris Tawfiq reminds us (as a former priest he used to preside over several funerals) that never had anyone said about the deceased "he had seventeen pairs of shoes" or "he had a really good job and went on holiday three times a year." Rather, people remembered the dead person as a loving father, or an honest worker, or a kind person. We are remembered by our character. An important and charismatic figure who played a pivotal role during the first phase of global environmental diplomacy was Mostafa K. Tolba (former Executive Director, United Nations Environment Programme, UNEP). He reminds us in his book *Global Environmental Diplomacy* that for example NGOs and we 'the public' influence negotiations to a significant degree.

Examples of action
129.   Get children back in touch with nature, in their *fitra*. In the UK try British Trust for Conservation Volunteers (BTCV, www.btcv.org.uk); in the US try *Children and Nature Network*, www.cnaturenet.org.

130.   Abdullah ibn Amr said, "There are four qualities such that if you were to be given them, you will not be harmed even if the world were to be taken away from you. They are: good character, restraint in food, truthful words, and upholding a trust." The Prophet ﷺ said: "Act in your life as though you are living forever and

250

act for the Hereafter as if you are dying tomorrow." Be the new NIMBY ('not in my back yard'): do what you can to get rid of pollution and regularly say 'not on my planet'.

131.   Contemplate on how you directly or indirectly may affect the lives of other creatures as the following incident shows how concerned Prophet Muhammad ﷺ was about taking care of animals, as narrated by Abdul Rahman bin Abdullah: "We were on a journey with the Messenger of God, and he left us for a while. During his absence, we saw a bird called hummara with its two young and took the young ones. The mother bird was circling above us in the air, beating its wings in grief, when the Prophet came back and said: 'who has hurt the *feelings* of this bird by taking its young? Return them to her'. If not, as Abu Masud Uqba reported that the Prophet ﷺ said, "Part of what people have learned from the words of prophethood is the statement: 'If you do not feel ashamed, do whatever you like."

Purification of the soul (tazkiyah)
"Verily, never will God change the condition of a people until they change what is in themselves." (Ar-Rad/ The Thunder [13] 11)

I used to find it difficult to understand that 'cleanliness is half of your *iman* (faith)' as I understood it referred to personal hygiene only. The main reason I found it hard to understand is that surely half the effort for being selected to end up in heaven was more than just washing your hands and trying to stay in state of ablution? After further study I now, God willing, believe I understand it better: the 'cleanliness' refers to so much more. For example, cleanliness of body *and* mind are stressed in the Quran (An-Nisa/ The Women [4] 43). Humans are outdoor creatures. However, we now often spend at least 80 per cent of our time indoors. The US Environmental Protection Agency (EPA) has found that indoor air quality is often five times worse (but can be up to 100 times worse) than the air outdoors.

Islam has three dimensions or levels, which in Arabic are called *islam*, *eman*, and *ihsan*. Islam (submission) refers to having the correct actions, that is, ones that are in accordance with the Quran and *sunna*. *Eman* (faith) refers to having the correct beliefs (*aqidah*). *Ihsan* (excellence) refers to having the correct motivations. Much attention is given to Islam and *eman* and to matters of Shariah and *aqidah*. But *ihsan* is important too. Having the correct motivations means purifying our souls from hypocrisy, caprice, heedlessness, and everything else that keeps us from serving God for His sake alone. This purification of the soul is called *tazkiyah*: purity of the body is a prelude to the purity of the soul. And on the importance of this Abu Malik al-Harith bin Asim al-Ashari relates that God's Messenger 🙲 said: "Purification is half of faith". Each one of us goes forth in the morning as a vendor for his soul. He either achieves its emancipation or brings it to perdition. Al-Nawawi points out that the word used for "half" in the *hadeeth* (*shatr*) does not have to be understood as a half in the literal, mathematical sense. Al-Uthaymin (author) also favours looking upon purification in a far broader sense. He writes: "Purification is half of faith in that faith is either to act upon something or to abandon something. To abandon something is to purify oneself of it and to act upon something is to bring it about. Purification is half of faith in that it means the abandonment of polytheism, since polytheism is an impurity. It has been said that the *hadeeth* means that purification for prayer is half of faith, since prayer is faith and it cannot be accomplished without purification. However, the first meaning is better and more universal. In this way, the Prophet ﷺ encouraged us to purify ourselves both physically and spiritually."

Another dimension of the Islamic approach to cleanliness is apparent in the Divine name of 'Most Holy' (*Quddus*), one of God's most beautiful names. In his explanations of this divine name, Bediuzzaman Said Nursi (Turkish thinker, 1878 – 1960 CE) points out the cleanness of the universe, and states that the face of the earth and such beings as the clouds, rain, flies, crows, maggots, earthworms, ants, various insects, and the red and white corpuscles in the human body all manifest the Name of Most Holy in their functions, and carry out duties as "cleansing officials." The Prophet ﷺ enjoyed the rain as Anas said, "Rain fell on us while we were with the Prophet ﷺ, he took off his garment so that the rain could fall on him. We said, 'Why did you do that?' He said, 'Because it has newly come from its Lord.'"

In addition, the Prophet ﷺ stated that cleaning rubbish and the like from streets is something which deserves divine reward. In this concern, the Prophet ﷺ said, "If you refuse but to sit in roads, then pay the road its right." They said, "What is the right of the road, God's

Messenger?" He said, "Lowering your gaze, returning greetings, and removing harmful things from the road".

According to a poem by Farid ud Din Attar (1119-1230? CE), translated by Andrew Harvey and Eryk Hanut, called *Four Things to Know* and includes: "Hatim al-Asamm said, "I have chosen four things to know and discarded all other things of knowledge. The first is this: I know that my daily bread is apportioned to me and will neither be increased or decreased, so I have stopped trying to add to it. Secondly, I know I owe to God a debt which no one else can pay for me, so I am busy about paying it. Thirdly, I know that there is someone pursuing me (death) whom I cannot escape from, so I have prepared myself to meet him. Fourth, I know that God is observing me, so I am ashamed to do what I should not."

Examples of action

132.　Try as Ibn Arabi (1165 – 1240 CE) advises: "Were it not for the excess of your talking and the turmoil in your hearts, you would see what I see and hear what I hear!" and thus live as Jafar ibn Muhammad ibn Ali ibn Husayn (702-765 CE) suggests: "Man should lead his life in such a way that he should not pollute his environment, because if he does so a day will come when it will be difficult and perhaps impossible for him to live on account of pollution." See if there are any patterns of waste that you are unaware of, such as regular trips to a shop that has become a habit rather than a need.

133.　Reflect on the wise words by Seyyed Hossein Nasr: "Men no longer want to climb spiritual mountains…

they now want to conquer all mountain peaks. They wish to deprive the mountain of all its majesty by overcoming it - preferably through the most difficult line of ascent... It is still our hope that as the crisis created by man's forgetfulness of who he really is grows and that as the idols of his own making crumble one by one before his eyes, he will begin a true reform of himself, which always means spiritual rebirth and through his rebirth attain a new harmony with the world of nature around him."

134. "But seek, with the (wealth) which God has given to you, the Home of the Hereafter, *But do not forget your portion in this world*: but do good, As God has been good to you, and seek not (occasion for) mischief in the land: For God loves not those who do mischief." (Al-Qasas/ The Story [28] 77). For one of the many inspiring examples to know how much you can achieve if you give it a try, is Abul Hasanat Mohammed Rezwan, an architect who set up *Shidhulai Swanirvar Sangstha* (self-reliance, www.shidhulai.org), designed a fleet of solar-powered boats to deliver education and supplies to remote regions of Bangladesh and in 2007 won an Ashden Award ('alternative Nobel') and UNEP Sasakawa Prize (www.unep.org/sasakawa).

135.   Hakim bin Hizam narrated: "I asked the Prophet ﷺ (for some money) and he gave me, and then again I asked him and he gave me, and then again I asked him and he gave me and he then said, "This wealth is (like) green and sweet (fruit), and whoever takes it without greed, God will bless it for him, but whoever takes it with greed, God will not bless it for him, and he will be

like the one who eats but is never satisfied. And the upper (giving) hand is better than the lower (taking) hand."

136.   Muhammad Kamal Al-Shareef advises that "[a] major element of being grateful to God for His favors is that believers should use these favors to improve their prospects in the life to come. This means that they use God's favors for good works and in ways that facilitate obedience to God. However, believers are urged not to neglect their portions in this life." Persist in your efforts in pleasing God with regards to supporting Creation, because as *Well taken, be taken by Islam* ("positive engagement for today's youth") reminds us: "Even if good environmental projects cannot continue, or disasters occur, a believing Muslim with knowledge should continue to do their best to apply Islamic principles, not losing heart, planning with optimism and hope for the future, with the conviction that God is watching and that the important thing is to keep doing their best. The earth is not eternal but our souls are."

Supplication (dua)

"If you would count the blessings of God you would not be able to reckon them" (Ibrahim/ Abraham [14] 34)

Abdullah ibn Abbas narrated that the Messenger of God ﷺ used to say, when he rose for prayer in the middle of the night, "O God, praise belongs to You. You are the light of the heavens and the earth and praise belongs to You. You are the Sustainer of the heavens and the earth and praise belongs to You. You are the *Lord of the heavens and the earth and whoever is in them.* You are the Truth, and Your words are true. Your promise is true, and the meeting with You is true. The *Garden is true* and the Fire is true and the Hour is true. O God, I submit to You and I accept You and I trust in You and I turn to You and I argue by You and I summon to You for judgement. Forgive me what I have sent before me and what I have left behind, what I have kept secret and what I have proclaimed, You are my god - there is no god but You."

Abdullah Quilliam (1856–1932 CE) stated that "If you will consider and try and reckon up all the blessings you have enjoyed in life, you will find that although you are a polyglot you will not have language enough to be able to thoroughly describe them all." The Prophet's companion Abu Dharr said, "Whenever the Messenger of God went to bed at night, he would say, 'In Your name do I die and am I given life again,' and when he awoke he would say, 'Praised be God Who gave me life after He caused me to die. And unto Him shall be the resurrection.'"

Suhayb narrated that the Prophet said: "The affairs of a believer are astonishing, and are all good; this is something which is true of him alone. For when something good comes to him he gives thanks, while when something bad comes he is steadfast, which is good for him also." Abu Hasan al-Kindi recited the following lines: "If you have been given blessings, then look after them for sins do away with blessings." Al-Junayd said, "I once heard al-Sari saying, 'Because to give thanks for blessings is itself a blessing, one can never cease to give thanks." Though bear in mind God "does not accept the *dua* of one whose heart is heedless of Him." Al-Numan bin Bashi relates that the Prophet ﷺ said: "Supplication is essentially what worship is", there is supplication through devotional acts. Our formal prayers are a form of supplication. The fasts that we observe are a form of supplication. When we undertake the pilgrimage, it is a form of supplication. The reason for this is that when a worshipper engages in one of these acts of worship, it is as if he is saying through his actions: "My Lord, You commanded me and I obeyed and hearkened to Your command. Here I am, offering you my worship, so please accept it from me." – so tending our garden etc is supplication.

If we would truly give thanks to the Creator, we are required to maintain the productivity of the soil, and not expose it to erosion by wind and flood; in building, farming, grazing, forestry, and mining, we are required to follow practices which do not bring about its degradation but preserve and enhance its fertility. For to cause the degradation of this gift of God, upon which so many forms of life depend, is to deny His tremendous favours. And because any act that leads to its destruction or degradation leads necessarily to the destruction and degradation of life on earth, such acts are forbidden. Abu Hurayra ﵁ reported that the Messenger of God ﷺ said, "Look at those who are lower than you and do not look at those who are higher than you. That is more likely to prevent you underestimating the blessing of God on you." In one variant, "When one of you sees someone who has been given more bounty in respect of wealth or physical strength, he should then look at someone who has less than him."

Examples of action

137. Count the blessings God has given you in greenery and consider working together for a 'green deen', like *Green Deen* in the US does (http://greendeen.blogspot.com); they are "a proactive effort of young Muslim activists from Southern California who have come together for the sake of *Allah* (*swt*) to raise awareness and change the current environmental conditions by promoting a healthier, greener and more environmentally conscious lifestyle."

138. Qais narrated "I heard Khabbab, who had branded his abdomen with seven brands, saying, "Had God's Messenger not forbidden us to invoke God for death, I would have invoked God for death. The companions of Muhammad have left this world without taking anything of their reward in it (i.e., they will have perfect reward in the Hereafter), but we have collected of the worldly wealth what we cannot spend but on earth (i.e. on building houses)."

139. Make *dua* for others to support your effort, but do not despair if they do not: Muhammad ibn Sahl Ibn Al-Marzuban (d. 956 CE) wrote a book called *The Superiority of Dogs Over Many of Those Who Wear Clothes: Ten Stories and Poems on the Dog* where the author and his friend contemplate the declining moral standards of the human race and sigh with nostalgia for 'the good old days', when one could depend upon the loyalty and friendship of one's fellow beings. An English translation is available thanks to the work of G. Rex Smith and M.A.S. Abdel Haleem.

Remembrance of God (dhikr)

"Those who remember God, standing, sitting and lying on their sides, and reflect on the creation of the heavens and the earth, [saying]: "Our Lord, You have not created this for nothing. Glory be to You! So safeguard us from the punishment of the Fire. Our Lord, those You cast into the Fire, You have indeed disgraced. The wrongdoers will have no helpers. Our Lord, we heard a caller calling us to faith: "Have faith in your Lord!' and we had faith. Our Lord, forgive us our wrong actions, erase our bad actions from us and take us back to You with those who are truly good. Our Lord, give us what You promised us through Your Messengers, and do not disgrace us on the Day of Rising. You do not break Your promise." Their Lord responds to them: "I will not let the deeds of any doer among you go to waste, male or female..." (Al-Imran/ The Family of Imran [3] 191-195)

Amherst D. Tyssen (1843-1930 CE) wrote a poem called *The Signs of God - Adapted from the Koran* includes the text: "Where'er we turn our reverent gaze, On fields or seas or skies, Signs of a wise Creator's hand greet our enquiring eyes." Remembrance of God brings cleansing and healing to the heart that is suffering disease, and it is the very spirit of righteous deeds. God promises success to those who remember God much: "… and remember the Name of God much, so that you may be successful." (Al-Anfaal/ Spoils of War [8] 45). The remembrance of God is greater than everything else, as God says: "… (and the remembering (praising, etc.) of (you by) God (in front of the angels) is greater indeed [than your remembering God in prayers etc.] …" (Al-Ankaboot/ The Spider [29] 45). This was the advice of the Prophet ﷺ to the man who thought that the duties of Islam were too much; he told him: "Keep your tongue wet with the remembrance of God." *Dhikr* pleases *al-Rahman* (the Most Merciful, one of God's 99 names) and keeps away the devil. It dispels worry and distress, and brings provision and opens the door to knowledge. It plants the seedlings of Paradise and helps one to avoid the evils of the tongue. It offers consolation to the poor who do not have the means to give charity; God has compensated them with remembrance of God, which takes the place of physical and financial acts of worship. Neglecting remembrance of God is said to cause hardness in the heart.

So the person who wishes to remedy his weakness of faith must increase his remembrance of God. God says: "… And remember your Lord when you forget…" (Al-Kahf [18] 24). God explains the effect that *dhikr* has on the heart: "… Verily, in the remembrance of God do hearts find rest." (ar-Rad/ The Thunder [13] 28). Ibn al-Qayyim stated, concerning the remedy of *dhikr*: "In the heart there is hardness which can only be softened by remembrance of God, may He be exalted. So the slave must treat the hardness of his heart with the remembrance of God, may He be exalted. A man said to al-Hasan al-Basri (642 – 728 or 737 CE), 'O Abu Said, I am complaining to you of the hardness of my heart.' He said, 'Soften it with *dhikr*.' The more forgetful the heart is, the harder it becomes, but if a person remembers God, that hardness softens as copper melts in the fire. Nothing can soften the hardness of the heart like the remembrance of God, may He be glorified and exalted. *Dhikr* is healing and medicine for the heart. Forgetfulness is a disease, the cure for which is remembrance of God. Makhool said: 'Remembrance of God is a cure and remembrance of people is a disease.'"

By means of *dhikr*, the believer can overcome the devil, just as the devil overcomes those who are neglectful and forgetful. One of the believers said: "When *dhikr* becomes well-established in the heart, if the devil gets too close, a person can defeat him. Then the devils gather around him (the devil who tried to get close to the heart of the believer) and say, 'What is wrong with this one?' and it is said, 'He was harmed by a human!'".

I remember when I was in Amman (Jordan) visiting Friends of the Earth Middle East in 2006. When I visited, there was also a volunteer from Iraq. I understood he used to be a pilot for many, many years. Not wanting to ask about the humanitarian situation (as a humanitarian aid worker in my day job being main contact point for Iraq at the time I knew all too well this was terrible and thus did not want to open any wounds), I asked the pilot to teach me something about the environment in Iraq … the poor pilot started to cry: he told me as a pilot he had seen his country's environment being raped and degraded beyond belief, that even if peace would come tomorrow, the people of Iraq and its environment would feel the consequences for many years to come. And as Mishkat Al-Moumin (human rights defender and former Environment Minister in the Iraqi Interim Government) put it: "environment is the third generation of a human right, and Iraqi people are entitled to a clean and a healthy environment".

Salman ibn Fahd al-Oadah (General Supervisor, IslamToday, www.islamtoday.net) refers to the fact that some scholars have said: "The signs to be found in God's Creation are too numerous to count, but few people benefit from those signs." A nice incident to clarify *dhikr* I found is: one day sixteenth century Turkish Sufi, Sunbul Efendi, founder of the Sunbuliyye Sufi order, sent out his disciples to bring flowers to the *zawiya* (retreat). While all of them returned with fine bouquets, one of them, Merkez Efendi, offered the master only a little withered flower, for, he said, "all the others were engaged in the praise of God and I did not want to disturb them; this one, however, had just finished its *dhikr*, and so I brought it'." Needless to say, he went on to become his master's successor as head of the *zawiya*. Practical *dhikr* is performed with one's obedient actions.

We are warned, as Ghulam Ahmad Parwez (1903-1985 CE) explains in his book *Islam: a challenge to religion*, that those who do not make proper use of their senses and mental powers sink to the animal level: "Many of the people, both civilised and nomads, live a life which dooms them to hell" (Al-Araf/ The Heights [7] 179). The reason for this is that "they have hearts wherewith they understand not, have eyes wherewith they see not, and have ears wherewith they hear not" (Al-Araf/ The Heights [7] 179). The result is that they cease to be rational beings. "These are like cattle: nay, but they are worse. These are the neglectful" (Al-Araf/ The Heights [7] 179).

Examples of action

140. Zaki Jalil from Singapore asks in his article *How green is Islam?*: "If being spiritual is doing what is pleasing to God, does that not make caring for His creation a spiritual activity?" Look around to God's

Creation in your area, or increase it if there is little…in January of each year, participate in the *Big Garden Birdwatch*, organised by the Royal Society for the Protection of Birds (RSPB), and the world's biggest bird survey, providing a vital snapshot of UK birds each winter. It is "fun, free and will only take an hour of your time": www.rspb.org.uk/birdwatch

141.   If someone tries to convince you to get the latest TV, go for quick weekend by flight abroad or delike, remember the Prophet ﷺ: "Take an informed opinion (literally, *fatwa*) from your heart. What is good puts your self and your heart at rest. What is wrong is never fully acceptable to yourself and wavers in your heart, even if people give you a different opinion (*fatwa*) and keep on giving it to you." Because, as Alastair McIntosh states in his 2008 book *Hell and High Water: Climate Change, Hope and the Human Condition*, states: "[t]o start to resolve what has become of the human condition we must get more real in facing up to despair and death. Only then will we discover the spiritual meaning of our troubled times."

142.   Do not be wasteful. Remember God when using anything of Creation, because as the leader of Libya, Muammar Al Qadhaf, says: "[y]ou can afford to give up and do without anything except the planet Earth ... Earth is the only thing you cannot afford to give up. If you destroyed any other thing you might not lose much. But be careful not to destroy the earth, because you would then lose everything. […] If you, for instance, ruined arable land, it would be the same as you wanting to cook after having smashed all your pots and pans. If

you ruined arable land, it would be the same as you wanting to drink from your only drinking vessel, which you had broken."

143.   As an article on Islam and ecology on the website of the Center for Religion and Democracy (CRD) in Azerbaijan suggests: "let us ponder over and over again on the following Koranic verses": "Have you considered what you sow? Is it you that cause it to grow, or are We the causers of growth? If We pleased, We should have certainly made it broken down into pieces, then would you begin to lament: Surely we are burdened with debt: Nay! we are deprived. Have you considered the water which you drink? Is it you that send it down from the clouds, or are We the senders? If We pleased, We would have made it salty; why do you not then give thanks? Have you considered the fire which you strike? Is it you that produce the trees for it, or are We the producers? We have made it a reminder and an advantage for the wayfarers of the desert. Therefore glorify the name of your Lord, the Great. But nay! I swear by the falling of stars; And most surely it is a very great oath if you only knew; Most surely it is an honoured Quran" (Al-Waqia/ The Event or The Inevitable [56] 63-77)

Education and cultivation (tarbiyah)
"But teach: for teaching benefits the Believers" (Al-Dhariyat/ The Winds That Scatter [51] 55)

One day, when going around my regular browse around the internet to see what the world was up to, I was intrigued by a title *Born in the Netherlands* (which I was too, but it being a fairly small country it is not that common a happening). I was even more intrigued (or perhaps quite worried) when "the highlights of the blog" included "If terrorists can do it, so can we". Fortunately it concerned a much more benign and exciting prospect. The author, Neale Donald Walsh (author of *Conversations with God*), was actually sharing a brainwave he had had during a talk in the Netherlands: if people could gather in small clusters around the world in "terrorist cells", then we, too, could gather in similar clusters across the globe in what he labels "creationist cells", with a purpose to "create a new reality on the earth, to create the possibility of a new tomorrow, a tomorrow without violence, without terror, without the use of force as a tool to get what we want and what we think is 'right'." This gave birth to his grassroots movement of the *The Group of 1000* (http://thegroupof1000.com). What a good idea. Especially as Muslims it would help us counter the hijacking of our beautiful religion by terrorists and support us in our implementation of our duty of *khilafah*, or guardianship of God's Creation.

Working for environmental causes is sometimes seen as a 'luxury', something for middle class people in the rich world. However, as Peace Nobel Laureate Wangari Maathai from Kenya stated in her acceptance speech: "In 1977, when we started the Green Belt Movement, I was partly responding to needs identified by rural women, namely lack of firewood, clean drinking water, balanced diets, shelter and income. [...] I came to understand that when the environment is destroyed, plundered or mismanaged, we undermine our quality of life and that of future generations."

On migrating to Medina, God's Messenger ﷺ organised the planting of trees and of date groves. These forests and green spaces were called conservation areas or sanctuaries (*hima*), where every sort of living creature lived. For example, a strip of land approximately twelve miles wide around Medina was proclaimed a sanctuary and made a conservation area (like in the UK's green belt around cities). It is known that he proclaimed other similar areas sanctuaries. According to Peter Vincent (Lancaster University) the *hima*, as a system, is "probably the oldest known organised approach to conservation anywhere in the world."

Way back in 961 CE, Muslim farmers published a *Calendar of Cordova*: a treatise where each month of the year had its tasks and timetable. It included, nearly nine centuries before Europe published similar ones, all science regarding soil use, irrigation, times for planting, harvests, actions against parasites and insects, farming administrative procedures, and all other details that regard farming in all its complexities. Why should Muslims (and non-Muslims of course for that matter) have to find out about this from a Muslim heritage source (www.muslimheritage.com), and not from actual practice and cultivation in our current gardens?

There is a fantastic initiative in Canada: *iEnviro* (www.ienviro.ca) where they "are working towards Revitalizing the Environmental Ethics in Islam through practical means, positive examples, mentorship, and lots of Encouragement and Cheers." And the US has a *Muslim Green Team* (http://muslimgreenteam.org) which claims to be "the first Muslim American grassroots environmental movement. Our goal is to educate and equip the Muslim community to live greener lives, and to demonstrate to the general public the Islamic environmental message." More at the forefront is Ayman Ahwal, a brother who, under the motto 'remember the Garden' does everything he can to save tropical rainforest and other elements of Creation. He now spends much of his time in Aceh (in Gunung Mas eco-village) and Belum in Malaysia. During a break back in the UK, he was so upset by the state of the urban environment in Muslim areas, he made the short film *Clean Medina* (available via IFEES). To read more about his work and find an opportunity to do some practical *tarbiyah*, check: www.upriverprojects.org.

Examples of action

144.   As Baba Dioum (a Senegalese poet) reminds us: "In the end, we conserve only what we love. We will love only what we understand. We will understand only what we are taught." So, set up a programme of 'Earth literacy' in your mosque, community centre or Islamic Society. For an idea, check the Centre for EcoLiteracy guide on *Linking Food, Culture, Health, and the Environment* http://ecoliteracy.org or get relevant readings from for example: http://greenbooks.co.uk or www.eco-logicbooks.com. Remember the Prophet ﷺ said: "There is no better gift a parent can give a child than good manners."

145. iEnviro (a Canadian Muslim initiative, www.ienviro.ca) plan to introduce recycling programmes in major mosques across Canada by 2010, God willing. Their target is to reduce waste in mosques

by 50 per cent – could you initiate or support something similar for your mosque? Remember: Aisha ﷺ narrated that the most beloved action to God's Messenger was that whose doer did it continuously and regularly. The American *Muslim Green Team*'s (http://muslimgreenteam.org) first ecofair included an 'electronic waste drop off' and an 'organic bazaar'.

146. If you are a homeschooler, like Inayet Sahin in the US, then include green and sustainable living into the curriculum (www.spiritualhomeschooling.com) or use *Love Allah, Unite to put the Planet-Ecology together*, Love God recycle story and follow-up teaching materials by Soumy Ana to support the education of your children (www.ummah.com/islam/taqwapalace/recycle.pdf). Or for more advanced studying, help Othman Llewellyn, working for the National Commission for Wildlife Conservation and Development (NCWCD) in Saudi Arabia, realise his dream: "I hope that before I die we will have established environmental *fiqh* [law] as a recognised discipline of Islamic law." (I was surprised to learn it was not yet the case)

147. Attend a 'sustainable living' course, for example Low Impact Living Initiative in the UK, www.lowimpact.org, www.sustainableliving.org.nz for New Zealand. Learn that 'fighting nature' (in your garden or at society level) is not the answer, as E. F. Schumacher (author of *Small is Beautiful*) said: "Man talks of a battle with Nature, forgetting that if he won the battle, he would find himself on the losing side." The answer is to work *with* nature/ Creation. To learn

about four remarkable stories of women, including Sahena Begum, check '*Sisters on the Planet* by Oxfam (www.oxfamamerica.org/sisters)

148. It is one thing to know, intellectually, that the sacred is present in creation. It is another to experience this in our heart, to feel it at the deepest level of our being. Reconnect to awe and beauty, sense the sacred in Creation. Organise a tree planting event in your community (see www.treeforall.org.uk to get a free tree for your school or community group) or go the full hog and implement urban farming: growing food on unused land and space and give it to the needy, see for example www.urbanfarming.org from Detroit, US. Prophet Muhammad ﷺ said, "If anyone cultivates waste land he will have a reward for it, and that which any creature seeking food eats of it will count as sadaqah to him." For a starting point on which vegetables are in season when, see: www.thinkvegetables.co.uk or www.muslimgrower.com.

149. To encourage environmental issues in schools (for example healthy local school lunches, growing plants on school grounds – I have fond memories of doing this-, organise 'walking buses', oppose selling off of school fields – something that is happening all too regularly), consider becoming a school governor. School governors make collective decisions as part of the governing body whose primary function is to help raise the educational standards and performance of a school by supporting the work of the headteacher and staff. The governing body is answerable to parents and

the wider community. For advice:
www.muslimgovernors.org , www.ecoschools.org.uk

Etiquette of eating

"Then let man look at his food, (and how We provide it): for that We pour forth water in abundance, and We split the earth in fragments, and produce therein corn, and grapes and nutritious plants, and olives and dates, and enclosed gardens, dense with lofty trees, and fruits and fodder, for use and convenience to you and your cattle." (Abasa/ He Frowned [80] 24-32)

According to Zaghloul El-Naggar (Professor of Geology, Head, Committee on Scientific Nations in the Glorious Quran and Purity Sunnah Supreme Council for Islamic Affairs, Cairo, Egypt), "the meaning of the term "look" here is not limited only to sight but goes beyond it. It is a kind of proverb. For food is one of the major necessities of life and no one can pretend that he has anything to do with the water cycle which is created and monitored by *Allah*, thanks to His knowledge, wisdom and capability." Also, M.L. Ghandi of the Nigerian Muslims Network reminds us, the encouragement to eat only good and pure foods is combined with warnings to remember God and avoid Satan. In this way, Muslims are shown that eating is not merely an action to satisfy the hungry body, but that, as in all of the human's actions, it has an effect on how well or how poorly a Muslim will serve God.

There are some general principles laid down by the Quran regarding food. The first condition is that it should be lawful (*halal*), which carries the double significance of being earned lawfully and not being prohibited to eat. As

271

the Islamic Food and Nutrition Council of America (IFANCA) warns us though: "there is no dearth of unscrupulous individuals willing to falsely claim their products as Halal". The second is that it should be good (*tayyib*) or fit for eating and wholesome, not unclean or such as offends the taste. It is further stated that the golden rule regarding what one eats and drinks is moderation. As underfeeding affects the build-up of man, so does also the overloading of the stomach.

Etiquette of eating: quantity

Eat and drink, but waste not by excess, for God loves not the wasters. (Al-Araf/ The Heights [7] 31)

Imran bin Husain said that the Prophet ﷺ stated: "The best people are my contemporaries [that is the Prophet's ﷺ generation] and then those who come after them [that is, the next generation]." Imran added: I am not sure whether the Prophet ﷺ repeated the statement twice after his first saying. The Prophet ﷺ added, "And after them there will come people who will bear witness, though they will not be asked to give their witness; and they will be treacherous and nobody will trust them, and they will make vows, but will not fulfil them, and fatness (obesity) will appear among them." According to the UK National Health Service (NHS), in England in 2006, 24 per cent of adults (aged 16 or over) were classified as obese (which is more than just being overweight). This represents an overall increase from 15 per cent in 1993. In the same year 16 per cent of children aged 2 to 15 were classed as obese, representing an overall increase from 11 per cent in 1995. 37 per cent of adults had a raised waist circumference in

2006 compared to 23 per cent in 1993 and women were more likely then men to have a raised waist circumference (41 per cent and 32 per cent respectively). For people aged 35 and over classified as having a raised waist circumference, men were twice as likely and women were four times more likely to have type 2 diabetes. In 2006, 1.06 million prescription items were dispensed for the treatment of obesity. Overall, the number of prescriptions in 2006 was more than eight times the number prescribed in 1999, when there were 127 thousand prescription items. According to the US Government Department of Health and Human Services, there has been a dramatic increase in obesity in the United States in the past twenty years: in 2006, only four states had a prevalence of obesity *less* than 20 per cent; twenty-two states even had a prevalence equal or greater than 25 per cent. According to the Organisation for Economic Co-operation and Development (OECD) this trend is spreading: half or more of the adult population is now defined as either being overweight or obese in no less than 15 OECD countries. And the dangerous thing is that, according to research by University College London, growing obesity in the population has increased what is perceived as 'normal' weight, which is leading to large numbers of people underestimating how fat they really are. As a result, more people are failing to recognise they are overweight, despite an increase in the prevalence of obesity in the population.

An article on *The four poisons of the heart*, based on the works of Ibn Rajab al-Hanbali (1335-1393 CE), Ibn al-Qayyim al-Jawziyya (1292-1350 CE), and Abu Hamid Al-Ghazali (1058-1111 CE), mentions eating too much food as one of the four poisons, quoting a warning from a man from the tribe of Israel: "Do not eat too much, otherwise you will drink too much, and then you will end up sleeping too much, and then you will lose too much."

You may wonder why I am including information about obesity in a book about environmental tips. Well, any excess of food that we eat puts an extra burden on the environment: it has to be grown, it has to be transported, more scraps will be thrown away putting a burden on landfill etcetera. This aspect is especially crucial as in the UK less than half of what we bought in 2008 was produced in the UK, meaning more than half of what we bought has been flown or shipped in from abroad and this figure is on the increase (air food kilometres rose by 11 per cent just in 2006).

Eating too much is also not only bad for the environment, but very expensive (taking up funds we could be putting to solving the environmental mess we got ourselves in): the current total annual cost to the UK National Health Service (NHS) (that us, us all as taxpayers) of overweight and obesity has been estimated at £1 billion, and the total impact on employment may be as much as £10 billion. By 2050 the NHS cost of overweight and obesity could rise to £6.5 billion and the associated chronic health problems are projected to cost society an additional £45.5 billion a year (at today's prices). And according to a report by the UK Government National Audit Office, obesity costs England 18 million sick days and 30,000 excess deaths per year. For example, researchers say there is "convincing" evidence that excess body fat can cause six different types of common cancers, including those affecting the breast, bowel and pancreas. The World Cancer Research Fund (WCRF) report is based on an in-depth analysis of 7,000 cancer studies from around the world dating back to the 1960s. The study also concluded that processed meat, such as sausages, was such a risk factor for bowel cancer that people should avoid it completely. But relying on pills to halt obesity epidemic seems no answers: Malaysian doctors have found that anti-obesity drugs and appetite suppressants are causing heart attacks.

Jacques Diouf (Director General, United Nations' Food and Agriculture Organisation, FAO) said in July 1999 (and I have found no information to conclude that this would no longer be true): "Globally, there is enough food to feed the world, but to our shame, we live in a world where food rots and people starve." For example in the UK we just throw away 6.7 million tonnes of food every year (1.2 million tonnes is simply left on our plates). According to a UK Government funded Waste and Resources Action Programme (WRAP) research published in July 2008. This reminds me of the *hadith* where Abu Hurayrah ﵁ narrated that God's messenger ﷺ said: "Surely God dislikes every ill-tempered person, foremost in eating, vociferous in the markets, a carcass in the night, a donkey by day, scholar in the affairs of the world and ignorant in matters of the hereafter."

The environmental costs of food waste are enormous: according to WRAP 20 per cent of the UK's greenhouse gas emissions are associated with food production, distribution and storage. If we stopped wasting food that could have been eaten, we could prevent at least 15 million tonnes of carbon dioxide equivalent emissions each year. The majority of these emissions are associated with embedded energy (energy in making the wasted food) but a significant proportion arises as a result of food waste going to landfill sites. According to research published in February 2008 by the Sustainable Development Commission (the UK Government's independent watchdog on sustainable development) 1.6 million tonnes of food goes to landfill each year. Once in landfill food breakdown produces methane - a greenhouse gas 23 times more powerful than carbon dioxide. According to research by the Government, the average UK household spends £420 a year on food that goes in the bin. Throwing food away wastes all of the energy and other inputs needed to produce, package and transport it. According to an article *Jihad against Food Waste* on the SoundVision website (www.soundvision.com), the food wasted in the US could feed 49 million people a year.

From the chapter on 'commodities' [*sic!*] by the UK Government Department for Environment, Food and Rural Affairs (DEFRA) *Agriculture in the UK 2006*, we learn that in the UK in 2006 there were almost 35 million sheep and lambs, some 10 million cows and claves and some 173 billion poultry (mainly chickens). As an example for the bowling fowls (chickens reared for meat) their "average producer price" [*sic!*] (in pence, per kilo) has gone down from 34.7 (1995-1997 average) to just 10.2 (2006). Around 90 per cent of chickens are reared for their meat to minimum welfare standards, which allow each chicken less space than a sheet of A4 paper – that is less space than is allowed for egg laying hens which are kept in cages (which reminds me of the saying of the Prophet ﷺ: "it is a great sin for man to imprison those animals which are in his power"; see also under chapter on mercy). They are bred to grow very quickly. The time from when they hatch to appearing as packaged meat in the shops can be only 39 days. This rapid growth can cause them a variety of health problems such as heart failure and lameness. They are kept in near constant dim light. This discourages activity to maximise their growth and they are only given a few hours of complete darkness each day to rest properly. It encourages the birds to eat more and therefore grow more quickly. This is against the recommendations presented at the conference on the *Islamic Principles on Animal Transport and Slaughter* as presented in October 2008: "Animals, including poultry, should not be kept in overly restrictive cages. They should be kept with sufficient space to carry out their natural behaviour. They should not be bred to grow so fast or for such high yields that their health and welfare are harmed."

The average number of eggs per chicken has gone from 283 to 298 between 1997 and 2006. – how would this all be possible without cutting corners on animal welfare? And the inefficient thing is: while we for example imported 30 tonnes of skimmed milk powder in 2006 from EU countries, in the same year we exported 35 tonnes to EU countries. And this is the same with many other items. Some recent more positive news are recommendations coming out of the *Conference on the Islamic Principles on Animal Transport and Slaughter* held in Cairo (Egypt) in October 2008. I pray all will take on board a key recognition that "all animals are sentient beings and that we should treat them with compassion throughout their lives until the point of death."

And should you be more interested in the direct effect on humans, according to a recent report conditions of intensively farmed birds could be contributing to avian flu virus mutation and infection. Plus effect on poverty: according to a report from November 2008 "If a population the size of North America replaced the meat in their meals with plant-based foods for just one day, it would save over 200,000 metric tonnes of human-edible grain. That amount of food could feed all of the estimated 2 million displaced people currently in urgent need of food aid in the Democratic Republic of Congo for at least six months, and the carbon emissions saved would be more than enough to cancel out the emissions from flying that food from the USA to Africa."

Examples of action

150.   When you eat, remember what Anas رَضِيَ اللهُ عَنْهُ narrated: "To the best of my knowledge, the Prophet ﷺ did not take his meals in a big tray at all [...]." Save cash and support Creation: buying and then throwing away good food costs us £10.2 billion every year, or £420 for the average UK household and £610 for households with children (some 11 per cent of the food we buy). The food we throw away is also responsible for the equivalent of 18 million tonnes of carbon dioxide emissions every year, the same as the CO2 emitted by one in every five cars on UK roads. Plus it is not just the methane that is released when the food goes to landfill that is the problem, but also the

energy spent producing, storing and transporting the food to us: every tonne of food we throw away is responsible for 4.5 tonnes of CO2 equivalent emissions. For tips on how to limit your food waste, check: www.lovefoodhatewaste.com. Having more than enough is also not an excuse to overeat, as Hamzah bin Abdullah bin Umar narrated: "Inspite of having abundant food, Abdullah bin Umar رَضِيَ اللهُ عَنهُ would never eat until his stomach was full."

151.   Eat the quantity the Prophet ﷺ suggested, as narrated Ibn Umar رَضِيَ اللهُ عَنهُ that God's Messenger ﷺ said, "A believer eats in one intestine (is satisfied with a little food), and one who has rejected faith or a hypocrite eats in seven intestines (eats too much)." And with global food price crisis, avoid unnecessary demand, as the Prophet ﷺ said: "He is not a man of faith who eats his fill when his neighbour is hungry." Sufyan al-Thawri رَضِيَ اللهُ عَنهُ said: "If you want your body to be healthy and to sleep less, then eat less." Al-Hakim narrated that Abu Juhayfah رَضِيَ اللهُ عَنهُ said: "The Messenger of God ﷺ said: "The more people eat their fill in this world, the more hungry they will be on the Day of Resurrection." Remember this when reading that in 1961 the average number of calories eaten per person in the UK was 2,254 kcals, while in 2003 it was 25 per cent higher at 2,809 kcals per person.

152.   Abu   Huraira   رَضِيَ اللهُ عَنهُ narrated   that   God's Messenger ﷺ said: "The food for two persons is sufficient for three, and the food of three persons is sufficient for four persons." Al-Miqdad ibn Maad

Yakrib narrated that he heard the Messenger of God ﷺ, say: "No human ever filled a container more evil than his belly. The few morsels needed to support his being shall suffice the son of Adam. But if there is no recourse then one third for his food, one third for his drink and one third for his breath."

153.   Do not waste food: Jabir reported God's Messenger ﷺ as saying: "When any one of you drops a mouthful he should pick it up and remove any of the filth on it, and then eat it, and should not leave it for Satan, and should not wipe his hand with towel until he has licked his fingers, for he does not know in what portion of the food the blessing lies." As we should not waste food (and avoid becoming fat), we should be careful in the quantities of food we prepare.

154.   If you are organising a celebration (*Eid*, wedding etc) and expect any quantity of edible food left, do not throw it away for it to end up in a landfill or incinerator, but contact a community food network (like FareShare, www.fareshare.org.uk, in the UK or Second Harvest, www.secondharvest.org, in the US) or contact your nearest homeless hostel directly. If it has gone off (or it consists of necessary by-product of food preparation (like peels): do not bin it, make compost - the worms will love you for it (plus you will save money in not having to buy compost to green your garden).

Etiquette of eating: quality
O you who believe! Eat of the good things wherewith We have provided you, and render thanks to God if it is

(indeed) He Whom you worship. (Al-Baqarah/ The Cow [2] 172)

The vegetables in the supermarkets look unblemished and we have the same choice all year round, but according to Bruce N. Ames (Professor, University of California, Berkeley, USA) a chronic shortage of vitamins and other 'micronutrients' in the diet may be responsible for triggering many of the ills of modern life such as cancer, obesity and the degenerative diseases of ageing, which means we would not be giving our bodies their rightful dues. Organic food in supermarkets are often sold under 'premium' ranges, giving the impression that growing organic is more expensive. Ultimately it is not, as a consumer you pay three times when you buy intensively farmed food, according to Jules Pretty (Professor for Environment and Society, Essex University, UK). Firstly, you pay at the shop till. Next, you pay for the same food through your taxes, as modern farming is subsidised through the tax system (farming subsidies cost the UK taxpayer about £3 billion pounds every year). Thirdly, the consumer pays again to clean up the damage to the environment caused during the growing and the raising of the food (the UK government spends £120 million of taxpayers' money every year just to clean up pesticide residues from farming which pollute our water. These are effectively hidden subsidies from water consumers to polluters).

I would guess very few Muslims in the UK today can honestly say they know where their meat comes from (or any other food for that matter, as less than two per cent of the UK population work in farming and we import more than half of our food into the UK), who reared the animal, what it was fed on and who slaughtered it. More worryingly, it seems many do not even care how it might be possible to buy "4 halal chickens for £5" (as seen in Birmingham, UK, in 2007 and 2008, meaning just £1.25 per chicken). In February 2008 I found a leaflet in my letterbox that a local butcher - 'under new management' – could now offer me a hen (chicken) for 99 pence), even if Tesco was rapped in that same February 2008 for hitting a "new low" for selling (non-halal) chickens for £1.99, Compassion in World Farming (CIWF) calling it "depressing" and just weeks after a big campaign on UK's Channel 4 had highlighted the general terrible life of battery-reared broilers. The mentality now seems that if the sign in the butcher's or restaurant says *halal* then it is fine to eat. We no longer question what we are putting in our bodies. I do not dare think about what animal welfare corners have been cut to achieve such 'rock bottom' prices. I am not tempted to buy these 'cheap' chickens etc, fearing I will quite likely have to pay the rest of the price on Day of Judgment. I agree thus with the Halal Monitoring Authority in Canada (and UK) who both include the following in their frequently asked questions (FAQ): "If I see a product marked as *halal* or I am given assurance, am I not supposed to believe him? The answer is that even then you must investigate. The main reason being is that today we are living in an era in which deceiving, cheating and being unfaithful has become prevalent within our society. This unfortunate state of affairs is something that was foretold by the Prophet ﷺ: Imran bin Hussain رضي الله عنه reported that God's Messenger ﷺ said, "The best of this nation is the generation within whom I have been sent then those people who will come after them. Then a people will emerge who will make vows and not fulfil them, they will deceive and they cannot be trusted…" When the current situation is such, we as Muslims have no choice but to be at the top of our guard and practice upon the following verse. "O you who have believed, if there comes to you a disobedient one with information then investigate…" (Al-Hujraat/ The Right Apartments [49] 6). Unfortunately today swearing oaths in the name of *Allah* is seen as a cheap bargain to earn a few dollars. Therefore when we have the right to be inquisitive and the resources to investigate, exercise them!" And even if you focus on *halal* only on the slaughter itself: at least two slaughterhouses in the UK that present themselves as *halal*, kill 6,000 chickens an hour, with only three slaughterers, which means each bird gets less than two seconds attention.

According to the UK Government's Office for National Statistics, average weekly household expenditure in the UK in 2005–06 was £443.40. The highest expenditure was on transport at £61.70 a week with the next highest expenditure on recreation and culture at £57.50 a week, followed by food and non-alcoholic drinks at £45.30. Average weekly expenditure on housing, fuel and power was £44.20 a week. Of the £61.70 spent on transport each week, close to half (45 per cent) was spent on the operation of personal transport (£27.90 a week), the majority of which was spent on petrol, diesel and other motor oils (£17.50 a week). Of the £45.30 spent on food and non-alcoholic drinks each week, £12.10 was spent on meat, £3.40 on fresh vegetables, £2.80 on fresh fruit, and £3.80 on non-alcoholic drinks. This means we spend more than 5 times more on petrol, diesel and other motor oils than on fresh vegetables and 6 times more on petrol, diesel and other motor oils than on fresh fruit. We spend more on recreation and culture (TV, DVD, video, cinema etc) than on food and drink. We spend only 10 per cent of our weekly incomes on food and drink. Even amongst households in the lowest income group, the proportion of expenditure on housing, fuel (gas) and power (electricity) plus food and non-alcoholic drinks was only 37 per cent together. So if we say 'organic'/ *tayyeb* food is so expensive, is that because it is factually true or because we have chosen not to prioritise it, possibly under media brainwashing that food is 'supposed to be cheap'?

At this point it may be of interest to share a response I received from a friend via my engagement in the Midlands Islamic Network for the Environment (MINE): "Noting your request for positive examples, I thought you might perhaps be interested in a scheme we run at work in which one of group of us buys a 20-25kg bag of potatoes from an independent seller (i.e. NOT from a supermarket) which we then share out amongst ourselves. We started this because:

i) We are concerned about the way in which supermarket chains dominate the market, force out small independent businesses and pay very low prices to farmers
ii) We wish to buy local where possible (from July to March we often buy from a farm in our county).

Perhaps surprisingly, the potatoes we buy are almost always cheaper and better tasting than their supermarket equivalents. In fact, they are SO cheap that we can afford to each chip in 50p to a charity box, use this money to periodically buy things from charity catalogues (considering our staff composition we rotate between a Muslim, a Christian and a non-faith-based charity) and STILL be cheaper than supermarket potatoes. Talk about a WIN-WIN scenario! Over the last three and half years we have bought over 1.5 tonnes of potatoes - that's a lot of mash! I wholeheartedly recommend this scheme to anyone who wants to make a real, tangible difference to their own and their friends/neighbours/work colleagues purchasing habits.

P.S: We have also branched out into Fairtrade Chocolate, Local Free Range Eggs and Sustainably Caught Tuna … but that is perhaps a story for another day!"

I also read of at least one Muslim who, in order to provide his children with "organic, ethical and halal" (which to me mean all and the same thing in this context) keeps 3 chickens which "don't need a run much bigger than you'd have for a rabbit or guinea-pig and make engaging pets." A friend, a lone parent with two young children, also got some chickens. And Muhammad Ridha and Nicola Payne have taken their faith, their belief in what '*halal* meat' really means to a next level. They have moved up sticks to Somerset in 2006 to try and start living a more eco-friendly, natural and self-sufficient lifestyle. They set up *Abraham Natural Produce* (www.organic-halal-meat.com) with a mission "to provide top-quality, naturally reared, 'organic' and ethically sourced *halal* meat through a business model that supports localisation and contributes to charitable causes through a fixed percentage donation from profits."

In an attempt to cut down on food miles and chemicals on my food, do some 'green gym' and more, I registered with an allotment scheme. For I believe some £20 I had a plot of land three times the size of my living room to work on. Unfortunately this was before I had bought my bike so it was half an hour's walk from my flat. I did go several times in the beginning and was received very positively and taken 'under the wings' of two elderly gentlemen (both in their eighties). One of them showed me how to rotate the land and then passed me the shovel. It looked so easy and if, at his age could do it, surely it should be a piece of cake for me: what a shock, my strength was very weak so a 'green gym' it truly became. On another occasion I came to inspect the progress of my efforts: the place looked a jungle (well, I had seen some of it coming as I had not done any weeding because I did not know which one was the consequence of what I had sown and which had been there before). So grandpa came to lend me a hand again: "where did you sow the onions?" "eehhh, I don't remember" "and where have you sown the radishes" "I don't remember that either". Lesson learned: mark anything you sow.

In a more successful attempt to cut down on my 'food miles', enjoy quality food and support local farmers, I registered with a vegetable box. Delicious! Every week is like a gift to see what I will be eating that week. Though freely admitting I am not the best cook around, I had thought myself relatively well reconnected with nature (especially since my fateful attempt to run an allotment). That is, until I found some vegetables I thought I had never seen before, and I realised it was part of the Dutch staple diet: beetroot. It reminded me of research published by

LEAF about that only a handful of youngsters nowadays know where milk comes from (they think it is just Asda or Tesco [2 major supermarket chains in the UK, the former owned by US-based Walmart], or perhaps a factory working for the supermarket), or where eggs come from. I remember when I first took out a vegetable (in summer: salad, not just lettuce) box a friend telling me: "now you are at the mercy of what the veg box man gives you", which made me think, but then I realised: I am not at the mercy of 'veg man', but at the mercy of what God makes ripe and ready in the area where I live (and as if in the supermarket you have so much choice: it looks like a lot, but is often basically the same vegetables all year round). To make life easy, in preparing any of the vegetables/ salad elements, if I do not know what it is, I just pretend it is something else and cook it (such as pretending half the items are potatoes, though they all taste wonderfully different). My box includes so many blessings not found in the shops: purple and orange bell peppers (not just the red, yellow and green ones), yellow tomatoes, brown mushrooms, butternut squash: all delicious.

Thank God, Islam gives priority to complete diets; it prefers for example the use of whole wheat over sieved flour as in the *hadeeth* where Umm Ayman reported that she sieved out flour and made bread out of it for the Prophet ﷺ who asked: "What's this?" She said: "Grain we harvest out of our land, out of which I have made bread for you". He said: "Put it (the bran) back in and knead it again". Or as M.L. Ghandi of the Nigerian Muslims Network put it "[a] balanced diet is not just about foods you should avoid, it is about foods you choose to include." Or as Yusuf ibn Asbat said, "When a young man worships, the devil says [to his minions], 'Look at his food.' *If they find his food to be from an impure source, he says, 'Leave him alone; let him worship long and hard, for he himself has ensured that your efforts are not needed.'*"

Hudhayfa al-Marashi once watched people hurrying to join the first row in a mosque, and said, "They should hurry likewise to eat lawful bread. When Sufyan al-Thawri was asked about the merit which attaches to praying in the first row, he replied, "inspect the crust of bread which you eat, and find out where it comes from, even if this means praying in the last row." He also said, "Look to see where your money comes from, even if you have to pray in the last row." Also Ibrahim ibn Hushaim was advised as follows by a friend of his before he left on a journey: "I advise you to act with righteousness, and to *eat what is wholesome*. A Godfearing man does not fear his God *until his food and drink are wholesome*; and until what he earns and owns are wholesome too and his speech is goodly and pleasant. This is God's law, as told by His Prophet ﷺ So may He bless him and grant him His peace!" As put so succinctly in an article under *Halal and Healthy* on Sound Vision (a US-based Islamic information and products website, www.soundvision.com): "our muscles, bones, lungs, liver, brain and secretions are made from the raw product we feed it. If we provide the factory with junk raw products, the factory will not produce tough bones, strong muscles, good pump (heart) and clean pipes (vessels)."

If suggesting to eat more locally grown food, you may ask 'what about the poor farmer in Kenya?!' SOS Faim, a Belgian development organisation that has analysed the effect of cheap chicken arriving in Africa, explains: "Two years ago we found that tens of thousands of people lost their livelihoods in Cameroon as a direct result of frozen legs and bits of chicken coming in from Europe and Brazil. It's chicken madness. Local producers just cannot compete." And what about Kenyans growing for themselves? Our world is now so upside down, where especially poor countries are 'encouraged' to grow cash crops for export, that Ethiopia even in 1984 (during its terrible famine) was *exporting* food to Europe and elsewhere in return for some cash to spend on international market.

With many goods as soon as we see the label *halal* somewhere on the product we seem to stop thinking. Though of course it is important we eat *halal*, I am not sure where the *tayyeb* (wholesome) is left when some sweets specifically sold as *halal* include amongst others the following ingredients: "Tartaric Acid, Flavouring, Colours; Tartazine (E102), Orange Yellow S (E110), Quinoline Yellow (E104), Carmoisine/ Azorubine (E122), Patent Blue V (E131), Brilliant Blue (E133), Caramel Colour (E150), Carbon Black, Vegetable Carbon (E153), Titanium Dioxide (Inorganic) (E171)." Note that research, published on the US Government National Institutes of Health website, has found that "[e]xposure to non-nutritional food additives during the critical development window has been implicated in the induction and severity of behavioral disorders such as attention deficit hyperactivity disorder (ADHD)." Four of the additives mentioned even feature in the top seven of those confirmed to increase hyperactive behaviour in susceptible children, especially when eaten together, as confirmed in scientific research published in September 2007.

In 2012 EU law will make it compulsory for chickens to have a minimum 750cm2 of space per chicken (now it is 600cm2, the way in which some 70 per cent of animals live). According to Compassion in World Farming (CIWF) 'enriched' cages still provide too little space and too little height to enable hens to perform many important basic movements such as wing-stretching, wing-flapping and turning without difficulty. Moreover, they do not allow hens properly to satisfy their behavioural needs to lay their eggs in a nest, dustbathe, peck and scratch at the ground and perch. Accordingly, CIWF believes that the use of 'enriched' cages should be prohibited." For Muslims we have long-standing advice. The classical thirteenth century CE Muslim jurist Izz ad-Din ibn Abd as-Salam formulated the following statement of animal rights in his book *Rules for Judgment in the Cases of Living Beings*: "The rights of livestock and animals upon man: these are that he spend on them the provision that their kinds require, even if they have aged or sickened such that no benefit comes from them; that he not burden them beyond what they can bear; that he not put them together with anything by which they would be injured, whether of their own kind or other species, and whether by breaking their bones or butting or wounding; that he slaughters them with kindness when he slaughters them, and neither flay their skins nor break their bones until their bodies have become cold and their lives have passed away; that he not slaughter their young within their sight, but that he isolate them; that he makes comfortable their resting places and watering places; that he puts their males and females together during their mating seasons; that he not discard those which he takes as game; and neither shoots them with anything that breaks their bones nor brings about their destruction by any means that renders their meat unlawful to eat."

Examples of action

155.   Eat the quality that the Prophet ﷺ suggested for *iftar* (breaking of the fast), for example when it is chicken, eat as I once read on a discussion list "a happy chicken is a yummy chicken, even if it's me cooking it!!" (see for example: http://halalmonitoring.com) And remember who has truly provided the food, so end all meals with: "All praises for God who gave us food and drink and made us Muslims (those who submit to God)". Initiatives like *Healthy Food for All* (www.healthyfoodforall.com) in Ireland focus on community food initiatives, supporting healthy and affordable food to poor communities.

156.   Eat the quality that the Prophet ﷺ suggested the rest of the year: Saad رضي الله عنه relates that God's Messenger ﷺ said 'O Saad, purify your food (and as a result) you will become one who's supplications are accepted. I swear by He in whose hands the soul of Muhammad ﷺ lies, verily a servant (of God) tosses a *haram* morsel in his stomach (due to which) no deed is accepted from him for 40 days." According to Basheer Ahmad Hafiz al-Masri (1914–1992 CE, former imam of Woking mosque, the first purpose built mosque in England, UK, in 1889): "If animals have been subjected to cruelties in their breeding, transport, slaughter and

general welfare, meat from them is considered impure and unlawful to eat." Should we still eat it, then beware of the advice of Ahmad al-Rashid of www.islamtoday.com: "Food has an affect not only on our health, but on our behavior. Good food will bring about a good affect on us and bad or impure food will bring about an ill affect." – are you sure about how the animals you eat are treated?

157.   Grow your own fruit and vegetable, in a garden, window box or allotment. According to the UK's Royal Horticultural Society just growing your own lunch can also save you £1,000 a year, as well as providing a supply of organic, tasty and healthy food. Of course growing your own costs time, but compare it with finding a job to earn money to go to the shop to buy food and it all becomes less of a chore. And with seed saving and sharing it is cheap too. For the best chance of success, grow indigenous fruits and vegetables, like Rasaq Qadirie is supporting the Afghan people with: www.theafghanseeds.org.

158.   For the freshest eggs, keep some chickens. You can get them from for example Omlet (www.omlet.co.uk) or provide a loving home for a battery hen alternatively destined for the slaughter house due to end of "useful life". The Battery Hen Welfare Trust (www.thehenshouse.co.uk) are specialised in this.

Etiquette of eating: type
"And the earth He has put for the living creatures. Therein are fruits and palms producing sheathed fruit-stalks; and also corn, with (its) leaves and stalks for fodder, and sweet-

scented plants. Then which of the Blessings of your Lord will you deny?" (Yunus/ Jonah [10] 10-13)

According to Syed Abul Ala Mawdudi the above quote from the Quran does not mean: "You are asking, instead of *manna* and *salva* [quail] which you get *gratis* [free], things for which you will have to till and cultivate the land", but it means: "You are neglecting that grand purpose the purification of your hearts and the preparation for the leadership of the world for which you are being made to travel in the desert: instead of this, you are after the gratification of your taste and palate and cannot forego those things even for some time."

Like a fellow convert opens an article *Compassion – the spirit of halal. A Muslim perspective* in Meeting Point (the newsletter of the New Muslims' Project) in May 2008, I too have rarely met a vegetarian Muslim (and noticed that *halal* choice on a flight has never been without meat). But why, I wonder? Perhaps because as Zakir Naik (1965- CE, Founder, Islamic Research Foundation) states that "[a]s far as Islam is concerned, it is not compulsory for a human being to have non-vegetables - a Muslim can be a very good Muslim, even by being a pure vegetarian. But... but when our Creator... Almighty God... *Allah (SWT)*, gives us permission to have non-vegetables, why should we not have it?" It is permitted, but are we eating meat as God meant meat to be? The US Union of Concerned Scientists (UCS) mention that "Under current [US] law, pigs, chickens, and turkeys that have been fed rendered cattle can be rendered and fed back to cattle - a loophole that may allow mad cow agents to infect healthy cattle. Animal feed legally can contain rendered road kill, dead horses, and euthanized cats and dogs. Rendered feathers, hair, skin, hooves, blood, and intestines can also be found in feed, often under catch-all categories like 'animal protein products.'" The Fiqh Council of North America at its meeting in May 2001 stated that "Should the above-mentioned information [a report received before May 2001] be further verified, it may make the meat of livestock and chicken subject to prohibition from the *shari'ah* standpoint." When I visited the UCS statement, it was last revised in May 2007. Animals in the US and UK are also regularly fed GM feed (see under GM).

Although the Quran explicitly allows the eating of the meat of certain animals (Al-Maidah/ The Table Spread [5] 1), I agree with Hamza Yusuf (Founder, Zaytuna Institute, US) that "meat is not a necessity in *Shari'ah*, and in the old days most Muslims used to eat meat, if they were wealthy, like middle class - once a week on Friday. If they were poor - on the *Eids*." And according to Karen Armstrong in her book *A History of God*, "The Koran does permit meat-eating, but it also encourages healthful foods (which many Muslims conclude does not include animal products). Given these traditions, many Shi'ite Muslims and Islamic mystics, such as Sufis, see vegetarianism as the Islamic ideal and choose this diet." By the way, the word vegetarian(-ism) is not derived from vegetable (potentially implying making non-vegetables *haram*): the first Vegetarian Society founded in 1847 claims to have created the word vegetarian from the Latin *vegetus* meaning 'whole, sound, fresh, lively' (which is how these early vegetarians claimed their diet made them feel).

Also, traditionally Muslims were semi-vegetarians. And the proof of that is, again according to Hamza Yusuf, clearly in the *Muwatta* - when Umar ﷺ says, 'Beware of meat, because it has an addiction like the addiction of wine.' And the other *hadeeth* in the *Muwatta* - there is a chapter called *Bab al-Laham*, the chapter of meat. Both are from Umar ﷺ. And Umar ﷺ during his Caliphate, prohibited people from eating meat two days in a row. He only allowed them to eat [it] every other day. One day he saw a man eating meat every day, and he said to him, 'Every time you get hungry you go out and buy meat? He said, 'Yes, *Amir al-Mumineen*, I love meat. And Umar ﷺ said, 'It would be better for you to roll up your tummy a little bit so that other people can eat.'

If we study the modern meat industry, you will find out that a lot of the famine in the world is a direct result of the over-consumption of meat in countries like the US, Canada and Europe, because the amount of grain needed to produce one pound of meat (cows rarely get fed grass, their natural diet; read for example www.greenzabiha.com for an Islamic view from the US) is much greater than the amount you need to produce grain itself. As a Muslim it reminds me of following 'incident': Yahua ibn Saeed narrated that Umar ibn Khattab ﷺ [second Caliph after Prophet Muhammed ﷺ] met Jabir ibn Abdullah who had with him one who carried his meat, so he [Umar ibn Khattab] said: "Does one of you desire to fill his belly for his neighbour and his cousin? Have you forgotten this verse [from the Quran]: And on the Day that the Unbelievers will be placed before the Fire, (It will be said to them): "You received your good things in the life of the world, and you took your pleasure out of them: but today shall you be recompensed with a penalty of humiliation: for that you were arrogant on earth without just cause, and that you (ever) transgressed.'" (Al-Ahkaf/ The Dunes [46] 20)"

And for those who think we need to eat animals to keep the balance (fearing that if we stop eating them we will be overrun by animals): according to the Worldwatch Institute "[f]actory farming is the fastest growing method of meat production worldwide. Unlike animals raised on pasture, the millions of chickens, pigs, and cattle raised in factory farms are housed in often crowded, unsanitary, and inhumane conditions." Even the reproduction is done by artificial insemination. For a shocking summary of facts, watch *The Meatrix* (http://themeatrix.com), "a classic, spin on *The Matrix*, but instead of exposing the fake human reality exposes the our misguided perception of factory farms".

If one diet is much more wasteful than another, should we not choose for less wasteful one as God hates the wasters? According to research, a person consuming a mixed diet with the mean American caloric content and composition causes the emissions of 1,485 kg CO2-equivalent *above* the emissions associated with consuming the same number of calories, but from plant sources. Far from trivial, at a US national level this difference amounts to over six per cent of the total US greenhouse gas emissions. And a typical European omnivorous diet requires five times the amount of land required for a varied vegan diet. Or that we should not put so much pressure on the market so as to out-price our brothers and sisters elsewhere (in 1900 just over 10 per cent of the total grain grown worldwide was fed to animals; by 1950 this figure had risen to over 20 per cent; by the late 1990s it stood at around 45 per cent)? This becomes particularly urgent when as we saw in the first part of this book, world population is heading for 11 billion.

Studying the Quran, I was happy to learn it does not view animals as mere resources but as individuals and communities in their own right, as we read from the Quran verse at the start of this chapter, some of which we can eat, if we so wish (Say: "I find not in the message received by me by inspiration any (meat) forbidden to be eaten *by one who wishes to eat it*, unless it be dead meat, or blood poured forth, or the flesh of swine, - for it is an abomination - or, what is impious, (meat) on which a name has been invoked, other than God's". But (even so), if a person is forced by necessity, without wilful disobedience, nor transgressing due limits, - your Lord is Oft-forgiving, Most Merciful." (Al-Anam/ Livestock [6] 145). Research published by the UN Food and Agricultural Organisation (FAO) in November 2006 states: "the livestock sector emerges as one of the top two or three most significant contributors to the most serious environmental problems, at every scale from local to global. The findings of this report suggest that it should be a major policy focus when dealing with problems of land degradation, climate change and air pollution, water shortage and water pollution, and loss of biodiversity. Livestock's contribution to environmental problems is on a massive scale and its potential contribution to their solution is equally large. The impact is so significant that it needs to be addressed with urgency." This impact is especially worrying as "Global production of meat [*sic!*] is projected to more than double from 229 million tonnes in 1999/ '01 to 465 million tonnes in 2050, and that of milk to grow from 580 to 1,043 million tonnes.

The environmental impact per unit of livestock production must be cut by half, just to avoid increasing the level of damage beyond its present level." However, the good news is that "major reductions in impact could be achieved at reasonable cost."

Bearing in mind the saying of the Prophet ﷺ said "He has not affirmed faith in me (that is, he is not a true follower) who eats to his satisfaction and sleeps comfortably at night while his neighbour goes hungry - and he is aware of it.", Musa Ibrahim Menk (*sheikh*) says of this saying "How astonishing that such a wide gap has occurred between these teachings and traditions and the actual conduct of the Muslims as a whole! It is extremely difficult for an unknowing person to believe that such, really, were the teachings of the Holy Prophet of Islam ﷺ." In an increasingly populated 'global village' our choice of diet will more and more directly impact what options are left for others. For example, according to an article in *The Ecologist* from 1996, Egypt now grows more food for animals than for humans - almost 40 per cent of the total agricultural land is under animal fodder crops. Human supplies of grain have been made up through (US) imports which contributed to Egypt's external debt; in 1988, the country's debt was five times the value of its exports. The consistent beneficiaries of Egypt's switch to livestock production have been large US grain merchants such as Cargill which have exported US grains at hugely subsidised prices to Egypt.

In 'developed countries' 50 per cent of agricultural output is to feed farmed animals. Until recently, a large proportion of livestock in developing countries were not raised for food, but for providing draught power and manure and as capital assets that were only disposed of in times of emergency. Livestock were an integral part of agricultural systems, distributed among many owners and raised close to their feed supplies. This pattern is changing rapidly. Almost all of the growth in livestock production is now occurring in industrial systems, where meat production is no longer tied to a local land base for feed inputs or to supplying animal power or manure for crop production. And what is perhaps more worrying is that the according to the FAO the diversity of livestock breeds is severely under pressure: in the past six years a breed a month has become extinct and inbreeding amongst the most 'marketable' breeds is causing increasing worries.

Eating meat leaves behind an environmental toll that generations to come will be forced to pay. While 40 million tonnes of food would eliminate the most extreme cases of world hunger, 540 million tonnes are fed to animals in Western countries every year. The world's cattle alone consume the same amount of calories as it takes to nourish 8.7 billion people - more than the entire current human population on Earth. This reminds me of the *hadeeth*: Yahya related from Malik from Yahya ibn Said that Umar ibn al-Khattab ﷺ saw Jabir ibn Abdullah carrying some meat. He said, "What is this?" He said, "*Amir al-muminin*. We desired meat and I bought some meat for a *dirham*." Umar ﷺ said, "Does one of you want to fill his belly apart from his neighbour or nephew? How can you overlook this *ayat*? 'You squandered your good things in the

life of this world and sought comfort in them.'" (Al-Ahqaf/
Winding Sand-tracts [46] 20).

It takes 2,500 gallons of water to produce a pound of meat,
but only 25 gallons to produce a pound of wheat. A totally
vegetarian diet requires 300 gallons of water per day, whilst
a meat-eating diet requires more than 4,000 gallons of
water per day. 10,000 litres of water needed to produce one
kilogramme of beef, compared with only 500 litres of water
for a kilogramme of potatoes. Since 1950, half of all of the
world's rainforests have been destroyed to make way for
grazing animals. After just six or seven years, the soil is
often so damaged that it can no longer support grass. It
turns to dust. Indigenous people are forced to move on as
their habitat is sold off to the meat industry. In the UK,
hedgerows are being cut down for the same reason, and 98
per cent of the forests that once covered most of the British
Isles have been cut down.

Desertification (mainly caused by overgrazing) is one of the
world's most alarming processes of environmental
degradation. The amount of land currently degraded by
desertification has doubled over the past 20 years,
translating into an annual loss of 58,000 km2 of productive
land or, as estimated by the United Nations Environment
Programme (UNEP), a value of $42 billion in yearly
agricultural potential, which is four times the total
development assistance to agriculture. The UN estimates
that if current trends of land degradation continue unabated,
about 8 billion acres of grazing land, irrigated zones and
cropland will be at risk by the end of the century,
threatening the livelihood of 1.2 billion people. The risks of
desertification are thus substantial and clear: it contributes

to food insecurity, famine and poverty, and can give rise to social, economic and political tensions that can cause conflicts, further poverty and land degradation. The great scope and urgency of this challenge led the UN General Assembly to proclaim 2006 to be the 'International Year of Deserts and Desertification'.

Of all agricultural land in the UK, 90 per cent is used to raise animals for food, and we still need more food, so we import it from developing countries which often cannot even feed themselves. Using precious land to raise animals for food is wasteful. On 10 hectares, you can produce meat to feed just two people, maize to feed 10 people, grain to feed 24 people or soya to feed 61 people. Overgrazing of livestock has led to desertification around the globe. Raising animals for food causes water pollution as slurry leaches into the waterways. In some parts of Europe, slurry is the single greatest cause of acid rain. The methane produced by the world's cows is a major contributor to global warming.

Ibn al-Arabi (1165- 1240 CE) said: "Our scholars said: 'the rule with the animal is its impermissibility, and it does not become permissible except when killed in due form, or through hunting, however, if there was doubt in the hunter, or the slaughterer, then it becomes impermissible.'" (this is the rule with the Maliki school). Imam Nawawi (1234-1278 CE) said: "the basic rule with an animal is its impermissibility, until it can be established that it was killed in due form." This is similar to what has been stated by Ibn Hajar Al-Asqalani (1372-1448 CE); this rule is followed by the Shafi school. Ibn Qudama (b. 1147 CE) said: "the basic rule is impermissibility, they only become lawful if killed in due form by a qualified person."

God has made it allowed for us to eat meat and fish, but that does not mean we have to eat it, or eat it as often. God has also made all vegetables allowed for us, so why not give them more chance? Richard Foltz stated "[i]t cannot be denied that, since the inception of Islamic civilization fourteen centuries ago, a dietary norm of meat-eating has gone largely unquestioned by Muslims, who have interpreted the traditional sources in ways that have affirmed a carnivorous diet. But from the standpoints of human health, social justice, ecological stewardship, and compassion toward non-human creation, it can be seen that a vegetarian lifestyle may in fact be preferable for Muslims. Such a lifestyle is not incompatible with the teachings of the Islamic tradition, which can actually be read in ways that fully support vegetarianism." Or as Ezra Ereckson put it an article *Halal and Tayyib in the Here and Now*: "simply because a permission is given for an action [meat eating], does not make that action required, nor does it make it the best or most appropriate action in all conditions."

Benazir Bhutto (murdered former Prime Minister of Palistan) once said: "When British Prime Minister John Major used the words "mad, bad, and dangerous," he was talking about the European ban on British cattle. Frankly, he just as easily could have been referring to our world's insatiable desire for red meat. […] So, the next time you want to improve your life, take a look at what's on your plate. A little less beef may not be such a mad idea."

Perhaps a reason we eat more and more meat is because we buy it nicely sanitised from the shop, we forget that our kebab or chicken curry are from 'communities just like us'. Next time you buy meat, try to remember the words of Muhammad Raheem Bawa Mahaiyaddeen (died in 1986 CE), who appealed to Muslims to reflect on the meaning of slaughter. When describing Islamic slaughter in his *Ninety Nine Beautiful Names of Allah*, he said that the knife-bearer should "... look into the animal's eyes, he has to watch the tears of the animal, and he has to watch the animal's eyes until it dies – hopefully, his heart will change."

Fish

"And He it is Who has made the sea subservient that you may eat fresh flesh from it and bring forth from it ornaments which you wear, and you see the ships cleaving through it, and that you might seek of His bounty and that you may give thanks." (Al Nahl/ Bees [16] 14)

People are exposed to pesticides by eating contaminated fish. In an extensive study by the United States Geological Survey (USGS), pesticides show up more than 90 per cent of the time in fish samples taken from agricultural, urban and mixed land-use areas. Many of these pesticides have been banned or restricted, yet still pose a concern in terms of fish consumption. Although USGS only tested for persistent chemicals, current practices also lead to fish contamination with other pesticides. Used to kill unwanted insects and plants, pesticides are widely applied to lawns and landscapes, playing fields and parks, home yards and schoolyards, gardens and farms, and sprayed over communities. The pesticides then run off or drift into surface water or leak into groundwater. Rain and snow melt washes pesticides into streets and gutters. From there, the pesticide-contaminated water makes its way to drains, which empty into water bodies. The US Environmental Protection Agency (EPA) states that: "By their very nature, most pesticides create some risk of harm to humans, animals, or the environment because they are designed to kill or otherwise adversely affect living organisms." For more information on this see Beyond Pesticides (www.beyondpesticides.org) including fact sheets on alternatives.

Everything from the sea is normally *halal*, but nowadays the majority of fish does not come from the sea, but intensive fish farms, a worldwide industry worth $78.4 billion in 2005 according to the UN Food and Agriculture Organisation. Fish farming's (also referred to as aquaculture, so it does not sound so bad) contribution to total global fish production has increased from 5.3 per cent by weight in 1970 to 40 per cent in 2005. Invasive techniques are used to remove eggs and sperm from for example Atlantic salmon and rainbow trout. Atlantic salmon and rainbow trout are often starved for several days, sometimes for two weeks or more, before slaughter to empty the gut. In Scotland, average survival rates tend to be below 80 per cent. The global industry uses gender reversal to produce batches of all-female fish, as in several species females mature later than males, thereby enabling the fish to be grown to greater weights. Gender reversal involves feeding the male hormone testosterone to young female fish. It is often claimed that fish farming may take the pressure off stocks of wild-caught fish by providing an alternative. However, for carnivorous species that rely on a high degree of fishmeal and fish oil in their diet the reverse can be true. Over three tonnes of wild-caught fish are needed to produce one tonne of farmed salmon.

Farmed fish are not bred in their natural state (*fitra*). Farmed fish get bred so that they grow much bigger, for example they get less space to move around so they 'waste' less energy on this. Because they are grown in much higher concentrations, much disease control is needed. As a result the fish are fed astaxanthin (a colour additive, nowadays mainly made in synthetic form from petrochemicals, for some reason exempt from need for certification by the US Food and Drug Administration when fed to fish) so they still look the way we expect them to look when they arrive in the shops. What is most staggering, while this additive constitutes a tiny portion of salmon feed (50 to 100 parts per million), it represents a major share of the cost of breeding fish, up to 20 percent. So what are we paying for? Note in the EU use of such additives has to be mentioned on the label (as E161g), though only if added after the fish's death, not if added to feed. And how many people know that farmed fish diet includes 'poultry-by-product meal' (bone and blood) and poultry manure is used as fertiliser in fish ponds (risking spread of avian flu)?

Islamic law has exempted fish, whales, and other sea creatures from the category of 'dead animals'. When the Prophet ﷺ was asked about the sea, he replied, "Its water is pure and its dead are *halal*." My question is: is this still halal today with our way of using the seas? I have not been able to find much scholarly information on this topic. Do get in touch if you do. The majority of fish sold in the West now comes from fish farms. Degradation of water quality by shrimp farm effluent also has serious implications in terms of depletion of wild fish and shrimp stocks. Even the seemingly reasonable assumption that aquaculture is an efficient way to produce new protein is undermined by the continued use of wild-caught raw fish and fish meal and oil in feeds for growing shrimp. Farming shrimp intensively or semi-intensively can require fish inputs of more than double the weight of the shrimp produced, leading to a net loss of protein and additional pressure being placed on marine reserves for direct human consumption. Fish do not actually produce omega-3 fatty acids (the reason we are encouraged to eat fish), they capture it from the food chain. One out of every three fish that is caught right now is used to make feed for other fish.

According to the UK's Royal Commission on Environmental Pollution (RCEP) report *Turning the Tide - Addressing the impact of Fisheries on the Marine Environment*, published in December 2004, at the global level, aquaculture is growing faster than any other means of animal food production. Worldwide, aquaculture production is expected to nearly double in the next two decades, climbing from 29 million tonnes in 1997 to 54 million tonnes in 2020 (though in 2006 it already reached 51.7 million). Within Europe, the output of marine fish farming has grown a thousand-fold since 1970. Today, the UK is the largest aquaculture producer in the EU, producing 30 per cent by volume of the EU's total production; 90 per cent of this effort is concentrated in Scotland, where the industry has an annual turnover of around £500 million. It states that the prospects for further growth within the industry will depend on many factors, but environmental concerns could prove a key constraint. For example, it takes millions of tonnes of wild fish fed to carnivorous fish to support the aquaculture industry: it takes on average 3 kilogrammes of wild caught feed grade fish to produce 1 kilogramme of salmon, and 12 kilogrammes of fish to produce 1 kilogramme of fish oil. This fact means that farming carnivorous fish relies on wild capture fisheries, and thus still removing a large number of smaller species of fish from the food chain can have adverse ecosystem affects.

Organic methods explicitly prohibit the use of pesticides, genetic modification, drugs and antibiotics. They also require minimum welfare standards for animals raised for organic meat. The largest and most well known organic body in the UK is the Soil Association (www.soilassociation.org; Organic Trade Association in the US: www.ota.com) and you will probably have seen their logo on products in the shops. They are so strict, their certification standards run to 110 pages. They will not even certify organic bread that has been baked on the same tray as non-organic bread. Labelling is strictly regulated by UKROFS, a government authority, so we can be pretty sure that an organic product is what it says it is.

Genetic modification (GM)

"Verily, I [Satan, speaking to God] will mislead them, and surely, I will arouse in them false desires; and certainly, I will order them to slit the ears of cattle, and indeed I will order them to change the nature created by God." (Al-Baqara/ The Cow [2] 119)

Besides indirect and unwanted consequences of man's behaviour there is the major issue of man's direct

307

intervention in God's Creation, most far reaching and un-understood is genetic modification. A genetically modified organism (GMOs in plural) is defined as an organism, with the exception of human beings, in which "the genetic material has been altered in a way that does not occur naturally by mating and/ or natural recombination", so the argument by the pro-GM lobby that "mankind has been manipulating the genetics of crops for around 10,000 years" is incorrect. It is seen as a solution by some to famines and is thus promoted in several African countries. Others, including me, fear that monopoly of business on start of food chain is a dangerous step, aside from the religious reason. Abu Huraira narrated: I heard the Prophet ﷺ saying, "God said, 'Who are most unjust than those who try to create something like My creation? I challenge them to create even a smallest ant, a wheat grain or a barley grain.'"

We rightly carefully do our best to avoid eating pork and drinking alcohol, but it can be most challenging to avoid GM as it is included in many products and listed as for example 'modified maize'. However, note that products produced with GM technology (cheese produced with GM enzymes, for example) do not have to be labelled. Also, products such as meat, milk and eggs from animals fed on GM animal feed also do not need to be labelled.

The US Department of Agriculture estimated that in 2007 GM accounted for 73 per cent of the US maize crop, 87 per cent of the cotton crop and 91 per cent of the soya bean crop. The second largest producer of GM soya beans, by volume, after the US is Brazil, where GM accounts for 65 per cent of the crop. 40 per cent of Brazil's cotton production is GM. In Argentina, 99 per cent of soya plantings and 65 per cent of maize plantings are GM. GM now constitutes 69 per cent and 66 per cent, respectively, of Chinese and Indian cotton output. The UK routinely imports soya bean meal, maize gluten feed and cotton meal from all of these countries. According to information from the UK Food Standards Agency (FSA), in 2007 the global area of GM crops was 114.3 million hectares in 23 countries (up from 102 million hectares in 22 countries in 2006 and 90 million hectares in 21 countries in 2005). This was the twelfth consecutive year of increase in the area devoted to GM crops, with much of the increase being in developing countries, who were responsible for 43 per cent of the world's GM crop production. GM crops now occupy over 8 per cent of the world's cultivable arable land, an area equivalent to approximately five times the size of the UK.

Fortunately, attempts to introduce genetically modified foods in Europe onto our shop shelves have, so far, been met by a consumer revolt. Corporations like Bayer, Monsanto and Syngenta are proclaiming the global benefits of their products. Syngenta is claiming to be concerned with ending world hunger, and is promoting 'Golden rice' as an example of how GM crops could feed the world (for example Syngenta mentions its products "reduce human mortality"). This overlooks the fact that the world currently produces more than enough food for everyone. Hunger occurs primarily when people do not have access to land or the resources to buy the food that is already there. In this respect it may be relevant to mention that according to the World Health Organisation that although there were over 800 million chronically hungry people in the world 2007, at the same time there are over one billion people who were overweight or obese. As the UN Food and Agriculture Organisation of the UN states in a report in 2002: "Hunger is not a natural condition: it is produced by human action (or lack of it) and, in a world that can produce more than enough food for everyone, its root cause is poverty. Remarkably, in the early 1990s nearly 80 percent of all malnourished children lived in developing countries that produced food surpluses."

GM crops have environmental and health risks that outweigh any alleged benefits. GM life forms create the pollution you can never put back. Pollen from crops that are wind and insect pollinated can travel up to 4 kilometre, therefore polluting and potentially interbreeding with non-GM crops and wildlife across a large area. The science about long-term safety and health implications is imprecise and relies on the companies' own research (one recent independent study has shown significant worries on impact of GM on health). Many GM crops are designed to withstand greater pesticide use with attendant health risks. A major problem with GM seeds is that they are sterile and thus make it impossible for farmers to save seeds from year to year, but made dependent on massive corporate companies whose aim it is to bring 'shareholder return'. GM crops hand even more control over food production to corporations. To read more, check Genewatch which monitors genetic technologies: www.genewatch.org.

Though presented as a "solution to world hunger" by major agro-chemical companies, the introduction of GM foods and crops has triggered worldwide concern, uniting consumers, small farmers, especially in the developing world (for example 'Poor don't want GM'), and the environmental movement. Questions have been raised about potential health effects, environmental safety, agronomic and economic impacts, and about the power of corporations to control what we grow and what we eat. There is also concern about the extent to which commercial interests are driving the science and the regulatory system. Remember, there is *no* food shortage: 40 million tons would solve world hunger, but we feed 540 million tons to farmed animals that we would like to eat.

A key question remains why such an enormously powerful technology, about which there are still deep uncertainties, has been introduced so rapidly without meaningful public consultation. And there is an obvious religious concern of meddling with God's Creation. A useful website on the topic has been set up by Muzammal Hussain (www.islamicgmfocus.org) where he reminds us that "genetic modification aggressively disrupts the expression of genes, thereby preventing the 'modified' plant/vegetable from functioning as a wholesome form of life" and "the actual physical blueprint of the food is changed from its original/ natural state (*fitra*)".

During Southern Africa's 2002 food shortages, the Zambian government rejected food aid from the US because it was genetically modified and several other governments are keen to protect their farmers and agricultural sectors from becoming dependant on big foreign biotechnical companies. A study by the African Centre for Biosafety, in cooperation with Friends of the Earth Nigeria, found that GM crops have not benefited consumers, farmers or the environment - only the biotechnology industry itself. Similar news comes from genetically modified Bt cotton experiments in India. Though Monsato mentions that "Two Studies Show Benefits of BT Cotton in India", the Institute for Science in Society (I-SiS) reported the outcomes as a "fraud", reminding readers that "for which it [Monsanto] was recently fined US$1.5 million for bribery and corruption in Indonesia." Not just were the cotton experiments not successful with regards to cotton yield "at least 1,800 sheep reported dead from severe toxicity after grazing on Bt cotton fields in just four villages in Andhra Pradesh India". Most promisingly, and a blessing from God "organic cotton is more environmentally friendly, better for the health of the community and for the local economy than GM cotton", according to a study by the Centre for Sustainable Agriculture in Andhra Pradesh (www.indiagminfo.org).

In March 2005, the journal *Nature* discovered that "between 2001 and 2004, Syngenta inadvertently produced and distributed several hundred tonnes of *Bt*10 corn - a different genetic modification that has not been approved." This raises serious concerns: either the company does not care properly for its activities or, even more worryingly it may have done it deliberately. And as to impact on health, in a study commissioned by the Austrian government - one of the very few long-term feeding studies ever conducted with GM crops, the fertility of mice fed Monsanto's GM Bt maize was found to be severely impaired. Juergen Zentek (Professor of veterinary medicine, University of Vienna and lead author of the study presented in November 2008) summarised the findings: "Mice fed with GE maize had less offspring in the third and fourth generations, and these difference were statistically significant. Mice fed with non-

GE maize reproduced more efficiently. This effect can be attributed to the differences in the food source."

An April 2008 the UN International Assessment of Agricultural Knowledge, Science and Technology for Development (IAASTD) report, the work of over 400 international scientists, on the future of global food production under the challenges of climate change and population pressure concluded that GM crops did not have much to offer – instead promoting an 'agro-ecological' approach. Confirming an earlier UN Food and Agriculture Organisation's conference's conclusions, the IAASTD report acknowledged organic farming's real potential to help feed the world in an era of increasing oil prices and the urgent need to cut greenhouse gases. According to the Soil Association, "the GM industry reps stormed out of the process and their PR machine has been in overdrive ever since!"

Not convinced of negative matters regarding GM? Rosli Omar also has a wise note to share: "because there is no [there is now] evidence of negative impacts on some aspects of GMOs, GE [genetic engineering] proponents take the advantage to say, "there is no evidence" of such and such impacts, whereas that evidence is lacking because research is lacking, not because we know for sure there is no impact. Absence of evidence is not the same as evidence of absence."

Plant-based foods
"O Moses, we cannot endure one and the same sort of food. Pray your Lord to bring for us the products of the earth

313

green herbs, vegetables, corn, garlic, onions, pulses and the like." (Al-Baqara/ The Cow [2] 61)

Though Muslims in the UK comprise a very diverse faith community, minority ethnic backgrounds are overrepresented. According to the Health Survey of England (UK, 1999) as summarised by the Muslim Health Network (www.muslimhealthnetwork.org): "Bangladeshi men and women were least likely to eat fruit six or more times a week (15 per cent men, 16 per cent women), and Pakistani men (7 per cent) and women (11 per cent) were least likely to eat vegetables with this frequency." Also, "among men the proportion with a high fat consumption score was greatest among Irish and Bangladeshi men (22 per cent and 21 per cent respectively)". Among women "the highest proportion with a high fat score was found among Bangladeshi women (27 per cent), followed by Irish and Pakistani women (14 per cent and 13 per cent)". Finally even "the proportion with a low fibre score was greatest among Bangladeshis (79 per cent of men and 82 per cent of women had low fibre intake)." So not just for the environment, for health reasons the Muslim Health network concludes that "[i]t is quite clear that we need to implement some drastic changes in our activity and eating habits. We sometimes take food for granted and abuse the abundant supply of food whilst trying to satisfy our desires for good taste at the expense of nutrition and health."

And for an extra reason to eat a more plant based diet: according to the World Cancer Research Fund (WCRF) "For better health [30 to 40 per cent of all cancers are linked to the foods we eat, the amount of exercise we take and our weight], we should try to base all our meals around plant foods, such as fruit, vegetables, tubers (potatoes, yams), wholegrain cereals (bread, pasta and rice) and pulses (beans and lentils). To do this, we should think of plant foods as the main focus of our meals. We can then add smaller amounts of other foods, such as fish, chicken or lean red meat, as the accompaniment to our dishes."

Examples of action

159.　Considering the information about the diet of animals, the Fiqh Council of North America (FCNA) feels that it is advisable to take the following precautions: "Abstaining or reducing temporarily the intake of meats [...and...] attempting, seriously, to buy meats of animals that are fed a totally vegetarian diet, without the use of any animal protein, hormones, antibiotics or preservatives." The good news is also that the Prophet ﷺ said: "Where there is an abundance of vegetables, a host of angels will descend on that place."

160.　Rafeeque Ahmed (Founder of Muslim Vegan/ Vegetarian Society) suggests to go further: "Every Muslim is supposed to mould his life according to Qur'an and Sunnah and judging by the teachings in Islam, I do not see how a good Muslim can be anything other than vegan/ vegetarian." (unless need necessitates eating meat). By doing so, as Yahya Monastra writes in an article in Crescent Life "I'm not making meat "harâm." I just don't wish for any, thank you." The Vegetarian Society (www.vegsoc.org) and Vegan Society (www.vegansociety.com) have useful resources about food, nutrition and environment.

161.   The Prophet ﷺ said: "Whoever kills a sparrow or anything bigger than that without a just cause, God will hold him accountable on the Day of Judgement. The listeners asked, O Messenger of God, what is a just cause? He replied, that he kill it to eat, not to simply chop off its head and then throw it away." From now on, think twice when you buy meat so as to avoid waste. Or, eat more like a vegetarian, as Dora Roper wrote in 1916 in her book *Food for the Traveler*: "It is possible for normal individuals under fairly normal conditions of life to nourish perfectly their bodies on a vegetarian diet, provided they are willing to live mainly on sun-kissed foods instead of on a mass of sloppily-cooked, devitalized, starchy vegetables, and soft nitrogenous foods that burden the digestive organs and produce obesity and slow consumption." Eating vegetarian does not imply making meat *haram*, it is just choosing other elements of God's edible bounties.

162.   The Prophet ﷺ said "Every intoxicant is *khamr*, and every *khamr* is *haram*." He ﷺ also said "Beware of meat because it has an addiction like the addiction of wine." I found it interesting to read that to this day, in some parts of Yemen, they call meat "*khamr al-mumineen*" (the wine of the believers). Are you addicted? Eat more plant-based food as, according to Mirza Arshad Ali Beg (President, Pakistan Environment Assessment Association), "the good food, according to the Quranic and Hadith descriptions, is one that contains the essential elements that include the well known anti-oxidants beta-carotene, vitamin C and vitamin E." According to Shahid Athar (Chair, Medical

Ethics, Islamic Medical Association of North America) "[t]here is no doubt that a vegetarian diet is healthier and beneficial to health in lowering weight, blood pressure, cholesterol, and blood sugar. Our Prophet [ﷺ] was mostly vegetarian..." Perhaps he was mainly vegetarian because he did not want to kill unnecessarily? Iftekhar A. Hai (Director, Interfaith Relations, United Muslims of America) reminds us that "[t]he Muslim defence army was diverted and made to travel a different route at the time of the attack from the Crusaders so as not to trample the ant hill, next to trees that also contained beehives. The needless intrusion, noise and commotion were considered cruel and not in line with the sacred relationship that humans enjoy with the animals and insects as part of God's Creation."

163.   The Messenger of God ﷺ said, "When you hear the crowing of cocks, ask for God's Blessings for (their crowing indicates that) they have seen an angel." In intensive, factory farming, cocks are killed at the age of one day as they are considered 'useless'. Buy less, but free range so you do not contribute to unnecessary killing of God's creatures. Also, tell shops you visit, farmers, slaughterers and politicians (who make animal welfare laws) why you prefer animals which are enabled to lead a natural (*fitra*) life.

164.   Remember advice from Prophet Jesus ﷺ: Yahya related to me from Malik that he had heard that Isa ibn Maryam (Jesus ﷺ, son of Mary) used to say, "O Banu Israil! You must drink pure water and the green things of the land and barley bread. Beware of wheat bread,

for you will not be grateful enough for it." Or as Imam Ali ﷺ said, "Do not make your stomach the graveyard for the animals."

165.   For some help changing to eating less meat, read an interesting cookbook, *Cooking with Muhammad*, written by a reformed character (troubled youth turned health and nutrition consultant), American Aubrey M. Muhammad: "This cookbook offers the person seeking healthy living a wide range of foods and meat alternatives that cleanse our digestive system instead of clogging it up and poisoning it with nutrient depleted processed foods." www.myspace.com/muslimcooking

166.   We may think 'out of sight, out of mind', but our waste will come back to haunt us. Achim Steiner (UN Under-Secretary General and UNEP Executive Director) tells us: "Worldwide, vulnerable people including pregnant mothers and babies are warned not to eat fish such as tuna, which can contain high levels of the metal [mercury]. And women of child-bearing years are advised not to eat pike, perch, burbot and eel at all, and the rest of the population only once a week." Mercury can damage the neurological development of foetuses and infants. On the topic of mercury: almost half of tested samples of commercial high-fructose corn syrup (HFCS) contained mercury, which was also found in nearly a third of 55 popular brand-name food and beverage products where HFCS is the first or second-highest labelled ingredient, according to two US studies including one by the Institute for Agriculture and Trade Policy.

167. Avoid eating GM: God has made so many varieties to eat, but though the UN Food and Agricultural Organisation (UN FAO) estimates that there are roughly a quarter million plant varieties available for agriculture, less than 3 per cent of these are in use today. Try something different for dinner today: according to International Development Research Centre (IDRC), the world's food supply depends on about 150 plant species. Of those 150, just 12 provide three-quarters of the world's food. More than half of the world's food energy comes from a limited number of varieties of three "mega-crops" designed for intensive farming: rice, wheat, and maize. Note most GM is engineered to be herbicide resistant: when growing organically no chemical herbicides are used in the first place.

168. It is important to eat whole foods (grains, vegetables and fruits) because they contain all the nutrients that we need to thrive as human beings in their natural form. The more we change them from their original state, the less benefit we get from them. According to *Medicine of the Prophet* (authored by Al-Akili), the Prophet ﷺ himself was known to eat fruits and vegetables grown in the region in which he lived and in season. By eating local, you eat fresher and save food miles too. An easy way to eat locally grown vegetables is to grow them or to sign up to a vegetable box delivery scheme. Check your local options for example via www.green-england.co.uk/category/Vegetable_Box_Delivery_Scheme.

169. The Prophet ﷺ enjoyed vegetables: Anas bin Malik reported that a tailor invited God's Messenger ﷺ to a meal which he had prepared. Anas bin Malik said: I went along with God's Messenger ﷺ to that feast. He presented to God's Messenger ﷺ barley bread and soup containing pumpkin, and sliced pieces of meat. Anas said: I saw God's Messenger ﷺ going after the pumpkin round the dish, so I have always liked the pumpkin since that day." Attend farmers markets, which are independent producers and suppliers selling organic food locally or delivering it straight to your door. National Association of Farmers' Markets (NAFM) exists to promote farmers' markets and can help you find one near you on www.farmersmarket.net. There are nearly 500 farmers' markets in the UK, of which about half are members of the NAFM, so it is always worth checking your local news for markets which are not members of the national association. www.bigbarn.co.uk is a virtual farmers' market where you can search by your postcode for nearby independent suppliers and producers.

170. Eat less meat, as Abdullah bin Abi Aufa narrated: We were in the company of the Prophet ﷺ on a journey and he was fasting, and when the sun set, he addressed somebody, "O so-and-so, get up and mix sawiq [according to Aisha Bewley sawiq is "a mush made of wheat or barley"] with water for us." He replied, "O God's Messenger! (Will you not wait) until it is evening?" The Prophet ﷺ said, "Get down and mix Sawiq with water for us." He replied, "O God's Messenger! (If you wait) until it is evening." The

Prophet ﷺ said again, "Get down and mix Sawiq with water for us." He replied, "It is still daytime." The Prophet ﷺ said again, "Get down and mix Sawiq with water for us." He got down and mixed Sawiq for them. The Prophet ﷺ drank it and then said, "When you see night falling from this side, the fasting person should break his fast." To help yourself eat more vegetables, take out a box from a vegetable box scheme. The Soil Association publishes the Organic Directory which lists retailers, box schemes, farm shops, manufacturers, restaurants and accommodation, and can be ordered from www.soilassociation.org. The website also contains much free information about local organic markets www.gustoguide.co.uk contains an address search engine that will help you find your local organic box scheme as does www.realproduce.co.uk.

171. Eat more locally produced food to avoid unnecessary 'food miles' as Sayed Azam-Ali (Professor of tropical agronomy at the University of Nottingham, UK) told the Television Trust for the Environment's Earth Report programme in February 2008: "I think the environment is going to be more unpredictable, so we need crops that are going to be safe. We can't rely on importing and moving crops around the world indefinitely. I think we have to be more reliant on locally sourced food." The Soil Association certifies organic food in the UK and their website (www.soilassociation.org) lets you search for local markets. Or start your own food co-op. Though I cannot condone racism, I do appreciate the efforts of the *Nation of Islam* to provide cheap wholesome food to

some of the poorest in the US: www.muhammadfarms.com.

172.   I wonder: if Qurbani is such a special occasion, why do we slaughter animals/ eat meat every day in current life? We know that the Prophet ﷺ said that "the excellence of Aisha over other women is like the excellence of *tharid* [broth, according to Aisha Bewley] over other types of food", but to 'degrade' his most special dish to a staple dish?! Change this habit, try to be more like the Prophet ﷺ, God willing.

173.   Avoid animal cruelty, even indirectly by eating meat from 'battery chickens', as according to the Prophet's ﷺ saying: "It is a fact that in the next life you will render their rights to those to whom they are due. The hornless sheep even will receive its right by way of retaliation from a horned sheep that butted it." And "an act of cruelty to an animal is as bad as an act of cruelty to a human being."

Etiquette of drinking
"Consider the water which you drink. Was it you that brought it down from the rain cloud or We? If We had pleased, We could make it bitter." (Al-Waaqeah/ The Inevitable [56] 68-70)

Just two companies control 77 per cent of the soft drinks market: Coca-Cola and PepsiCo. A key active ingredient is phosphoric acid (for coke flavoured) or citric acid (for citrus flavours). Until the 1980s, soft drinks obtained nearly all of their food energy in the form of refined cane sugar or corn syrup. Today, high-fructose corn syrup (HFCS) is used nearly exclusively as a sweetener because of its lower cost. However, HFCS has been criticised as having a number of detrimental effects on human health, such as promoting diabetes, hyperactivity, hypertension, and a host of other problems.

Most importantly though for this book, from an environmental perspective, soft drinks (and bottled water, see under *wudu*) use too much water. Even a report commissioned by Coca-Cola themselves, after a US university was requested to cancel its contract with the company by its students, concluded that "Coca-Cola bottling plants in India are contributing to water scarcity and often fail to meet the company's regulations on the treatment of wastewater." As a result thousands of farmers across the country are struggling to make a living because of crop failure as a result of the water shortages. And before you think that by changing from soft drinks to water would not change water stress: one litre of soft drink uses 1. 54-2.7 (according to the companies, the former in the UK for Coca-Cola) - 4 (according to NGOs) litres of water.

Before you then take the first milk that you come across: the "average yield per dairy cow" went from 5,094 litres of milk per year (1989- 1991 average) to 7,627 (2007). So in some 15 years the yield increased by a 50 per cent. If we would be talking about a new machine that over time is made more efficient, that is one thing, but here we are talking about an animal, a part of God's Creation. It reminds me of the following saying included in Malik's *Muwatta*: a man came to Abdullah ibn Abbas and said to him, "I have an orphan and he has camels. Can I drink from the camels' milk?" Ibn Abbas said, "*If* you search for the lost camels of his *and* treat the camels' mange *and* fill in the cracks in their water basin *and* give it water on the day it drinks, then drink it *without doing harm to the suckling camels by milking them excessively*." (my emphases). The farm gate price of milk has gone from 24.87 pence per litre in 1996 to just 17.9 pence per litre in 2006. The reason the yield increased so much was by giving cows a different (non-*fitra*) diet. Scientists at Newcastle University did a study which found that organic milk (where cows get fed their natural diet) contained 67 per cent more antioxidants and vitamins than ordinary milk. To be on the safe side for animal welfare, I personally prefer organic soy milk (plus it tastes nice).

Examples of action

174.   If you find a fly in your drink, do not waste it as the Prophet ﷺ, as narrated by Abu Hureira, said "If a house fly falls in the drink of anyone of you, he should dip it (in the drink), for one of its wings has a disease and the other has the cure for the disease."

175.   Save money and avoid all the chemicals in fizzy drinks (which makes children jumpy anyways): Sahl narrated that Abu Usaid As-Saidi came and invited God's Messenger ﷺ on the occasion of his wedding. His wife, who was the bride, was serving them. Do you know what drink she prepared for God's Messenger ﷺ? She had soaked some dates in water in a bowl overnight. It is cheaper to buy organic cordial (to dilute with tapwater) than endless bottles of "juice drinks" (which in several countries need only contain one per

cent of fruit juice to be called so, no matter how fancy the impression from the photo on the package). Also, Abu Al-Juwairiyya narrated: "I asked Ibn Abbas about Al-Badhaq. He said, "Muhammad prohibited alcoholic drinks before it was called *Al-Badhaq* (by saying), 'Any drink that intoxicates is unlawful.' I said, 'What about good lawful drinks?' He said, 'Apart from what is lawful *and good*, all other things are unlawful and not good."

Etiquette of dress
"Tell the believing men to lower their gaze and be modest. That is purer for them. God is aware of what they do. And tell the believing women to lower their gaze and be modest [...]. (Al-Nur/ The Light [24] 30-31)

According to TRAID (Textile Recycling for Aid and International Development, a charity working to protect the environment and fight global poverty through its clothes recycling), every year UK consumers purchase 2.15 million tonnes of new clothing, shoes and accessories, and, in that very same year, throw away more than 900,000 million items – yes, 900,000 million (with only 200,000 tons of this recycled, the rest ending up in landfill). Over the last ten years women's yearly clothing purchases have doubled contributing to the estimated £7.3 billion worth of clothes that British women own but do not wear. The average woman in the UK apparently buys 34 new items of clothes a year, a figure that has nearly doubled in the past decade. What made this possible is that, in that same time, the average cost of clothes has dropped by 36 per cent, with £1 in every £4 now spent on so-called 'bargain fashion'. But buying with an environmental thought in mind can make a difference: each 100 per cent organic cotton T-shirt you buy eliminates the use of 150 grams of agricultural chemicals (though of course not buying such shirt unless needed is even better).

The Prophet ﷺ said: "Whoever refrains from dressing (in fancy, expensive clothes) out of humility towards God, even though he is able to do so, God will call him on the Day of Judgment at the head of His Creation and will give him the choice of whatever garment of faith he wishes to wear." Abd al-Rahmaan ibn Awf could not be distinguished from his slave.

On the topic of clothes, I used to have a favourite brand: real wool, quality sweaters, timeless fashion, and I was swayed by their anti-racism and peace ads. So when travelling around Argentina in 1999, and intending to visit some family in the south of the country, I was kind of happy to hear that the family which owned the brand owned significant land there. However, when arriving there I hardly noticed any sheep. I learned that due to lack of long-term interest for the land as grazing land, the local farmers had been forced to overgraze the land to survive. Now the whole area had turned into a desert in all but name. Upon return I gave away most of my clothes of that brand and have not bought anything from them since.

Much of the clothing is made far away and out of sight, and under sweatshop conditions. When we can buy jeans or a shirt for just a few pounds, we think we got ourselves a bargain, but at what price? At such prices we are enticed to buy again as opposed to mend. While cotton growth is 2 per cent of agriculture, it uses 25 per cent of the world's pesticides. And then of course there is the workers' circumstances: how else is it possible to get your clothes so 'cheaply'? For some useful insight, see: www.cleanupfashion.co.uk.

Examples of action

176. The Prophet ﷺ said: "Take care of your clothes." This way they will last longer so you can afford better quality and avoid environmental and social pressures for high volumes of clothes. Or as Umar رضي الله عنه said: "By God, if I wanted I could wear the finest clothes among you, and eat the best food, and have the most luxurious life. But I heard that God will condemn people for some of their actions and said: "You received your good things in the life of the world, and you took your pleasure therein. Now this Day you shall be recompensed with a torment of humiliation, because you were arrogant in the land without a right, and because you used to rebel against God's Command (disobey God)" (Al-Ahqaf/ The Dunes [46] 20]. For clothes to last, buy quality and avoid child labour (check www.cleanclothes.org, an alliance of NGOs and others to support garment workers in their efforts to create substantive, sustainable improvements in working conditions).

177. The Messenger of God ﷺ said to his wife Aisha رضي الله عنها : "If you wish to join me (in the Hereafter), be satisfied with worldly things to the extent of a rider's provision, avoid sitting with the rich, and do not consider a garment worn out until you patch it."

178. Donating your clothes is good; buying your clothes from charity shops 'closes the loop' (what can charities do if nobody buys donated clothes too?) and can give you three good deeds in one: supporting a good cause, not supporting a potential sweatshop and your clothes will have most likely travelled less miles. Most clothes items can be reused, even tights (check www.tightsplease.co.uk and check under 'recycle for charity': helping poor Ethiopian women who have suffered a fistula injury due to complications in child birth.

179. In the Prophet's ﷺ time a man remarked, "But a man likes his clothes to be nice and his sandals good." The Prophet ﷺ said, "verily, God is beautiful and loves beauty. Arrogance is refusing to acknowledge what is right and considering others beneath one." The Prophet ﷺ also said: "Eat, drink and clothe yourselves without extravagance or arrogance".

180. Copy Uganda, which on 1 July 2007 joined a number of countries that prohibited plastic bags. Have a cloth bag ready in your handbag for any impulse buys, for example a *Keep it Halal* (in Latin/ Arabic wording) eco-friendly bag made from natural fibres as designed by *Visual Dhikr* (see www.islamicdesignhouse.com). Ireland was the first country to introduce a plastic bag tax (or plastax) and led to a drop from 328 plastic bags used per head to just 21 (proving we do not *need* plastic bags).

181.   Jabir bin Abdullah reported that God's Messenger ﷺ said: "[In the house] there should be a bedding for a man, a bedding for his wife and the third one for the guest, and the fourth one is for Satan." I assume that if there are children in the house, they could also have something. Idea is again to guard against excessive quantity: thus cheaper too.

Etiquette of the road/ travel

"And He has created horses and mules and donkeys that you may ride them, and as a source of beauty. And He has created other things of which you have no knowledge." (Al-Nahl/ Bees [16] 8)

Where I live, I have seen the *Navara Outlaw*, *Landrover Defender*, *Mitsubishi Animal*, but, no, I do not live in the African outback, I live in an inner city neighbourhood of a large city in the UK. According to the UK Government's Department for Transport traffic on our roads has more than doubled in the past thirty years and motor traffic in the UK has grown tenfold since 1950. The number of billion of kilometres made by cars and taxis versus bicycle in the UK in 1949 were 20.3 and 23.6 respectively. By 2005 these figures were 397.2 and 4.4 respectively. The total number of billion of kilometres of transport has risen from 218 in 1952 to 797 in 2005. In 1952, 27 per cent of the journeys were made by car, van or taxi and 11 per cent were made by bicycle. In 2005, 85 per cent of journey kilometres were made by car, van or taxi, while only one per cent of journey kilometres were made by bicycle. I read somewhere about the paradox around the feeling of independence derived from owning a car and our dependency on owning one to get around.

The number of visits abroad by UK residents using air travel has almost doubled between 1995 and 2005 (from 28,097 thousand to 53,626 thousand trips) and only 30 per cent of the 2005 figure (16,182 trips) is for business or visiting family and friends. The rest (seventy per cent) is for holidays. And what is scarier: the European plane maker Airbus predicted that 28,534 passenger and freight aircrafts would be flying in less than two decades' time - more than double the current total of 13,284, and Britain will be the third largest customer for their new aircraft. According to the *key facts* document accompanying the aviation white paper, there were 32 million passengers at UK airports in 1970, 189 million in 2002, between 350 and 460 million forecast in 2020. Due to this significant increase of passengers and the impact on the environment for us all, the centre-left think-tank Institute for Public Policy Research (IPPR) says flying is so unhealthy that adverts for flights should carry cigarette-style warnings.

According to statistics available from the UK Department for Transport, in 2005 taxpayers contributed £4,660 million towards road infrastructure (98.5 per cent of total), while taxpayers contributed £3,543 million towards rail infrastructure (82.9 per cent of total). This means that people using the train subsidise car drivers *more* than vice versa. I guess most people would have thought it was the other way round. At least I did.

Research presented in September 2008 found that friendships on busy streets are cut by more than 75 per cent, as per the title *No friends? Blame the traffic*. And more than affecting your social life, according to a 1998 report from the UK Ministry of Health, up to 24,000 people die prematurely in the UK every year as a result of air pollution, much of it pumped out by road traffic in our towns and cities. The number of 4x4s sold in the UK rose by nearly 13 per cent between 2003 and 2004, whereas sales of minis and super-minis fell by 4 per cent, so any technical gain in energy efficiency is more than undone by use of more energy hungry cars. And contrary to popular opinion, drivers and their passengers are not protected from the pollution they create - the air inside a car can be more polluted than for the pedestrian on the pavement.

13 per cent of the carbon emissions produced from transporting food in the UK come from individuals driving to and from the shops. With Tesco alone in 2008 commanding one third of the UK grocery market and the 'big four' supermarket chains in the UK commanding more than three quarters of the total grocery market, and them increasingly investing in big out of town stores, this can only rise (and greenhouse gas emissions by UK households from food shopping, storage and preparation rose by around 14 per cent between 2002 and 2006, almost half of this increase was due to shopping by car), unless we collectively do our part to stop them, for example by using your local independent shops.

Abu Hurairah رضي الله عنه , stated that the Messenger of God ﷺ said: "If anyone purifies himself in his house, and then *walks* to one of the houses of God to fulfil one of the obligations laid down by God, then [each one] of his steps will erase one of his sins and the next will raise his degrees." Anas bin Malik also narrated that the Prophet ﷺ went out on one of his journeys with some of his companions. *They went on walking until the time of the prayer became due.* They could not find water to perform the ablution. One of them went away and brought a little amount of water in a pot. The Prophet ﷺ took it and performed the ablution, and then stretched his four fingers on to the pot and said (to the people), "Get up to perform the ablution." They started performing the ablution till all of them did it, and they were seventy or so persons. Abu Musa reported God's Messenger ﷺ as saying: The most eminent among human beings (as a recipient of) reward (is one) who lives farthest away, and who *has to walk the farthest distance*, and he who waits for the prayer to observe it along with the Imam, his reward is greater than one who prays (alone) and then goes to sleep. In the narration of Abu Kuraib (the words are):" (He waits) till he prays along with the Imam in congregation." (my emphasis)

Two thirds of trips less are than two miles. To stay healthy doctors say we need 30 minutes of exercise five times a week. How realistic is it to have separate time five times a week to go to the gym? Integrating exercise into our normal routine is the best and most sustainable way to keep it up. I so much like the initiative of Paris: in July 2007 they scattered 10,000 self-service bicycles around the city centre, increased to 20,000 by the end of 2007. The Parisians call them *Vélibs* (short for *vélo libre* or freedom-bikes in French). Subscribers pay €29 (£20) a year, give their credit card details and leave a €150 credit card deposit to join the scheme. This buys half an hour's pedalling a day and a card to lock and unlock bicycles from automated stations spaced every 300 metres in the city's centre. An accompanying website (www.velivelo.com) allows you to find your nearest parking spot for the start and end of your journey plus a detailed plan on how to get from one to the other. The official website of the project is www.velib.paris.fr. Compare that with AUS$120-350 a week to own and run a car in Australia.

While doing research for this book I found a photo of a billboard from Scotland. The billboard included a call out on a car with the text: "don't blame me for global warming, I wanted to be 18 bicycles" and I thought that really brings the message home: it is not cars which are the problem (they do not have a will etc), it is people who want the cars (to be made). By our choice of means of transport, we have influence over our emissions, over what Creation we leave for those after us in this world.

When reading about the Prophet's ﷺ life I notice how often *hadeeths* start with or include "when I was *walking* with the Prophet..." (my emphasis), "Prophet was riding the horse of Abu Talha" (when it was dangerous), or "Prophet and his wife were riding together" (when travelling to Medina). Though he ﷺ did not have our current choices (nor do we practically have some of his choices – have not seen any camels on the roads in Birmingham, UK, lately), he seems to have adopted the right means of transport for the right occasion. An interesting website pondering this issue for our days is *What would Jesus [ﷺ] drive?* (www.whatwouldjesusdrive.org), initiated by the

Evangelical Environmental Network (www.creationcare.org) and Creation Care Magazine in the US "because transportation is a moral issue" because they "believe that individuals, families, churches, automakers, and elected officials all have important roles to play in loving our neighbo[u]rs through reducing fuel consumption and pollution from vehicles."

Car

From 17 August 1896, when Bridget Driscoll was the first person to die in a petrol-engined car accident in the UK; and 13 September 1899, when Henry Bliss was the first person killed by a car in the United States, the World Heath Organisation (WHO) has forecast that between 2000 and 2015 road accidents would globally cause 20 million deaths (second or third cause of death in half of the age groups!), 200 million serious injuries and leave more than one billion people killed, injured, bereaved or left to care for a victim. I have seen one village in Argentina nicely reminding car drivers of this risk: "*no nos sobra ningun habitante, maneje con precaución!*" (we have no spare resident, drive cautiously).

The number of licensed cars in the UK has grown by circa 25 per cent between 1997 and 2007. 25 per cent of car trips in the UK are less than two miles and 58 per cent are less than five miles. A car travelling in a city centre during 'rush' hours spends up to half the time (28 minutes stationary. According to the UK motoring organisation RAC the average car in 2008 cost £6,133 to run per year, a people carrier cost some £7,500 (and a Porsche over £19,000 per year). This cost reflects the cost of insurance, fuel, servicing, tax and breakdown membership. This is much higher than many people think...

Research published in a peer-reviewed toxicology journal in 2008 showed that diesel exhaust from heavy lorries can affect the way our brain works: it changes the way our brains function, though it is not (yet) clear if this necessarily impairs our abilities.

According to Austrian philosopher Ivan Illich (1926 – 2002 CE) "the model American male devotes more than 1,600 hours a year to his car. He sits in it while it goes and while it stands idling. He parks it and searches for it. He earns the money to put down on it and to meet the monthly instalments. He works to pay for gasoline [petrol in the UK, RtV], tolls, insurance, taxes, and tickets. He spends four of his sixteen waking hours on the road or gathering his resources for it. And this figure does not take into account the time consumed by other activities dictated by transport: time spent in hospitals, traffic courts, and garages; time spent watching automobile commercials or attending consumer education meetings to improve the quality of the next buy. The model American puts in 1,600 hours to get 7,500 miles: less than five miles per hour. In countries deprived of a transportation industry, people manage to do the same, walking wherever they want to go, and they allocate only 3 to 8 per cent of their society's time budget to traffic instead of 28 per cent. What distinguishes the traffic in rich countries from the traffic in poor countries is not more mileage per hour of life-time for the majority, but more hours of compulsory consumption of high doses of energy, packaged and unequally distributed by the transportation industry." Imagine if we all thus gave up cars and spend the time spent on affording the car on tending to God's Creation: some food for thought.

Though car engines have become more efficient, because we now do not just want four wheels, but air-conditioning, electric windows, a CD-player and so many other bells-and-whistles that the average *MPG* (miles per gallon) is all but the same (for example the Citroen's 2CV – produced from 1949 to 1990 - does a similar MPG as its latest C1). Ibn Umar ﷺ said that the Messenger of God ﷺ prohibited riding a camel which eats dung, or animal or human waste. According to a commentary I read on this *hadeeth* it refers to any animal which usually eats filthy things including human excrement. This filth becomes a part of his body and it stinks. After reading this, I wonder what the Prophet ﷺ would make of our car addiction with all the toxic fumes.

Cycling/ Public transport

If there is a will there is a way, as the German city of Berlin shows: in November 2004 the Berlin House of Representatives decided that bicycles should make up 15 per cent of city traffic by the year 2010 by adopting an ambitious *Bicycle Transportation Strategy for Berlin*. Results released from a 2007 traffic study of the Berlin Development Administration show that the goal could be reached early: the number of bicyclists has more than doubled in the last decade to 400,000 riders daily, accounting for 12 per cent of total traffic. As the Berlin City website summarises it: "by leaving your car at home and getting on your bike, you are not only helping to reduce pollution and minimise climate change. Cycling also helps prevent illnesses caused by lack of exercise. Bicycle travel is the quickest mode of transport for short journeys, the ideal way for busy city dwellers to get around. Many an unused bicycle is waiting to be taken out of storage and put back on the road this spring."

I feel disappointed and somewhat down when Muslims (usually men in big cars) shout some words I cannot understand at me when I cycle, as even though I cannot understand what they are saying (sounds like Arabic or Urdu) it is clear they seem to have one objection or other to me cycling. And, just in case you were wondering, I do not cycle in lycra shorts and other *Tour de France*-style gear. I wear my normal modest clothes and on top of that an oversized ex-army bright yellow and reflective striped raincoat (bought on eBay for a few pounds to help me be safe in traffic) plus a sarong-type wraparound, which makes some of my non-Muslim fellow environmentalists laugh. If somebody does not feel like cycling is for them, fine, but if the Prophet ﷺ thought it was OK for his wife Aisha ﵁ to ride a wild camel (we know because he once told her off for being somewhat rough with her animal. Aisha ﵁ herself narrates: "I was riding a restive camel and turned it rather roughly. The Prophet ﷺ said to me: 'It behooves you to treat the animals gently.'"), then personally I cannot see why I could not use a cycle (by the way: I have asked around and never heard a proper Islamic objection against cycling, especially not from those shouting at me from their cars – anyways never my source of knowledge).

Some people have said that cycling is easy for me as I am Dutch. Though I agree cycling is seen as far more 'normal' in the Netherlands than in some other countries, I have not yet heard of there being such a thing as a 'Dutch cycling gene'. Others say that cycling is OK for me as I enjoy it … when it is nice weather, I have the wind in my back and there is not too much other traffic, I indeed do enjoy cycling. However, for the rest of the time I just see it as a means to get from A to B which fortunately incorporates much of my physical activity (apparently I could be 10 years younger inside because of this), is kind to the environment and my wallet. Or as the British Medical Association puts it: "[c]ycling is an activity which, both as a leisure pursuit and as a means of transport, can have many benefits, not only for those who cycle, but for everyone". The board of science of the British Medical Association (BMA) has recognised this by in 1992 publishing a major report on cycling (*Cycling: towards health and safety*).

By the way, if you think you might be too old to go cycling, or a few miles is far: remember our Chechen under the *hajj* chapter? A man in his sixties so motivated he cycled from his home in the Russian Federation to Makkah … and back. Plus remember this: "I'm asking you for your good and for your Nation's security to take no unnecessary trips, to use carpools or public transportation whenever you can, to park your car one extra day per week, to obey the speed limit, and to set your thermostats to save fuel. Every act of energy conservation like this is more than just common sense - I tell you it is an act of patriotism." That is according to former US President Jimmy Carter in 1979 (later Nobel

Peace Prize winner and author of *Palestine: Peace Not Apartheid*). I tell you: they are acts of pleasing God.

Walking

Several *hadeeth* start with or include "I was walking with the Prophet ﷺ ..." (for example when he passed by some people near their palm trees.). According to the Ramblers "[w]alking is the most inclusive, sociable and sustainable means of transport, the closest thing to perfect exercise and the best way to access the outdoors." Perhaps it is easy to say that the Prophet ﷺ and the people at that time did not have cars and planes (implying he would most likely use them), which of course is true, but I would say that he did have many alternative means of transport, such as camel, horse and donkey, but still chose to walk.

Abu Hurairah رضي الله عنه says, "I did not see anyone more handsome than the Prophet ﷺ. It was as if the brightness of the sun had shone from his auspicious face. I did not see anyone walk faster than him, as if the earth folded for him. A few moments ago he would be here, and then there. We found it difficult to keep pace when we walked with him, and he walked at his normal pace."

Reading Jeremy Henzell-Thomas (on The Book Foundation http://thebook.org whose "mission is to bring to light the universal message of Islam as revealed in the Holy Qur'an and the lived example of the Prophet Muhammad ﷺ, as well as the finest elements of the Islamic tradition"), I may be naïve in expecting more to walk: "I have always been struck by what has seemed to me to be a reluctance by many, if not all, my Muslim friends to explore the natural world. By this I do not necessarily mean arduous trekking through vast natural wildernesses or scaling the highest mountain peaks but simply the joy of walking amidst virgin nature and contemplating its beauty and majesty." The reason I will still continue is not because I expect people to listen to me, but I pray more fellow Muslims will reflect on the Quran and the example of the Prophet ﷺ. Remembering there is no such thing as bad weather (for example rain is a blessing from God), just wrong clothes.

Examples of action

182.   If you have to use a car, remember this information from RAC published in February 2008: "Green driving [for example switching off air-conditioning and avoiding driving erratically] could not only help the environment but also save drivers up to £100 each year in wasted fuel. New RAC research shows that motorists who choose against 'eco-driving' contribute to a £2.2 billion wasted fuel bill each year."

183.   If you have to buy a car, do not only look at the purchase price, but also the running costs: better for your record on Day of Judgment and cheaper in this world. And when checking fuel use, unless you drive 50 per cent in urban setting and 50 per cent motorway/ highway, check the individual MPG as I have seen examples where the difference between city and motorway/ highway is almost 20 MPG (check www.greencarsite.co.uk, the Environmental Transport Association, www.eta.co.uk, or the Vehicle Certification Agency's (VCA) www.vcacarfueldata.org.uk.

184. Instead of driving to gym, pay entry, then exercise on stationary bike, then drive back home, why not buy a proper bike and use it for all your short and medium distance trips. Even if you are only paying £30 a month for your gym membership, there is still £360 worth of annual savings direct to be made for those who are willing to replace the exercise bike with the real thing (plus the savings in using less petrol, being ill less often). To get started, go along to *Bike Week* (www.bikeweek.org.uk). Their mission is to get 'more people cycling, more often'. It provides a unique opportunity to promote cycling as a great way to "have fun, get fit, and feel free". If you are employed in the UK, you could even get significant support to buy a bike/ bicycle to get to work: www.dft.gov.uk/pgr/sustainable/cycling/cycletoworksch emeimplementat5732.

185. Making fewer food shopping trips by car, or using other forms of transport will help cut emissions, help reduce congestion and local air pollution plus save you cash. And save your health too: according to research funded by the British Heart Foundation (BHF) diesel exhaust impairs two important aspects of heart and circulation health and therefore contributes to the development of heart disease (and air inside cars is four times as bad as outside). So as Sustrans (UK's leading sustainable transport charity) puts it: "Do you dream of a world with cleaner air, quieter streets and less congested roads? Do you want to get fit while you travel to work, to school or the shops? Change Your World one mile at a time" by cycling.

186.   When comparing modes of transport, be honest to compare true like with like. I once read "driving to work costs me £20 in petrol per month, the bus costs me £57 – the choice is a no brainer" – but is it (author implied that taking bus was not an option)? To drive the car you also need tax, insurance and more; with the bus, once you have a month's pass, you are done, plus no parking worries. Even if you include the occasional taxi, it is still greener and cheaper for most people.

187.   Walk or cycle for short distances (Zaid Shakir has said: "riding my bike and walking around the streets of Oakland and Berkeley, California, had drastically reduced the time I was spending sitting in a car and the result was that the back problems that initially led me to seek out a chiropractor had totally disappeared."). When choosing mode of transport for any journey, bear in mind Sustrans' finding that: "people always overestimate the time it takes to cycle or walk somewhere - so they tend to end up arriving on time or even early when they cycle, whereas people tend to underestimate how long it takes to drive somewhere." In Lebanon, Green Line (www.greenline.org.lb) started work on *On the move without your car* back in early 2001. Since then, Green Line and other NGOs have been lobbying members of the Lebanese parliament to enforce laws directed towards managing the land transport sector and decreasing the air pollution caused by motorised vehicles. Note: according to the World Health Organisation in high-income countries those most at risk of injury or death are drivers and passengers in cars; in low- and middle-income countries

these are pedestrians, cyclists, motorcyclists and users of informal modes of public transport.

188.   Learn more about the benefits of walking, discover the hidden spaces of your neighbourhood and follow the 12-week walking plan on one of the Ramblers free *Get Walking Keep Walking* programmes or DIY pack (www.ramblers.org.uk). Go on walking 'days out' or on a walking holiday. For ideas, see for example: www.go4awalk.com; www.walking-routes.co.uk.

189.   We could provide safe routes for all schools in England for about £1 billion. Widening the rest of the M25 to four lanes each way would cost an estimated £1.6 billion. Widening the M6 motorway costs £35,000 per metre; a cycle lane costs £180 per metre. Contact your member of Parliament (MP) and other elected officials and tell them your preference.

190.   Encourage your children to go to school walking by organising a 'walking bus' (www.foe.co.uk/resource/factsheets/walking_bus.pdf). For practical information like a 'walkability checklist', go to: www.saferoutestoschools.org or www.bikewalk.org.

Man's natural state (fitra)

"So set your face to the religion, a person of pure faith, God's original upon which He originated mankind. There is no changing God's creation. That is the right religion; but most people know it not." (Ar-Rum/ The Romans [30] 29)

According to Hyder Ihsan Mahasneh (biologist, Islamic scholar and the first African head of the Kenya National Parks Service, appointed by the Muslim World League to compile the Islamic Faith Statement for the Alliance of Religions and Conservation, ARC): "*Fitra* can be taken as perhaps the most direct injunction by *Allah* to man to conserve the environment and not to change the balance of His creation. This is specifically contained in the verse below: [followed by verse 30:29] Thus, Islam teaches that humanity is an integral part of the environment; it is part of the creation of Almighty God. We remain deeply locked into the natural domain despite the fact that there is talk of bringing the environment to the people as though we were independent of it."

According to Abdal-Hakim Murad, "The *fitra* tells us that nature is a medicine. The *Sunna* allows us to take it. And Islam liberates because it is rooted in our natures." For Muslims, as Francesca De Chatel clarifies, Prophet Muhammad ﷺ is the "perfect expression of this *fitra*, since his life depicts the Quranic teachings in action. In terms of environmental care, simple living, moderation, and respect and concern for all creation, his life abounds with examples of the Islamic environmental philosophy".

According to Soumaya Pernilla Ouis (Human Ecology Division, Lund University, Sweden): "*Fitra* is considered to be the natural state of man in harmony with nature, according to the Islamic ecotheology. The argument that people must "return" to another way of living with an understanding of the interconnectedness of everything in nature, has been proposed by environmentalists. *Fitra* is an idea compatible with this argument." Abdur-Raheem Green

(English Dawah Coordinator, London Central Mosque/ Islamic Cultural Centre) has written a poem which summarises it nicely, called *Box*, about how much we have distanced ourselves from our natural state: going from house box to car box, eating food from boxes, pills from boxes and at the end of the day sit shattered in front of 'the' box (TV). There is also a *nasheed* (religious song) called *The People of The Boxes* by Dawud Wharnsby Ali.

Examples of action

191. Suleman Dangor (Professor, University of Durban-Westville, South Africa) states: "In my view, Muslims should be in the forefront supporting programmes of Sustainable Development." Is this part of your natural state (*fitra*)?

192. In an article entitled *What Does the Islamic Concept of Fitra (Primordial Nature) Mean?*, Fethullah Gülen (1941– CE) states: "improving one's family and environmental conditions is vitally important if we want to produce good Muslims." If you have an unloved area in your neighbourhood, get together and convert it into a beautiful place. For inspiration, check *Converting a derelict site into an urban park* developed by the Aga Khan Development Network: www.akdn.org/publications/cairo_brochure2.pdf.

193. Or copy Woking (UK) and set up *fITRA*: fun Islamic Teaching, Reading and Activities. Woking's fITRA aims to "provide outward-looking Islamic Education in Woking, Surrey for local children, ensuring the children develop a happy and confident British Muslim identity." For some ideas of what these *fITRA* activities could

345

entail, check *The Big Green Idea* ("a dynamic new charity dedicated to showing people how sustainable living can be easy, healthy, inexpensive and fun", www.thebiggreenidea.org), which includes free fact sheets on for example *Nature Games and Activities* or check www.ecokids.co.nz.

Balance (mizan)

"He created man and taught him clear expression. The sun and the moon both run with precision. The stars and the trees bow down in prostration. He erected heaven and established the balance, so that you would not transgress the balance. Give just weight do not skimp the balance. He laid out the earth for all living creatures" (Ar-Rahman/ The Beneficent [55] 3-9)

According to Seyyed Hossein Nasr "[w]hen we speak of the environmental crisis […], we mean […] one that has upset the balance and harmony of the natural world which has surrounded and nourished human beings for as long as they remember […]. Not that there was no contention or strife between man and nature before, not that ten thousand years ago when man was becoming agricultural, that shift had no impact on the natural environment, but such shifts did not create a crisis for there was a remarkable ecological harmony which continued. Had there been a crisis of the dimension we have now at that time, it is most likely that we would not even exist today." So we can benefit from Creation, the issue is not to tip the balance, get into continual ecological debt.

Another example of this need for balance is that Abu Huraira ﷺ reported the Prophet ﷺ as telling of an incident that happened to another prophet in the past. This prophet was stung by an ant and, in anger, he ordered the whole of the ants' nest to be burned. At this, God reprimanded this prophet in these words: "because one ant stung you, you have burned a whole community which glorified Me". More recently similarly repeated by the World Association of Muslim Youth (WAMY) that there should be balance and moderation in all things: "Self-restraint and not extremism- neither uncontrolled capitalism and free markets, nor oppressive dictatorship; not taking everything from the soil without giving anything back; not taking all the valuable trees in a forest, but leaving and planting enough to allow those trees to regenerate...."

Research done as part of the World Values Survey asked people in Egypt in 2000 what they would give priority: the environment or economic growth. I was very happy to read that in a country facing such challenges 51.5 per cent still chose environment over economic growth (in 2001 in Pakistan only 7.4 made this same choice).

From Hanzalah al-Usayyidee who said Abu Bakr ﷺ met me and asked: How are you O Hanzalah? I replied: Hanzalah is guilty of hypocrisy! He said: Free is God and far removed from all defects! What are you saying? I said: When we are with God's Messenger ﷺ and he reminds us of the Fire and Paradise it is as if we were seeing it with our own eyes. Then when we depart from God's Messenger ﷺ and attend our wives, our children and our business, then much of this slips from our mind. Abu Bakr ﷺ

347

said: By God we also experience the same. So I went with Abu Bakr until we entered upon God's Messenger ﷺ. I said: Hanzalah is guilty of hypocrisy, O Messenger of God. So God's Messenger ﷺ said: And how is that? I said When we are with you, you remind us of the Fire and of Paradise and it is as if we are seeing it with our own eyes. Then when we depart from you and attend our wives, our children and our business then much of this slips from our minds. So God's Messenger ﷺ said: By Him in whose hand is my soul if you remained continually as you are when you are with me and in remembering (God) then the angels would shake hands with you upon your beds and upon your roads. But O Hanzalah, (there is) a time for this and a time for that, (there is) a time for this and a time for that, (there is) a time for this and a time for that.

As Hwaa Irfan (Managing Editor, Family and Cyber Counselor Pages, IslamOnline.net) concludes in an article: "We are intrinsically a part of the environment that *Allah (swt)* gave to support our needs. Maybe one day, we will realize that everything has a place within which we can achieve much, but only through balance. Only then will we begin to heal - physically, mentally, emotionally and spiritually."

Examples of action

194.   To help restore the Earth's balance, consider setting up a *Three Tonne Club* as proposed by the Women's Environmental Network (WEN, www.wen.org.uk). They have issued a handbook to help you calculate and control your carbon footprint. Three tonnes is the goal we need to achieve by 2030 in order to limit global

warming to 2°C and the handbook gives much information and tips on how to shed those carbon tonnes by getting together and having a good time (like a diet, but you can still eat chocolate cream cakes).

195. Read about the (un)balance of man and nature, about how man no longer feels any responsibility for nature, using it only as a source of materials. A good start is Seyyed Hossein Nasr's book *Man and Nature*. When feeling down that your contribution may not be enough, think of the following anonymous short story: an elderly man was picking up objects off the beach and tossing them out into the sea. A young man approached and saw that the objects were starfish. He asked, "Why in the world are you throwing starfish into the water?" "If the starfish are still on the beach when the tide goes out and the sun rises high in the sky, they will die," replied the elderly man. The young man countered, "That is ridiculous. There are thousands of miles of beach and millions of starfish. You can't really believe that what you're doing could possibly make a difference!" The wise old man picked up another starfish, paused thoughtfully, and as he threw it to the safety of the sea, he said, "It made a difference to that one."

196. Sahl bin Sad As-Said narrated that a man passed by God's Messenger and the Prophet ﷺ asked a man sitting beside him, "What is your opinion about this (passer-by)?" He replied, "This (passer-by) is from the noble class of people. By God, if he should ask for a lady's hand in marriage, he ought to be given her in marriage, and if he intercedes for somebody, his

intercession will be accepted. God's Messenger kept quiet, and then another man passed by and God's Messenger asked the same man (his companion) again, "What is your opinion about this (second) one?" He said, "O God's Messenger! This person is one of the poor Muslims. If he should ask a lady's hand in marriage, no-one will accept him, and if he intercedes for somebody, no one will accept his intercession, and if he talks, no-one will listen to his talk." Then God's Messenger said, "This (poor man) is better than such a large number of the first type (i.e. rich men) as to fill the earth." Live lightly, choose voluntary simplicity (learn to do more with less, or act consciously to reduce your need for purchased services or goods and, by extension, your need to sell your time for money). For the US a good starting point is www.simpleliving.net, for the UK we could learn from Christian website www.livinglightly24-1.org.uk (named after Psalm 24:1 - Because 'The Earth is the Lord's': there "must be more to life than working, consuming, acquiring and being sucked into a value system that we know is wrong").

197. Keep your balance between acquiring goods and your faith: as Abu Hurairah رَضِيَ اللهُ عَنهُ said that God's Messenger ﷺ said: "Richness is not having many belongings, but richness is the richness of the soul (contentment)." As American philosopher Richard B. Gregg (1885-1974 CE) mentions in his 1936 book *The Value of Voluntary Simplicity*: "Voluntary simplicity of living has been advocated and practiced by the founders of most of the great religion: Buddha, Lao Tse, Moses and Mohammed, - also by many saints and wise men

such as St. Francis, John Woolman, the Hindu rishis, the Hebrew prophets, the Moslem Sufis."

198.　　Balance your desires and duties, as Al-Alaa ibn Ziyaad said: a man asked Abdullah ibn Amr ibn al-Aas, saying: which of the believers is best in his Islam? He replied: He from whose tongue and hand the Muslims are safe. He asked: Then what is the best *Jihad*? He replied: He who strives against his own self and desires for God. He asked: Then which of those who migrates (performs *hijrah*) is best? He replied: He who strives against his own self and desires for God. He asked: Is it something you have said O Abdullah ibn Amr, or God's Messenger ﷺ? He said: Rather God's Messenger ﷺ said it.

199.　　After all your green hard work, balance it with a nice reward: treat yourself to some nice organic drink looking over your garden work.

Epilogue

"And that man shall have nothing but what he strives for"
(Al-Najm/ The Star [53] 39)

A friend told me about what she had heard a French sheikh say about Prophet Yusuf (Joseph) ﷺ, especially what was meant by chapter 12 (Yusuf/ Joseph) verse 36: people did not trust the prophet with their dreams because they had *heard* something from him (his talk perhaps), but because they had *seen* him *do* good action (walk his talk/ actions). So increase your number of good actions for Creation and, as the Prophet ﷺ says: "He who starts something good in Islam has its reward and the reward of those who practice it until the Day of Judgement, without lessening in the least the reward of those who practice it." Do I live by all the mentioned actions? Unfortunately not yet. Am I trying? Definitely. Am I making a difference? That is up to God; it is my duty to give it my best.

God willing the 199 practical actions mentioned is this book are a helpful reminder of opportunities to please God by *living* Islam. And after that, please encourage others to do the same, because as Anas ﵁ said, the Messenger of God ﷺ said "Help your brother whether he is the doer of wrong or wrong is done to him." They (his companions) said, O Messenger of God! We can help a man to whom wrong is done, but how could we help him when he is the doer of wrong? He said: "Take hold of his hands from doing wrong."

To conclude, I would like to encourage myself and my fellow Muslims to fear God in every aspect of our lives. We must make it our habit to always seek the truth and then act upon it. We should strive to acquire a better understanding of our religion. The Prophet ﷺ said: "When God intends good for a person, he gives him understanding of the religion." We must look for this understanding in the Quran and *Sunnah* and the understanding of our pious predecessors. We should neither accept nor reject anything without knowledge. When a matter is unclear, we must take recourse to reputable people of knowledge and obey the command of our Lord who says: "Ask those who possess knowledge if you know not." (Al-Nahl/ The Bees [16] 43). God says the following about those who disregard knowledge: "Recite unto them the tale of him to whom We gave Our revelations, but he sloughed them off, so Satan overtook him and he became of those who went astray. If it had been Our will, We should have elevated him with Our signs; but he inclined to the Earth, and followed his own vain desires. His similitude is that of a dog: if you attack him, he lolls out his tongue, and if you leave him alone, he still lolls out his tongue. That is the similitude of those who reject Our signs. So relate the story, that perchance they may reflect." (Al-Araf/ The Heights [7] 175-176)

And do not just take it from me, but from people like Mohamed Nasheed (President, the Maldives, a country just 1.5 metres above sea level): "People often tell me caring for the environment is too difficult, too expensive or too much bother. I admit installing solar panels and wind turbines doesn't come cheap. But when I read those science reports from Copenhagen [for Government negotiations in December 2009], I know there is only one choice. Going green might cost a lot but refusing to act now will cost us the Earth."

If after implementing one or more of the above ideas you get called a 'tree hugger', be happy, be very happy indeed as you are in great company, as narrated by Jabir bin Abdullah, the Prophet ﷺ used to stand by a tree or a date-palm on Friday. Then an Ansari woman or man said. "O Messenger of God! Shall we make a pulpit for you?" He replied, "If you wish." So they made a pulpit for him and when it was Friday, he proceeded towards the pulpit (for delivering the sermon). The date-palm cried like a child! The Prophet ﷺ descended (the pulpit) and embraced it while it continued moaning like a child being quietened. The Prophet ﷺ said, "It was crying for (missing) what it used to hear of religious knowledge given near to it."

The Prophet ﷺ said: "The believers with respect to one another are like a building, each one lending support to the whole." What kind of a building block are you being today, are you going to be tomorrow? Perhaps best to follow the advice of Abdullah Quilliam: "Do your best, God will do the rest."

And God knows best. In peace.

Sources & Resources

"Say [unto them, O Muhammad]: Are those who know equal to those who know not? But only men/ women of understanding will pay heed" (Az-Zumar/ The Troops [39] 9)

Islamic Foundation for Ecology and Environmental Sciences (IFEES), www.ifees.org.uk

Islamic Declaration on Sustainable Development (2002), www.isesco.org.ma/pub/Eng/Sust_Dev/P7.htm

Mohammad Assayed Jamil (translated by Lahcen Haddad), *A Study on Environmental Issues with Reference to the Qur'an and the Sunna*, Islamic Educational, Scientific and Cultural Organisation (ISESCO), 1420AH / 1999 CE, www.isesco.org.ma/pub/Eng/Env_QS/Menu.htm

The Islamic World and the Sustainable Development (Specificities, Challenges and Commitments), Islamic Educational, Scientific and Cultural Organisation (ISESCO), 1420AH / 1999 CE; www.isesco.org.ma/english/publications/Sust_Dev/Menu.php

Bagader et al. 1994, *Environmental Protection in Islam*, IUCN, Gland, Switzerland and Cambridge, UK; http://cmsdata.iucn.org/downloads/eplp20en.pdf

Abdul Karim Awad, *Messages through animals, Qur'anic context* (2008), published by Message of Islam; www.messageofislam.com

Al Hafiz Basheer Ahmad Masri, *Animal Welfare in Islam*, (2007) republished by Islamic Foundation (copyright Compassion in World Farming)

Islam and Ecology, edited by Fazlun Khalid with Joanne O'Brien, World Religions and Ecology, WWF, 1992

Islam and the Environment, edited by Harfiyah Abdel Haleem, Ta-Ha Publishers, 1998

Islam and Ecology, a bestowed trust, edited by Richard F. Holtz e.a., Harvard University Press, 2003

Earth Charter, www.earthcharter.org and *Earth Charter in Action*, www.earthcharterinaction.org (includes link to an open-source application for Evaluating Initiatives, Projects, and Organisations)

Al-Imam Abu Zakariya Yahya bin Sharaf An-Nawawi Ad-Dimashqi, *Riyad as-Salihin (The Meadows of the Righteous)*; www.sunnipath.com/Library/Hadith/H0004P0000.aspx

Towards an Islamic Jurisprudence of the Environment, Mustafa Abu-Sway, February 1998; http://homepages.iol.ie/~afifi/Articles/environment.htm

Islamic Perspectives on Natural Resources Management and Sustainability, Karim Hamdy, Oregon State University, Oregon USA; http://oregonstate.edu/dept/IIFET/2000/papers/hamdy.pdf

Surkheel (Abu Aaliyah) Sharif, *The Earth's Complaint*,
Jawziyyah Institute,
http://web.mac.com/jawziyyah/iWeb/The%20Jawziyyah
%20Institute/Reading%20Room_files/Earth.pdf

*Ecology in Islam: Protection of the Web of Life a Duty for
Muslims*, Hasan Zillur Rahim, Washington Report on
Middle East Affairs, October 1991, Page 65;
www.wrmea.com/backissues/1091/9110065.htm

Conservation International Indonesia (October 2005),
Islamic Boarding Schools and Conservation, The World
Bank, Faith and Environment Initiative;
http://siteresources.worldbank.org/INTBIODIVERSITY/21
4578-
1116622078457/20859316/Islamic_Boarding_Schools_and
_Conservation.pdf

Paola Triolo, *Climate Change Partnership Handbook*,
Alliance for Religions and Conservation,
www.arcworld.org/downloads/ClimateChange.pdf

Mohammed Alexander Russell Webb (1846-1916)
Foundation, www.webbfound.org

*Beyond Belief: Linking faiths and protected areas to
support biodiversity conservation*, WWF, Equilibrium and
the Alliance of Religions and Conservation (ARC),
www.arcworld.org/downloads/WWF%20Beyond
%20Belief.pdf

*The Meaning of Our Testimony that Muhammad ﷺ is the
Messenger of Allah*, Abd al-Aziz bin Abdallah bin

Muhammad Al-Sheikh, Grand Mufti, Saudi Arabia;
www.islamtoday.com/book/meaning/testimony.pdf

Abdullah Quilliam Society:
www.abdullahquilliamsociety.org.uk

1997 Seoul Declaration on Environmental Ethics, World
Environment Day 1997 (5 June 1997), www.nyo.unep.org/
wed_eth.htm

Jickling, B., Lotz-Sisitka, H., O'Donoghue, R., Ogbuigwe.
A. (2006) *Environmental Education, Ethics, and Action: A
Workbook to Get Started. Nairobi*: UN Environment
Programme (UNEP),
www.unep.org/training/downloads/PDFs/ethics_en.pdf

Environmental Protection in Islam, www.islamset.com/env/
contenv.html

The Hima: an ancient conservation system for the future,
Serhal, A. and Amer R. Saidi, A.R., Society for the
protection of nature in Lebanon (SPNL), October 2005,
www.iucn.org/places/wescana/documents/hima_spnl_positi
on_paper.pdf

*The book of nature, a sourcebook of spiritual perspectives
on nature and the environment* (2006), edited by Camille
Helminski, The Book Foundation, www.thebook.org

UK Royal Society (April 2007), *Climate change
controversies: a simple guide*,
www.royalsoc.ac.uk/page.asp?id=6229

Worldwatch, www.worldwatch.org

GreenBooks, http://greenbooks.co.uk

Millennium Ecosystem Assessment (MA) Synthesis Report, released 30 March 2005: www.millenniumassessment.org/documents/CbdSynthesisFinal.pdf

Global Footprint Network www.footprintnetwork.org

Sustainable development indicators in your pocket 2008, An update of the UK Government Strategy indicators, UK Department for Environment, Food and Rural Affairs (DEFRA); www.defra.gov.uk/sustainable/government/progress/documents/SDIYP2008_a6.pdf

National Renewable Energy Laboratory, www.nrel.gov

Arab Environment Monitor, environmental news from the Arab world, www.arabenvironment.net

Religion and Nature, www.religionandnature.com

Forum on Religion and Ecology, www.religionandecology.org

Ibrahim Ozdemir, Turkey (site with articles on Islam and nature), www.ibrahimozdemir.com

Earth Policy Institute, www.earthpolicy.org

Johannesburg Renewable Energy Coalition:
http://europa.eu.int/comm/environment/jrec/index_en.htm

International Energy Agency's World Energy Outlook:
www.worldenergyoutlook.org

Salman bin Fahd al-Oadah, *Walking the Straight Path,
Constancy, Renewal & the Contemporary Muslim*;
www.islamtoday.com/book/walking/walking.pdf

Community Carbon Reduction Project, www.cred-uk.org

Sustainable Development Commission, www.sd-commission.org.uk

About the author

With a long-standing interest in the environment, Rianne C. ten Veen enjoys being engaged in challenging (sustainable) projects, including volunteering on management team of Islamic Foundation for Ecology and Environmental Sciences (IFEES) and Steering Group of Faith and Climate Change project initiated with Birmingham Friends of the Earth. A humanitarian aid worker in her day time job with particular experience in working with complex emergencies, she is a keen researcher on the relation between poverty and the environment and our Islamic duty to do something about it.

Rianne has studied, lived, worked and/ or travelled in over 30 countries in 4 continents. She has a Master's degree in Law (from Leiden University, the Netherlands), a Master's degree in International Politics (from CERIS, Belgium/ Paris XI University, France) and a Post-Graduate Diploma in Environmental Policy (from the Open University, UK). Her aims are to continue researching Islamic injunctions to look after our surroundings near and far and work together with like-minded people as a means of practical worship. She would be interested to hear your ideas and experience of looking after Creation in our guardian role.

To get in touch:

riannetv@care2.com

www.greencreation.info

Lightning Source UK Ltd.
Milton Keynes UK
12 November 2009

146114UK00001B/80/P